JAVA™ STYLE

PATTERNS FOR IMPLEMENTATION

ISBN 0-13-085086-1

90000

9 780130 850867

Titles in the PH/PTR *essential* series:

Series Editor Alan McClellan is co-author of the best-selling *Java by Example*, *Graphic Java: Mastering the AWT*, and *Automating Solaris Installations: A JumpStart Guide* (Sun Microsystems Press/Prentice Hall). He is an award-winning software technical writer with over ten years of experience in the computer industry.

essential

JAVA STYLE

PATTERNS FOR IMPLEMENTATION

JEFF LANGR

Prentice Hall PTR
Upper Saddle River, NJ 07458
http://www.phptr.com

Library of Congress Catalog-in-Publication Data

```
Langr, Jeff.
    Essential Java style : patterns for implementation / Jeff
Langr.
    p. cm. --   (PH/PTR essential series)
    ISBN 0-13-085086-1
    1. Java (Computer program language) I. Title. II. Title: Java
style III. Series.
    QA76.13.J38 L357 1999
    005.13'3--dc21                                        99-34858
                                                              CIP
```

Production editor and compositor: *Vanessa Moore*
Acquisitions editor: *Gregory Doench*
Editorial assistant: *Mary Treacy*
Development editor: *Ralph E. Moore*
Technical editor: *Jerry Jackson*
Series editor: *Alan McClellan*
Marketing manager: *Bryan Gambrel*
Manufacturing manager: *Alexis Heydt*
Cover design director: *Jerry Votta*
Cover designer: *Scott Weiss*
Cover photo: *Christine Langr*
Project coordinator: *Anne Trowbridge*

Prentice Hall books are widely used by corporations and government agencies for training, marketing, and resale. The publisher offers discounts on this book when ordered in bulk quantities. For more information, contact Corporate Sales Department, Phone: 800-382-3419, Fax: 201-236-7141, Email: corpsales@prenhall.com
or write: Prentice Hall PTR
            Corporate Sales Department
            One Lake Street
            Upper Saddle River, NJ 07458

Printed in the United States of America
10   9   8   7   6   5   4   3   2   1

ISBN 0-13-085086-1

Prentice-Hall International (UK) Limited, *London*
Prentice-Hall of Australia Pty. Limited, *Sydney*
Prentice-Hall of Canada, Inc., *Toronto*
Prentice-Hall Hispanoamericana S.A., *Mexico*
Prentice-Hall of India Private Limited, *New Delhi*
Prentice-Hall of Japan, Inc., *Tokyo*
Prentice-Hall (Singapore) Pte. Ltd., *Singapore*
Editora Prentice-Hall do Brasil, Ltda., *Rio de Janeiro*

This book is dedicated to
Kathleen, Katie, Tim, and Anna.

CONTENTS

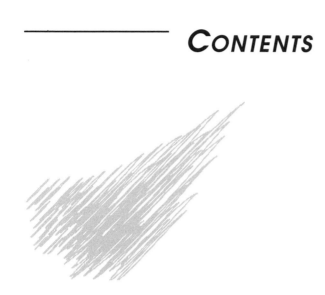

CHAPTER 1   BEHAVIOR — METHODS   1

CHAPTER 2   BEHAVIOR — MESSAGES   45

CHAPTER 4   COLLECTIONS   123

APPENDIX B   PATTERN SUMMARY   257

INDEX   273

INTRODUCTION

Each time I learned a new language, I began to recognize and identify specific things that I was doing over and over in my code. Back in my COBOL days (the early 1980s), these repeated bits of code weren't known by the now-ubiquitous buzzword "patterns," but they were most certainly coding constructs that I was aware of and that I actively reused. Since then I have worked extensively with Pascal, C, C++, Smalltalk, and now Java. The specific constructs may have changed, but the concept of a reusable pattern has remained.

To remember these constructs, I typically would save off snippets of code into small, stand-alone demonstration programs. When I encountered the need for a construct that I had already coded, I searched my directory of code chunks, and hopefully found the one that would work well in my new coding challenge. If I was fortunate, I achieved object nirvana — reuse! Organizationally speaking, though, this is a less-than-ideal system, and certainly other developers would have a difficult time finding anything useful in my grab-bag of example programs.

Somewhat sadly, I still use this technique in Java today, with only minor improvements. The better Java IDEs today support the concept of a scratch pad or workspace, something that Smalltalk has had for years. These scratch pads allow you to quickly code and test snippets of code on the fly without requiring you to create a new project, open a new file, type all the supporting code, save the code, and so forth. But in the end it's still a random list of solutions that is of little value to other developers.

With this book, then, I offer an improved solution. I intend to fill a void that most of the innumerable Java books available do not address. I explain neither how the language works nor how to use the class libraries. Instead, I describe low-level coding patterns that describe how to properly write Java code. If used appropriately, these patterns can be used as the standard for building *cost-effective, universally maintainable systems.*

Coming to Java from Smalltalk, I am already encountering what I have experienced too often before with C++ and other languages:

- Widely varying coding style;

- Overly procedural code that is difficult to understand;

- Inconsistent, overly terse and misleading method, identifier, and class naming;

- Widely different techniques for common operations, such as instance creation and lazy initialization.

These practices are unfortunate and only drive up the cost of code maintenance. In comparison, the Smalltalk development community has a very established, embedded culture. This culture promotes standards and practices that you adhere to without the enforcement of a compiler. The benefit of adherence to these standards is considerable, as I no longer need to figure out individual programmer styles in order to effectively understand their code.

My hope is to someday see in the Java community the amount of consistency and clarity for which the Smalltalk community strives. This book is my effort to provide such a basis for clear code communication.

Patterns

If you are a developer and are not aware of the driving force that patterns have become in the industry, you have probably been sleeping in your cubicle. There are dozens of books available on the topic. *Design Patterns*[1] is the father of all software pattern books. Unfortunately, as buzzwords go, too many things today are expressed in terms of patterns, whether or not it makes sense. "Patterns" is to the late 1990s as "client/server" was to the early 1990s.

The best advantage to using patterns, from my experience, is that you now have a clear means of communicating common design concepts. Used properly, patterns allow you to communicate not just within your workgroup, your company, or your industry, but within the entire development community.

---

1 Gamma, E., Helm, R., Johnson, R., and Vlissides, J. *Design Patterns*. Reading, Massachusetts: Addison-Wesley Publishing Company, Inc., 1995.

Other industries have long adopted patterns and appropriate names for them. Without names for their patterns, architects would have to tell you they were designing "a small, open hall immediately inside the front entrance to the house that will act as a waiting area" instead of just using the word "foyer." For Java development and maintenance to be most cost-effective, the development community similarly needs to adopt a common language of coding patterns.

When hiring a plumber to install a new bathtub, you assume he or she knows how to get it to mesh with your house properly, regardless of whether you use copper plumbing, PVC, or a large bucket to fill your tub. Similarly, a new Java maintenance programmer coming on board should be able to maintain the system by first assuming that the common pattern language has been used. Once this assumption has been proven correct, the programmer should be able to rapidly look at existing code to determine its intent and structure.

The patterns contained within this book are very specific coding-level patterns. They are generally not subsystem design patterns like those contained in *Design Patterns*. My main intent (and *intent* is a key word when considering patterns) is to present a guidebook for a common Java coding style defined in terms of patterns.

Other books on style have a significant shortcoming — the styles are not named. For rules to be useful, they must somehow be internalized by all developers involved. Without the benefit of descriptive names, it is difficult to understand and communicate specific rules. (What was rule #121 again?) *Essential Java Style*, and patterns in general, rectify this by providing a precise set of names for the rules.

Regarding intent, the most important thing to do when you are coding is to ensure that someone else will be able to quickly understand what the heck you were thinking. Too often a maintainer has to try to read the mind of a programmer who may be long gone. Clairvoyance is a good skill to have, but unfortunately it is not prevalent in the software development industry. Comments sometimes help, but more often than not the comments are inaccurate, out of date, or don't add value to what the code already states.

If you follow the patterns in this book, the amount of your code that will need commenting should decrease significantly. While the promise of self-documenting code is rarely fulfilled, these patterns give you the best opportunity to allow your code to declare just what it is doing. If you are writing lots of comments to explain things, then your code is not declaring its intent in a simple fashion and could use some cleaning up.

This emphasis on clean, understandable code is extremely important, because maintenance is the costliest part of a typical development shop. The ability to rapidly fix, amend, or enhance code is one of the chief promises of object-oriented development. The reality will only come when coders learn to express themselves clearly and consistently.

Essential Java Style: Implementation Patterns

What are these patterns? Are they about style or standards? Or neither?

Style is an imprecise word. The word *style* connotes flash, panache, coolness. On the opposite end of the spectrum, the word *standards* connotes stodginess, inflexibility, tedium. Neither term accurately describes the goal of this book, which is why it has a subtitle: *Patterns for Implementation*. I also think that people only reluctantly buy books on standards, so that was left out of the title completely.

There are few hard-and-fast programming rules. Most of these patterns reflect just one possible solution to recurring implementation questions. So the patterns cannot be absolute standards. Yet the patterns do decide what should be the usual and expected solution to a problem. The preferred solution identified by each pattern is generally the simplest, not the most creative. So this book is not about style in the classic sense either.

What these patterns do is provide guidelines for development and a common language with which to communicate these guidelines. All of the patterns have specific names to assist you in internalizing them. The collection of pattern names is the vocabulary for the pattern language.

This book uses a pattern itself for the naming of its patterns. The bulk of the patterns described are the same as those contained within *Smalltalk Best Practice Patterns*[2] by Kent Beck. Obviously, there are some key differences between the two languages, but other than syntax, *Smalltalk* has more in common with Java than either C or C++. Many of the extremely useful concepts presented in Beck's book translate very closely to Java. With generous thanks to Beck, I have reused his set of patterns where applicable.

Who This Book Is for

If you program, read, test, or document Java code, *Essential Java Style* is for you. It is not intended as a programming primer or a class reference, but some of the patterns contained in it will explain Java concepts where necessary. I assume the reader has some minimal knowledge of Java programming, but the reader does not need to be a Java expert to use this book effectively.

Essential Java Style is especially geared toward team development. The patterns provide a common language for communication of implementation concepts. But even if you are the only one who ever looks at your own code, the patterns within will still help you improve your development efforts.

On a personal basis, I have been exposed to Java for three years, working in depth with the language over the past year. I do not consider myself a Java expert, but I do have considerable experience in various other languages. Clean coding is something I have striven for throughout my career. Code almost never exists in a vacuum — someone will be reading or main-

---

2 Beck, Kent. *Smalltalk Best Practice Patterns*. Upper Saddle River, NJ: Prentice Hall PTR, 1996.

taining your code in the future. Unlike a muddled movie, which can be walked out on, some poor soul may have to understand your code, like it or not. If you respect your fellow developer, you will strive for clear code.

What You'll Need

Essential Java Style is intended to be a manual of style. To get started, all you really need is a Java toolkit or IDE and this book. The latest JDK can always be downloaded from http://www.javasoft.com.

While I recommend you work with JDK 2 or later, most of the examples in this book will apply to any version of the JDK. The bulk of the chapter on Collections (Chapter 4) is specific to the Collections Framework in JDK 2. For the rest of the patterns, differences in implementation between JDK 1.1 and JDK 2 are highlighted.

You should have a basic knowledge of Java programming, including how to edit, compile, and run Java programs. A modest amount of object-oriented experience is expected. I also assume that you have done some sort of actual development before.

While this book refers to other books on design-level patterns, knowledge of those patterns is not necessary. The footnotes list several books that are referred to within the text.

There is no CD-ROM provided with this book. The patterns are short. Demonstrations of the patterns can be typed quickly. As such, I believe you will learn more from typing in the patterns yourself, or applying them to your own work, rather than from executing a test program from a CD.

How This Book Is Organized

The core patterns in this book are contained within six chapters:

> Chapter 1, "Behavior — Methods"
> Chapter 2, "Behavior — Messages"
> Chapter 3, "State Patterns"
> Chapter 4, "Collections"
> Chapter 5, "Classes"
> Chapter 6, "Formatting"

A final Chapter 7, "Development Example," provides a small example that demonstrates how these patterns might be pieced together in actual software development. Appendix A presents a discussion of performance issues related to the patterns.

Each pattern starts on a new page to help you quickly locate specific patterns. A summary box is provided at the start of each pattern. The summary heading for COMPOSED METHOD is provided below as an example. After the PATTERN NAME, the specific problem to be solved by the pattern is stated in the form of a question (*Answers the Question*). The *Solution* is then briefly stated, and the *Category* to which the pattern belongs is reinforced. *Related Patterns* are listed as a jumping off point to other patterns that may be useful.

COMPOSED METHOD

Answers the Question	How do you divide a class into methods?
Solution	Create small methods that, each of which accomplishes a single task that is concisely represented by the method name.
Category	Behavioral
Related Patterns	Method Comment Intention-Revealing Method Name

I highly recommend reading all of the patterns first to get a good overview of what is available. However, there is no reason why you cannot open the book randomly and choose a pattern to delve into. Many of the patterns, especially core patterns such as COMPOSED METHOD, refer to other patterns or use them as prerequisites.

At the minimum, you should read Chapter 1, "Behavior — Methods," which forms the core of how your classes should be organized. Many of the patterns contained within that chapter are closely coupled; there is a yin-yang relationship between them.

How to Use the Patterns

Once you get the feel of a few patterns, go back to your own code and see if the patterns can be applied to make it clearer. The more you implement the patterns in actual code, the easier it should be for you to add new patterns to your mental library.

The ultimate test, though, is not how well you can understand your code, but how well another developer can understand it. Where these patterns are most useful is in a team development environment. If you code for yourself, these patterns may have limited usefulness. In a team environment, though, the patterns should greatly assist your development team in achieving common coding habits. Part of your team's *lingua franca* is this pattern language.

Most team development environments use reviews for code quality assurance. These can be in the form of simple peer reviews, structured walkthroughs, or inspections. Reviews tend to have the following problems:

- They are random in nature. Different perspectives glean different programming defects. While this can be helpful, it can result in missed spots. Inspections typically have this problem.

- They provide inadequate coverage. Often in crunch mode, a single successful peer programmer review is enough to put something into production — the absolute worst time to shrink the scope of review.

- They are extremely time-consuming and tedious. Every developer I have met dreads the classic walkthrough. Half a dozen people gather in a windowless conference room, each armed with stacks of printouts, and slug their way through the code, line by line, while the producer diligently explains and defends his code. This takes hours if not days.

I hope that these patterns will play a significant role in expediting and improving your review processes. If you use inspections, the benefit of a common guideline should help in leveling the varied points of view. You should also achieve more consistent and complete results, even if the number of inspectors is limited.

With walkthroughs, if everyone involved is familiar with the patterns, inappropriate solutions are identified more rapidly and are expressed more precisely. The developer getting beat up immediately understands what the problem is and how to fix it. ("You need to refactor `processFile()` using COMPOSED METHOD, and apply a GUARD CLAUSE to handle the null exception condition.")

I recommend that you initially use a checklist to make passes against code as you look for places where the patterns can be applied. While there are a great number of patterns, developers and reviewers should be able to internalize them quickly. Many of the patterns should already present familiar concepts, so that your goal becomes more of standardizing according to a single solution and communicating that solution with the appropriate pattern name. The patterns will become second nature as your development efforts begin to standardize around cleaner, more maintainable code.

Conventions Used in This Book

This book uses many snippets of code to explain its concepts. Code is always presented in a `fixed font`, as follows:

```
public static void main(String[] args)
```

When the name of a `method()` is referenced within the text, it will similarly appear in a `fixed font`.

Usually, code that runs more than a line or two is presented in a separate numbered listing. Each listing number begins with the chapter number and is followed by a sequence number that runs consecutively through the chapter. For example, **Listing 3.5** is the fifth listing in Chapter 3.

Listing 3.5 *DEFAULT VALUE CONSTANT with LAZY INITIALIZATION*

```
public int getHoursPerWeek()
{
    if (hoursPerWeek == 0)
        hoursPerWeek = defaultFullTimeHoursPerWeek;
    return hoursPerWeek;
}
```

(1)

When specific lines of code in a listing are mentioned in the text, they are bracketed. In the listing itself, the line number (e.g., line [1]) appears in parenthesized bold italics to the left of the pertinent line of code. As with the listings themselves, line numbers are consecutive throughout the chapter.

Also, a `methodName()` referred to within the text will not usually explicitly list its parameter types, unless it is necessary to do so to uniquely identify or explain the method (e.g., `methodName(String)`).

A ClassName in the text is capitalized per Java standards. Note that a generic instance of a class, or an English-reference to what the class represents, will appear in lowercase. Thus, I may state, "the Employee class contains the `terminate()` method" but explain that "an employee can be terminated."

The name of an *Essential Java Style* pattern will always be in small capitals. Patterns from other texts (*Design Patterns*, for example), will be capitalized.

Demonstration code often will contain a line-comment followed by ellipses:

```
// ...
```

This is used to indicate that portions of code not pertinent to the example have been omitted.

In the preparation of the patterns for this book, the Java Language Specification (JLS), the JDK core packages, and industry-accepted standards have all been taken into account.

Key Terms

I am not inclined to provide a glossary, because they usually appear at the end of a book and are often overlooked. *Essential Java Style* also assumes you are familiar with basic OO (object-oriented) concepts and terminology. There are few terms unique to this text. Some of the important terms that may be unfamiliar are defined here:

Client: Developers or other objects that use the classes you develop. You are developing objects that will be publicly consumed by other developers' code (clients).

Grunt: A low-level, nonmanagement worker-bee employee.

Message: Something sent to an object to get it to invoke a method.

Receiver: An object receiving a message.

Refactor: To reorganize code. Methods can be refactored into the superclass or out of the implementing class. Long methods can be refactored into smaller methods within the same class.

A Final Note

If you have read this far and have decided to purchase *Essential Java Style*, I offer my thanks. My sincere hope is that you take the patterns to heart and help make the code in this world a little cleaner.

Acknowledgments

I would like to thank my wife Kathleen and children Katie, Tim, and Anna for their support and understanding during this book-writing process. Giving up computer time, husband time, and dad time has not been easy for them. Kids, keep working on your books and someday you can monopolize the computer.

Jerry Jackson, co-author of *Java By Example*, played a critical role as the technical reviewer for this book. I give great thanks to him for ensuring that this book doesn't expose me as being full of it.

Without Alan McClellan, editor of the series, this book would not have been possible. Thank you, Alan, for making this project happen so quickly, and for providing invaluable guidance and assistance along the way.

Thanks as well to my developer friends for reviewing portions of the book and for coming up with good examples. Eric Wessbecker. Andrew Washburn, Al Weber, Bob Smolarek, Jerry Huber, and David Clark in particular provided valuable input. There's nothing better than having someone who will bluntly tell you when your work stinks.

Many thanks to the fantastic support at Prentice Hall, especially Ralph and Vanessa Moore. Thanks also to Greg Doench for making this a smooth and enjoyable process.

Final thanks go to:

- Tim O'Connor, who did more than anyone to shape my career and personal development, and was a respected mentor;
- My high-school math teacher, Ed Brune, one of those teachers you never forget; and
- Mom and Dad, who never said a word of discouragement to me in my entire life.

About the Author

Jeff Langr is a software developer with more than 16 years of experience. He has worked for Marriott Corporation and MCI, and is currently employed by ChannelPoint, Inc. in Colorado Springs as a professional services consultant.

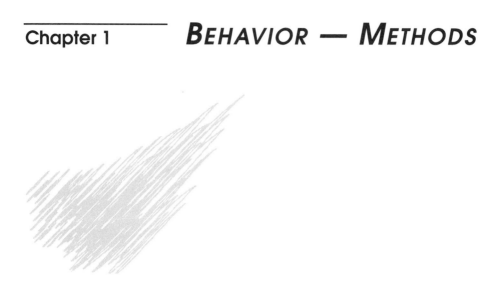

Chapter 1   *BEHAVIOR — METHODS*

Your classes are defined to the world in terms of their behavior. Even your state is declared in terms of behavior — you use public methods to allow clients to access your instance variables (unless you violate virtually every book on object-oriented [OO] and Java programming and make your instance variables public). You do this because the principle of encapsulation states that classes should hide their data. So while objects are partnerships between individual instance data and behavior, the behavior gets all the glory, while the data hides behind the scenes.

Behavior is a two-way street. Implementation of behavior is done with methods; invocation of behavior is made by calling those methods, also referred to as sending a message. This book prefers the term "message" in the pure sense that when you make a method call, you are sending a message to an object to ask it to perform some behavior. How messages are sent and how the corresponding behavior is implemented in methods are very closely related.

This chapter and the next define a series of behavioral patterns that will aid you in organizing your class appropriately. You should already have defined your public methods during your object design phase, so that your work is partly done. You could implement those public methods and conceivably be done with the development of your class. It would work, but it probably would not be very maintainable.

Applying these behavioral patterns will result in the creation of additional private or protected methods. This will help your class better declare how it accomplishes its published goal. It will also make your class more flexible. You achieve this by breaking up the tasks representing the public methods into understandable pieces. You also use consistent patterns to help guide an educated reader of the class through its intent.

Methods

The history of software development started with writing single programs that executed from the top down, start to finish. This progressed to the ability to define subroutines, or functions, which were scoped either globally, to a source module level, or even to another function. Finally, with object-oriented languages, we have moved to class-scoped methods. In Java, *all* code is scoped to a class. There is no such thing as a global function like there is in C++. And to build a class, you must code methods.

It would be entirely possible to code a complete class within its constructor method or a complete application within a `main()` method. Java does not restrict you from being so obnoxious — the Java *language* allows you to code as you wish. But the Java *class library* demonstrates that classes must be broken into separate methods to be useful. If you are coding an applet, for example, you may need to code `init()`, `stop()`, `start()`, `paint()` and `destroy()` methods. Each of these methods provides an important chunk of functionality to the applet.

I too will do my best to get you to code lots of methods. There is a distinct advantage to breaking up code within your class in specific ways. With long methods, you increase code duplication, limit reuse, and make your class difficult to decipher and maintain.

You might be thinking, "Doesn't performance suffer if you have lots of short methods?" Indeed, invoking a method in Java is a moderately expensive operation. Ironically, though, if you have performance problems in your code, you cannot effectively measure the source of your performance problems with large methods. Small methods give you the granularity you need to be able to isolate performance bottlenecks. For an in-depth discussion of how performance relates to *Essential Java Style* patterns, refer to Appendix A.

There is also a point at which an excessive number of methods makes a class too cumbersome to manage. But the possibility also exists that if your class has too many methods, another class may need to be defined.

In summary, there is a happy medium between lots of very small methods and few very long methods. Coding methods is about organizing your class to achieve the goal of optimal flexibility and maintainability. This section provides patterns for proper method organization.

COMPOSED METHOD

Answers the Question	How do you divide a class into methods?
Solution	Create small methods, each of which accomplishes a single task that is concisely represented by the method name.
Category	Behavioral
Related Patterns	Method Comment Intention-Revealing Method Name

The COMPOSED METHOD pattern is the centerpiece of this book. If you absorb one thing from *Essential Java Style*, make it how to use COMPOSED METHOD to organize your classes. Good class organization is what effective maintenance is all about.

A simple mantra to remember for class development is, "make it run, make it right, make it fast." COMPOSED METHOD and the remainder of the patterns in this book are the "make it right" part of the mantra. Your development should follow all three steps as described under the next three subheadings.

Making It Run

Making it run (correctly) is your most important goal in developing any software. If the code is beautiful but does not run, it is utterly useless.

Your initial class development should take the following steps:

1. Determine and name your public methods. Classes are about providing behavior to client objects. If you don't understand how your class will expose its behavior to other classes, you have missed an important step in object design.
2. Define the attributes that class instances will store in terms of instance variables.
3. Code the public methods. Typically there will be few additional methods at this point, because the most rapid way to code a method is top down, through to completion.

At this point, you will have a class that can be used by client code — "make it run." Is that enough?

While your class may run just fine, you will not have a class that can be easily maintained or extended. The methods that you have coded in step 3 will be fairly long. Are these long methods inherently bad? Code in the method itself can answer this question. I take the view that code speaks volumes, and if you don't like what it's saying, there is a problem.

First, aesthetics of presentation are important. If I cannot easily read code, my ability to rapidly maintain it will be diminished. White space, consistent indentation, and breaking things up into legible chunks go a long way towards improving readability. If I have a several-hundred-line method that spans multiple screens or pages and seems to go on forever with many things going on like this overly long sentence, it will take the reader considerably longer to even scan the method to get the whole picture. Page up, page down, bookmark, page up, page down, return to bookmark — What's going on here?

If I had condensed all the paragraphs in this book into a single paragraph, eliminating all of the paragraph headers, I guarantee that you would not have purchased the book. As it is, you may regret having bought this book, but at least it is organized well enough so that you can find your way around. The book speaks its intent by its chapter and topic organization.

Having long methods also means that the methods are doing lots of different things. This leads to negative side effects such as the need for excessive comments (see METHOD COMMENT) or generic, bland method names (see INTENTION-REVEALING METHOD NAME).

More importantly, though, coding long methods violates good object-oriented design principles by lumping scads of tasks into a single method. Your capacity for reuse within the class is diminished — the more tasks within a method, the more specialized it will be. Specialization minimizes the potential for inheritance and reuse and can also increase the amount of code duplication.

Small methods, which limit the number of things going on, end up being vastly more readable and easily replaceable or extensible. Smaller methods are also tested more easily. To properly test a method, you must prove that it produces the expected results for all possible inputs and initial object states.[1] These expected results include not only the return value of the method, but also the resultant object state. This is an excruciatingly painful task, as you might expect, and most people have neither the time nor the patience for it. Nevertheless, the fewer things that are going on within a single method, the less there is to prove.

Making It Right

After you have completed the first three steps in the development cycle and you have a handful of lengthy methods, your job is to "make it right." Making it right means applying the patterns in this book to your class to make it as easily readable and maintainable as possible. COMPOSED METHOD is the starting point.

---

1 Arbib, M.A., Kfoury, A.J., Moll, R. N. *A Basis for Theoretical Computer Science.* New York, NY: Springer-Verlag, New York Inc., 1981, p. 104.

Listing 1.1 provides an example of a fairly short method that does too much.

Listing 1.1   Composed Method *Example — Before*

```
public void createCustomerCSV()
    throws IOException
{
    String tempFilename = null;
    for (int i = 0; i < 1000; i++)
    {
        String filename = "temp." + i;
        File file = new File(filename);
        if (!file.exists())
        {
            tempFilename = filename;
            break;
        }
    }
    if (tempFilename == null)
        throw new IOException(
            "Could not create temp file");

    FileWriter output =
        new FileWriter(tempFilename);
    try
    {
        Iterator iterator = customers.iterator();
        while (iterator.hasNext())
        {
            Customer customer =
                (Customer)iterator.next();
            output.write(customer.getName()+",");
            output.write(customer.getCity()+",");
            output.write(customer.getCountry()+"\n");
        }
    }
    finally
    {
        output.close();
    }
}
```

This `createCustomerCSV()` method is doing three separate tasks. It derives a legitimate temporary file name for output, loops through a list of customers, and writes information from each customer to the output file in a CSV (comma-separated values) format. If I were to comment the chunks in this method properly, I would need three comments just to guide the reader along.

Using COMPOSED METHOD to reorganize, or "refactor," the method, you might end up with the three methods shown in **Listing 1.2**.

Listing 1.2 Composed Method *Example — After Refactoring*

```java
public void createCustomerCSV(String filename)
   throws IOException
{
   FileWriter output =
      new FileWriter(filename);
   try
   {
      Iterator iterator = customers.iterator();
      while (iterator.hasNext())
         writeCustomer(output,
                       (Customer)iterator.next());
   }
   finally
   {
      output.close();
   }
}

public String getTempFilename(String prefix)
   throws IOException
{
   for (int i = 0; i < 1000; i++)
   {
      String filename = prefix + "." + i;
      File file = new File(filename);
      if (!file.exists())
         return filename;
   }
   throw new IOException(
      "Could not create temp file");
}

private void writeCustomer(
   FileWriter output,
   Customer customer)
   throws IOException
{
   output.write(customer.getName()+",");
   output.write(customer.getCity()+",");
   output.write(customer.getCountry()+"\n");
}
```

The benefits of this reorganization are many. Client code will have the flexibility to create the CSV file with whatever filename is desired, or it can call getTempFilename() to provide the filename parameter to createCustomerCSV(). If the algorithm in getTempFilename() is deemed inadequate, it can be easily overridden with a better one in a subclass. Also, if more fields from Customer are required to be written to the CSV record, the maintenance programmer can easily locate the single method (writeCustomer()) that manipulates the customer data.

Finally, and most importantly, the code in each of the three methods in **Listing 1.2** can be immediately understood. Not only is the code brief enough to visually recognize, but conceptually the method name tells us what each method is accomplishing. Conversely, if you cannot look at a method and rapidly determine what it is doing, then it is doing too much.

After applying this pattern, the bulk of your Java code (excluding repetitious processing, such as doing user interface layouts and setup) will be divided into short, concise methods. Most of my methods are from 5 to 10 lines of code each.[2]

Making It Fast

It's to be hoped that you will not have to pay homage to this part of the mantra very often. But sooner or later, someone will come along and complain about the speed. It is Java, after all.

If you do encounter performance problems, the biggest mistake you can make is to assume you know where the problem is. I have incorrectly assumed that a specific method was the bottleneck. I spent lots of time fixing the presumed source of my performance problem, only to make my code uglier and to find out that my assumption was incorrect. As my high school math teacher Mr. Brune often repeated, "When you assume, you make an *ass* out of *u* and *me*."

Use a tool to monitor performance. If your code was "made right," performance tests will point out the precise source of the problem. With large multipurpose methods, you will have no way of determining just which piece of a method is causing the bottleneck.

Modifications to increase performance usually are made at the expense of easily understood code. You will need to add comments to explain why things were done that way. Your code will become less maintainable. The implication of these downsides is that you should always save performance modifications until the last step. Even then, only implement them as a last resort.

For more information on performance issues, refer to Appendix A, "Performance."

---

2 Surprise — pretty much all that we are doing here with Composed Method is classic functional decomposition. Not that there's anything wrong with that.

CONSTRUCTOR METHOD

Answers the Question	How do you represent instance creation?
Solution	Provide a constructor for each valid way to create an instance; do not provide constructors that allow creation of invalid objects.
Category	Behavioral
Related Patterns	None

All classes have the capability to produce new instances. If you do not provide any constructors, Java provides what is known as the default constructor.[3] The default constructor is a no-argument method with the same name as the class; it returns a new instance of the class.

However, if you explicitly code *any* constructors, that's all you get — a "no-arg" constructor is not available to you, and any attempts to refer to one will result in a compile-time error. This is nice to know if you want to prohibit the creation of objects with no parameters. Line [1] in the main() method of **Listing 1.3** tries to call a nonexistent no-arg constructor to create a new Customer object.

Listing 1.3 *Missing No-Arg Constructor Example*

```
// BROKEN CODE!
public class Customer
{
    public static void main(String[] args)
    {
        Customer customer = new Customer();
        customer.display();
    }

    String name = "<no name provided>";
    public Customer(String _name)
    {
        name = _name;
    }
    public void display()
    {
        System.out.println(name);
    }
}
```

(1)

---

3 The term "default constructor" is a bit overloaded, so I am compelled to provide the appropriate definition. You will find other sources that use the term "default constructor" to refer to a constructor with no arguments. This use of "default" is misleading — a default anything is the fallback in case something is not provided. JavaSoft calls arguments with no constructors simply "no-arg constructors," which isn't a great term but is at least accurate. In this book, a default constructor is the no-arg constructor that is provided if none is explicitly defined.

Compiling **Listing 1.3** will result in the following error, because the constructor `Customer(String)` was provided but `Customer()` was not:

```
Customer.java:5: No constructor matching Customer()
found in class Customer.
     Customer customer = new Customer();
                         ^
```

So what kind of constructors should you provide? Usually your design will lead to the need for only a few constructors in each of your classes, and often only a single constructor is needed. The question that you must answer is: "At what point is my class valid?" In most cases, the set of CONSTRUCTOR METHODS should be all the ways to produce valid classes.

You might choose to provide only a no-arg constructor, allowing the individual attributes of a new object to be populated via its setter methods. This technique is shown in **Listing 1.4**.

Listing 1.4 *Setting Attributes After Instance Creation*

```
Manager manager = new Manager();
manager.setName("Blow, Joseph");
manager.setSSN("999-13-1349");
manager.setContractedRate(40);
```

As long as the resultant object of the no-arg constructor is in a valid state, this is fine. Normally, though, your object requires additional data to be set in order for the object to be in a valid state.

In **Listing 1.4**, what if the client neglects to set the contracted rate? Calculations against the manager that require the rate will either produce incorrect results or cause an exception. Somehow, you have to alert client developers as to which fields need to be set, and hope they follow your comments.

Instead of trusting client developers, provide a set of constructors that represent the ways to create only valid instances. Required data is passed into the object via constructor parameters. Two examples of how to create the Manager object are shown in **Listing 1.5**.

Listing 1.5 *Constructors Creating Valid Instances*

```
public Manager(String name,
               String ssn,
               int contractedRate)
public Manager(String name,
               String ssn,
               int contractedRate,
               boolean hasGoldenParachute)
```

CONSTRUCTOR METHOD answers the question: "How do I create a valid instance of this class?" for client developers. If you follow javadoc conventions, their answer is the list of methods available in the Constructor Summary of the javadoc pages produced for your class.

CONSTRUCTOR PARAMETER METHOD

Answers the Question	How do you set instance variables from the parameters to a CONSTRUCTOR METHOD?
Solution	Use DIRECT VARIABLE ACCESS; create a private set() method if more than one constructor needs to set common parameters.
Category	Behavioral
Related Patterns	Indirect Variable Access Direct Variable Access Default Parameter Values

Many of your constructors will take parameters of some sort. But what is the best way to set the object state from these parameters?

If you are using INDIRECT VARIABLE ACCESS, you might be tempted to use your setter methods to store the parameter data from the constructor in the object, as in **Listing 1.6**.

Listing 1.6   *Setters Used for Constructor Initialization*

```
public Manager(String name,
               String ssn,
               int contractedRate)
{
    super(ssn, name);
    setContractedRate(contractedRate);
}
```

(2)

In [2] of this example, the operation of setting the `contractedRate` attribute is delegated to the `setContractedRate()` setter method.

Occasionally, you will come across the special case where attributes need to be set differently on object instantiation than after the object has been created. An example is the distinction between an empty object being populated from a database versus an object being newly created by an application. In the first case, you simply want to use the data retrieved from the database to directly set the attributes. In the second case, you might create a partially complete object and then trigger a database update operation when attributes are set.

With this in mind, you should avoid using the setters within the constructor. Instead, use DIRECT VARIABLE ACCESS to set the attributes (**Listing 1.7**).

Listing 1.7 *DIRECT VARIABLE ACCESS in Constructor Initialization*

```
public Manager(String _name,
               String _ssn,
               int _contractedRate)
{
   ssn = _ssn;
   name = _name;
   contractedRate = _contractedRate;
}
```

If you have more than one constructor or more complex operations are required to set the attributes, provide a private CONSTRUCTOR PARAMETER METHOD. This method takes all of the parameters from the constructor and does whatever operations are necessary to directly set the parameters. Call this method set(). **Listing 1.8** demonstrates the use of CONSTRUCTOR PARAMETER METHOD for the Manager example.

Listing 1.8 *CONSTRUCTOR PARAMETER METHOD Example*

```
public Manager(String name,
               String ssn,
               int contractedRate)
{
   set(name, ssn, contractedRate);
}

private void set(String _name,
                 String _ssn,
                 int _contractedRate)
{
   name = _name;
   ssn = _ssn;
   contractedRate = _contractedRate;
   baseSalary = contractedRate * 2000;
}
```

If you need to provide constructors that use default values for required attributes, use the pattern DEFAULT PARAMETER VALUES instead.

DEFAULT PARAMETER VALUES

Answers the Question	How do you set parameters to default values?
Solution	Overload the method with all combinations of required parameters. Delegate from the more specific methods with fewer parameters to the methods with more parameters, ultimately delegating to the method that does the actual work.
Category	Behavioral
Related Patterns	Constructor Parameter Method

If you are a C++ developer, you are familiar with the ability to define default arguments:

```
int setCursorTo(int x=1, int y=1)
{
    // ...
}
```

This capability is a shortcut for supplying function overloading. In this example, setCursorTo() can be called in three different ways:

```
setCursorTo();      // both x and y default to 1
setCursorTo(5);     // x is set to 5; y defaults to 1
setCursorTo(5, 4);  // x is set to 5; y is set to 4
```

Java does not provide this feature by design. A possible substitute solution in Java would be to test each parameter and initialize the parameters that are passed in as null. This is a poor solution, as it adds a lot of code and overhead to your methods. DEFAULT PARAMETER VALUES defines a better technique for accomplishing this: you provide multiple methods representing all possible initialization scenarios.

To accomplish this, first create a method that takes all possible parameters and does the actual work. Overload this worker method with methods, each of which takes one less parameter than the previous one, and delegates back to the method with the next-most parameters, supplying defaults as required. This sounds like a mouthful; a demonstration using the setCursorTo() example should clear things up:

```
int setCursorTo(int x, int y)
{
    // ...
}
int setCursorTo(int x)
{
    return setCursorTo(x, 1);
}
int setCursorTo()
{
    return setCursorTo(1, 1);
}
```

If you have any sort of conscience, you will use either the DEFAULT VALUE pattern or the DEFAULT VALUE METHOD pattern to help explain why x and y default to the value 1.

DEFAULT PARAMETER VALUES can also be used to provide default values, for instance, creation, as shown in **Listing 1.9**.

Listing 1.9 DEFAULT PARAMETER VALUES *Example*

```
public class Employee
{
    public Employee(String name)
    {
        this(name, 40);
    }
    public Employee(String name,
                    int hoursWorkedPerWeek)
    {
        // ...
    }
}
```

You will need to properly organize your method cascades. Determine which parameters are optional and which must be provided by client code.

First, code the method that takes all parameters, including defaults. Required parameters will appear to the left in the argument list, followed by the defaultable parameters. Then code the method with the next fewer default parameters; repeat until all methods have been provided. For javadoc presentation purposes, the method list is usually the reverse of how you will code things: start with the shortest method signature and move to the one with the most arguments.

SHORTCUT CONSTRUCTOR METHOD

Answers the Question	How can you simplify the construction of objects?
Solution	Provide a method that creates an instance of a new object, using its parameter as an initialization value.
Category	Behavioral
Related Patterns	Converter Method

This pattern is a bit more useful in C++ or Smalltalk, where you have the capability to do operator overloading. Operator overloading, a confusing feature at best in C++, is a powerful construct in Smalltalk that can make your code considerably more expressive. It can be abused, of course, as can just about any construct in any language, including Java.

In Java, without the benefit of operator overloading, there are not many good examples for SHORTCUT CONSTRUCTOR METHOD. The concept of the pattern is that you implement a shortcut method in one class that constructs and returns an object of another class. Information required to construct the new class may come either from the source class or from parameters passed to the SHORTCUT CONSTRUCTOR METHOD.

An example in VisualWorks Smalltalk is the shortcut creation of an Association object. An Association is simply an object that contains a key and value pair. A similar construct in JDK 1.2 is the Map.Entry interface obtained by enumerating a Map. In Smalltalk, you can create an Association object by sending it the message -> with any other object as a parameter. The method in Smalltalk is:

```
-> anObject
   ^Association key: self value: anObject
```

Client code to create an Association looks like the following:

```
x -> y
```

In Java, consider a word processor application. Suppose you have instances of the class Word representing the individual words captured by a word processor. As words are typed, they are combined with other words to form a Sentence object.

Without SHORTCUT CONSTRUCTOR METHOD, to concatenate a word to an existing sentence and create a new sentence, you would code:

```
new Sentence(existingSentence, word);
```

Using SHORTCUT CONSTRUCTOR METHOD, you implement a method in Sentence that takes a Word as a parameter and returns a new Sentence object. **Listing 1.10** demonstrates how this is accomplished.

Listing 1.10 *SHORTCUT CONSTRUCTOR METHOD* **Example**

```
public Sentence cat(Word word)
{
    return new Sentence(this, word);
}
```

Concatenate is abbreviated as `cat`. It would be great if you could overload the + operator. Too bad Java won't let you. Using this SHORTCUT CONSTRUCTOR METHOD, your client code becomes:

```
existingSentence.cat(word);
```

This pattern is useful only if the operation is performed frequently in code, otherwise you are sacrificing understandability for little gain. Using this pattern makes it appear that your code is doing a little bit of magic, unless you are familiar with the idiom. Understanding that a method is creating a new object of a different class is not necessarily intuitive.

CONVERTER METHOD

Answers the Question	How do you represent simple conversion of one object to another with the same protocol but a different format?
Solution	Prefer the use of CONVERTER CONSTRUCTOR METHOD if possible. If not, create a method `asTargetClass()` and have it return a new instance of the target class.
Category	Behavioral
Related Patterns	Converter Constructor Method Shortcut Contstructor Method

If you are required to convert an object from a target class to a source class, you might be tempted to provide converter methods within the source class. For instance, to convert from a Grunt to a Manager (a promotion!), your solution might be the following method on Grunt:

```
public asManager()      //  AVOID THIS TECHNIQUE
{
    initialContractedRate =
      Math.round(getSalary() / 2000);
    return new Manager(name,
                       ssn,
                       initialContractedRate,
                       false);
}
```

But using this solution means that your source class, Grunt, is now dependent on the target class, Manager. If the constructors for Manager change, the Grunt class will have to change as well. If you add a new class, such as Contractor, you would now need to add an `asContractor()` method to Employee, and you would also want the same method on Manager. This increases coupling between classes from a code maintenance standpoint and tends to clutter your classes.

Often you will not have the ability to change the target class, in which case the use of CONVERTER METHOD cannot be avoided. If this is the case, provide a method name that follows the pattern `asTargetClass()` and have it return a new instance of the target class.

If you are able to modify the target class, the preferred solution is to provide a CONVERTER CONSTRUCTOR METHOD. If your conversion is used heavily within code, you may still opt to provide a CONVERTER METHOD on the source class as in **Listing 1.11**.

Listing 1.11 CONVERTER METHOD **Example**

```
public asManager()
{
    return new Manager(this);
}
```

The asManager() method in **Listing 1.11** should never need to change and is only used to slightly reduce the amount of code.

CONVERTER CONSTRUCTOR METHOD

Answers the Question	How do you represent the conversion of an object to another, possibly with a different protocol?
Solution	Provide constructor methods in the target class that take the source object as a parameter.
Category	Behavioral
Related Patterns	Converter Method

The ideal solution for converting one object to another is to simply overload the constructor of the target object. In other words, for each source to be converted from, provide a constructor in the form:

```
public TargetClass(SourceClass sourceParm)
```

Listing 1.12 provides an example that supports the promotion of a Grunt to a Manager.

Listing 1.12 CONVERTER CONSTRUCTOR METHOD **Example**

```
public Manager(Grunt grunt)
{
    name = grunt.getName();
    ssn = grunt.getSSN();
    contractedRate = grunt.getSalary() / 2000;
    hasGoldenParachute = false;
}
```

CONVERTER CONSTRUCTOR METHOD makes the target class dependent only on the technique for conversion. As long as the Grunt class provides the appropriate public methods, any changes to the conversion process are isolated to the constructor of Manager. The Manager class bears sole responsibility for understanding how a Grunt gets "promoted" to a Manager.

Provide a constructor in the target class for each source class to be converted from. Its sole parameter is the source class object.

A Note on Converting Strings and ints

Java provides several different ways to convert ints (and other numeric quantities) to Strings and vice versa. Choosing the correct technique can be confusing.

ints to Strings

To convert an int `iSource` to a String, there are at least three techniques:

```
"" + iSource;
```

or

```
new Integer(iSource).toString();
```

or

```
String.valueOf(iSource);    //  PREFERRED
```

Let's eliminate what we can. The first solution, which concatenates the int to an empty String, is just silly. It certainly involves less typing, but every time I have seen this technique, I have had to look twice to figure out what was going on.

In the second solution, creating an Integer first from the int and then using `toString()` to return its printable representation is considerably more expensive. It also declares a misleading intent: it performs a conversion by using a method intended to provide a printable representation of an object.

The class method `String.valueOf(int)` is the fastest implementation and provides the clearest code as well. The `valueOf()` method is also preferred as a generic solution for converting Object subclasses to strings, as it can handle the `null` object. The message `toString()`, on the other hand, will generate a NullPointerException if sent to the `null` object.

Strings to ints

For converting a String `sSource` to an int, there are also three solutions:

```
new Integer(sSource).intValue();
```

or

```
Integer.valueOf(sSource).intValue();
```

or

```
Integer.parseInt(sSource);    // PREFERRED
```

The first solution, creating a new Integer object and retrieving its intValue(), is a bit indirect.

Ideally, we'd like to have a technique for converting a String to an int that mirrors converting an int to a String. Consistency is always a noble goal. No dice, though — ints are not objects. If they were, we would have the method int.valueOf(String). Unfortunately, we are stuck with Integer wrappers, as used in the second solution. We must first convert the String into an Integer, and then derive its intValue(). So the second solution also ends up being indirect.

It turns out that the Integer.valueOf(String) class method actually calls the parseInt() method to do its dirty work and then wraps the resultant int in an Integer object. By definition, unless some good optimization is going on, parseInt() will thus perform fastest. Use the third solution to convert Strings to ints.

QUERY METHOD

Answers the Question	How do you represent testing the property of an object?
Solution	Provide a method named like a query: Prefix the property to be tested with a form or variant of the verb "be": `isOpen()`, `hasDependents()`, `wasDeleted()`, for example. Return a `boolean` from the method.
Category	Behavioral
Related Patterns	Enumerated Constants

Many classes define attributes that hold simple true-false (boolean) values or enumerated constants in a short range. For example, in tracking employees you might have the need to store whether or not the employee works part-time, full-time, or flex-time, whether the employee is tax exempt, or whether the employee is a relative of the CEO.

The employee class might also need to provide testing that depends on combined criteria or calculated information. For instance, full-time status might be calculated from the number of hours worked per week.

Regardless of whether the object property is a state variable or a derived value, means of testing the condition should be the same. For booleans, this simply means that you return the attribute directly:

```
public boolean wasHiredByCEO()
{
    return wasHiredByCEO;
}
```

For enumerated data, the instance variable representing the attribute should not be directly exposed to client developers. Instead, provide a QUERY METHOD for each possible state of the instance variable. For example:

```
public boolean isFullTime()
{
    return status == FULL_TIME;
}

public boolean isPartTime()
{
    return status == PART_TIME;
}
```

These QUERY METHODS should be named starting with a form of the verb "be" — something like "is" or "was." For example:

```
isFullTime(), isPartTime(), wasHiredByCEO()
```

These method names also improve client code readability:

```
if (employee.isFullTime())
```

You should provide converse testing methods if possible, especially for true boolean attributes. For example, if you store a boolean attribute isTaxExempt, you should provide methods isTaxExempt() and isTaxable(). Whenever possible, be positive about things. Negativity is not good for the spirit and in general is more difficult to understand. Thus for a CD player application you might have methods isTrayOpen() and isTrayClosed() (instead of isTrayNotOpen()) to represent the single boolean attribute isTrayOpen.

If you have a domain that spans more than two or three values, or if you know that the range of your domain is likely to expand, use the ENUMERATED CONSTANTS pattern instead. For example, the employee status could be represented by many values. You might implement a subclass that provides constants for full-time, part-time, flex-time, and shift-time employee status values. Refer to ENUMERATED CONSTANTS in Chapter 3, "State Patterns," for more information on this option.

COMPARING METHOD

Answers the Question	How do you order objects with respect to each other?
Solution	Implement the Comparable interface within the objects to be ordered and call Collections.sort (List). Use Collections.sort (List, Comparator) if the elements are to be sorted in a non-natural sequence.
Category	Behavioral
Related Patterns	Equality Method

One feature that was sorely missed from Java — until version 2 — is built-in sorts. How disappointing. Coming from other languages, it's been more than a decade since I had to write my own sort. Even C libraries provide the qsort() function.

Version 2 provides a merge sort as part of its Collections Framework. You may wonder why quick sort, the ever-popular sort of choice, wasn't included. The reason quick sort is so prevalent is that it is very simple to write (almost as easy to write as the justly maligned bubble sort) and gives O(n log n) performance in most cases. However, in the worst case, when the data is already sorted, performance goes to O(n^2). Merge sort is not trivial to write, but it is a stable[4] sort that is guaranteed to provide O(n log n) performance.

To sort in Java, either you must initialize the sort with a Comparator object, or the objects being sorted must implement the Comparable interface. Your sortable objects (usually your domain objects) should always define a natural sorting order — the specific order in which the objects are most often required. For a set of employees, this sort order is typically by the employees' full names. To implement a natural sorting order, declare that your class will implement the Comparable interface and provide its required compareTo() method.

The compareTo() method takes a single parameter, the object to which this is to be compared. compareTo() should return one of three domains of values. For the example x.compareTo(y):

If	Return
x < y	a negative integer
x == y	0
x > y	a positive integer

---

4 A stable sort does not reorder equal elements, which is important when you are sorting the same list repeatedly using different attributes.

There are also three important requirements that this comparison method must meet. The JDK states the requirements as following:

JDK Terms	In English, Please
sgn(x.compareTo(y)) == -sgn(y.compareTo(x)) for all x and y	If x is less than y, then y must be greater than x, and vice versa. If x is equal to y, then y equals x must also be true.
x.compareTo(y) > 0 and y.compareTo(z) > 0 implies x.compareTo(z) > 0	If x is greater than y and y is greater than z, then x must be greater than z.
x.compareTo(y) == 0 implies sgn(x.compareTo(z)) == sgn(y.compareTo(z)), for all z	If x is equal to y, then the comparisons between x and any other object return the same result as the comparison between y and the same object.

The JDK also highly recommends that if `x.compareTo(y)` returns 0, then `x.equals(y)` returns true. If this is not the case, you probably should define a Comparator object instead. Comparators are objects used to provide special case ordering for a collection. A comparator must implement the `compare(Object, Object)` method, which works the same as the `compareTo()` method except that the objects to be compared are both passed as arguments. In most cases, you want to provide an `equals()` method for your Comparator. Otherwise, the Comparator uses the default implementation of `equals()` — object identity — to compare elements.

REVERSING METHOD

Answers the Question	How do you code a smooth flow of messages?	
Solution	Add a new method to the class of a parameter. The new method takes the original receiver as a parameter and sends a "reversing" message back to the original receiver with this as a parameter.	
Category	Behavioral	
Related Patterns	None	

One of the nice features about Java is that it allows for message chaining — using the resultant object of one message send as the receiver to a subsequent message send:

```
iterator.next().toString().toLowerCase();
```

This line of code sends the message next() to an instance variable presumably containing an Iterator object; the result is an Object. This resultant object is sent the message toString(), which returns a string. This string finally gets sent the message toLowerCase() and returns another string.

Of course, this is also a not-so-nice feature if it is abused. Sending long chains of messages can make it difficult to understand what is going on. Breaking up these chains with appropriate uses of EXPLAINING TEMPORARY VARIABLE can go a long way toward making your code clear in intent.

What if you want to send a series of messages to the same receiving object? Java does not provide special syntax for this. You must explicitly code multiple statements to achieve this effect, known as cascading.

Listing 1.13   *Nice-Looking Cascade*

```
list.add("string 1");
list.add("second string");
list.add("3rd string");
list.remove("second string");
```

With the help of the text being left-aligned, as demonstrated in **Listing 1.13**, it is clear what is going on in this code. The code has a nice flow to it and is understandable at a glance. While many developers discount the value of visual considerations in code, it is extremely valuable to make your code as readable as possible. Humans generally consume things in chunks of a reasonable size; the smaller a chunk is and the more organized it is, the quicker it is interpreted by the human brain. If I throw nine coins on the floor and they fall in a random pattern, it will take you longer to count them than if they were in three rows of three.

Code is the same way. With larger methods — perhaps 10 or more lines — it will take longer to comprehend the code unless it makes judicious use of white space. Early BASIC coders would cram as much code on a single line as possible. No one with any sense does this any more; We all are good little coders because we put each statement on a separate line. You should strive to break up methods into understandable chunks, or better yet, into separate methods.

REVERSING METHOD is a visual enhancing pattern that is almost a formatting pattern. But because it involves altering behavior, it remains in this chapter. REVERSING METHOD helps you keep that flow of cascading messages looking pretty.

Occasionally you will be coding a cascading series of statements and find out that your clean flow has been rudely interrupted by a message send that has to go to a different object. **Listing 1.14** gives an example of this unfortunate code.

Listing 1.14 *Not-as-Nice-Looking Code*

```
canvas.moveTo(3, 4);
canvas.drawLineTo(7, 11);
bulletArt1.drawOn(canvas);
canvas.drawLineTo(12, 13);
bulletArt2.drawOn(canvas);
```

Using REVERSING METHOD, you first implement a `draw()` method in the class that created the canvas object. Then you simply *reverse* things and call the original `drawOn()` method, passing `this` as the parameter. The code is shown in **Listing 1.15**.

Listing 1.15 *REVERSING METHOD Example*

```
public void draw(Art art)
{
    art.drawOn(this);
}
```

Listing 1.16 shows the clean, concise cascade that is now possible, thanks to REVERSING METHOD.

Listing 1.16 *The Improved Cascade*

```
canvas.moveTo(3, 4)
canvas.drawLineTo(7, 11);
canvas.draw(bulletArt1);
canvas.drawLineTo(12, 13);
canvas.draw(bulletArt2);
```

If you want to do this with Java system classes, such as the Graphics class, you will need to create your own specialized subclasses so you can make the necessary modifications.

METHOD OBJECT

Answers the Question	How do you code a method where many lines of code share many arguments and temporary variables?
Solution	Define an inner class named after the method. Declare an instance variable in the class for each temporary variable in the original method; pass the temporary variables into the class via a single constructor. Define a method `compute()`, which triggers the process defined in the original method. Apply COMPOSED METHOD within the METHOD OBJECT.
Category	Behavioral
Related Patterns	Composed Method Parameter Object Collecting Temporary Variable

Occasionally you will come across a very long, very ugly (VLVU) method that uses a good number of stack variables and parameters as integral parts of its computation. If you attempt to apply COMPOSED METHOD to the method, you end up needing to pass the original parameters plus the large number of stack variables from method to method as parameters. You no longer have a VLVU method, but instead you have VLVU method signatures. You typically do not want to define these variables as instance variables. Not only would they clutter the definition of the class unnecessarily, but they violate the principle of instance variables by representing something other than object state.

I have come across the need for METHOD OBJECT a few times. Most of the time I solved it with PARAMETER OBJECT. But METHOD OBJECT goes one step further than PARAMETER OBJECT. It not only encapsulates the variables needed in a separate object, it also encapsulates the behavior that represents the complex method.

An abbreviated example follows. You might not bother implementing METHOD OBJECT for such a short example. Extrapolate, though, and imagine that the following method has several hundred lines involving several more tasks and several more stack variables.

A portion of the VLVU method is presented in **Listing 1.17**.

Listing 1.17   A VLVU Method

```
private void calculatePay(Employee employee,
                          int payPeriod)
{
   int baseSalary = employee.getBaseSalary();
   int contractedRate =
         employee.getContractedRate();
   boolean isContracted = contractedRate > 0;
   int hoursWorked =
         employee.getHoursWorked(payPeriod);
   String state = employee.getState();
   List taxItemizations = new ArrayList();
   List preTaxDeductions = new ArrayList();
   List postTaxDeductions = new ArrayList();

   // calculate bi-weekly pay amount
   double basePay =
      isContracted ?
         contractedRate * hoursWorked :
         baseSalary / 26;

   // calculate FICA tax
   double baseFICA = basePay * .0751;
   double ytdFICA = employee.getYtdFICA();
   double maxFICA = Payroll.getMaxFICA();
   if (ytdFICA > maxFICA)
      ficaTax = 0.0;
   else
      if (ytdFICA + baseFICA > maxFICA())
         ficaTax = maxFICA() - ytdFICA();
      else
         ficaTax = baseFICA;
   taxItemizations.add(new LineItem("FICA Tax",
                                    ficaTax));

   // calculate local tax
   boolean hasLocalTax = isInTaxDistrict(employee);
   //  yadda yadda yadda....

   // calculate state tax

   // out of state adjustments?

   // calculate federal income tax

   //  calculate medicare tax

   //  pre-tax deductions
   //     code for 401K, health care contrib, etc.
   //  post-tax deductions
   //     code for stock purchase plans,
   //       meal plans, etc.
}
```

As you can see, this is potentially a very large method. Don't bet that payroll systems you come across will have cleaner code than this. Most payroll systems I have come across seem to take pride in their inscrutable nature.

The parameters `employee` and `payPeriod` will be required in most of the computations. The COLLECTING TEMPORARY VARIABLES `taxItemizations`, `preTaxDeductions`, and `postTaxDeductions` will each be required in many separate computations. These five variables would have to be passed around to all of the various methods that would result from applying COMPOSED METHOD.

Using METHOD OBJECT instead, create a new class PayCalculator named after the original method (`calculatePay()`). Define its instance variables and constructor as in **Listing 1.18**.

Listing 1.18 *Instance Variables and Constructor for* METHOD OBJECT

```
private int payPeriod;
private Employee employee;
private List taxItemizations = new ArrayList();
private List preTaxDeductions = new ArrayList();
private List postTaxDeductions = new ArrayList();

protected PayCalculator(Employee _employee,
                        int _payPeriod)
{
   employee = _employee;
   payPeriod = _payPeriod;
}
```

Next, create a method within PayCalculator called `compute()`, and copy into it the code from the original VLVU `calculatePay()` method. The declaration of the COLLECTING TEMPORARY VARIABLES can be eliminated, as they now are available as instance variables. **Listing 1.19** shows the results.

Listing 1.19 METHOD OBJECT `compute()` *Method*

```
public compute()
{
   int baseSalary = employee.getBaseSalary();
   int contractedRate =
         employee.getContractedRate();
   boolean isContracted = contractedRate > 0;
   int hoursWorked =
         employee.getHoursWorked(payPeriod);
   String state = employee.getState();

   // calculate bi-weekly pay amount
   double basePay =
      isContracted ?
         contractedRate * hoursWorked :
         baseSalary / 26;
   //  ... rest of the method here
}
```

The original `calculatePay()` method becomes the code in **Listing 1.20**.

Listing 1.20   *Cleaned-Up VLVU Method*

```
private void calculatePay(Employee employee,
                          int payPeriod)
{

    PayCalculator calculator =
       new PayCalculator(employee,
                         payPeriod);
    calculator.compute();
}
```

Once this is in place, the next-to-last step is to ensure that the `compute()` method works. Testing must show that it mirrors the original behavior of `calculatePay()`.

Finally, apply COMPOSED METHOD to clean up the `compute()` method in PayCalculator. Almost every chunk of code identified by individual comments in the original `calculatePay()` method would become its own method. The modified `compute()` method, along with a couple of its refactored methods, would look something like **Listing 1.21**. Once again, you must test to ensure that you have not changed the required behavior.

Listing 1.21   *After Applying COMPOSED METHOD*

```
public compute()
{
    double basePay = calculateBasePay();
    calculateFICA(basePay);
    if (isInTaxDistrict())
       calculateLocalTax(basePay);
    calculateStateTax(basePay);
    calculateOutOfStateAdjustments(basePay);
    calculateFederalIncomeTax(basePay);
    calculateMedicareTax(basePay);
    calculatePreTaxDeductions();
    calculatePostTaxDeductions();
}

private double calculateBasePay()
{
    int contractedRate =
            employee.getContractedRate();
    boolean isContracted = contractedRate > 0;
```

```
if (isContracted)
    return
        contractedRate *
        employee.getHoursWorked(payPeriod);
  else
    return employee.getBaseSalary() / 26.0;
}


private void calculateFICA(double basePay)
{
  double baseFICA = basePay * .0751;
  double ytdFICA = employee.getYtdFICA();
  double maxFICA = Payroll.getMaxFICA();
  if (ytdFICA > maxFICA)
    ficaTax = 0.0;
  else
    if (ytdFICA + baseFICA > maxFICA())
      ficaTax = maxFICA() - ytdFICA();
    else
      ficaTax = baseFICA;
  taxItemizations.add(new LineItem("FICA Tax",
                                   ficaTax));
}
```

PARAMETER OBJECT

Answers the Question	How do you code a method where many lines of code share many arguments and temporary variables?
Solution	Apply COMPOSED METHOD; use an inner class to store the parameters that need to be passed from method to method. Access the parameters within the PARAMETER OBJECT directly from the COMPOSED METHODS.
Category	Behavioral
Related Patterns	Method Object Composed Method

This pattern is the converse of METHOD OBJECT.

Again, assume you have a VLVU method that uses a good number of stack variables and parameters as integral parts of its computation. Instead of creating a METHOD OBJECT to contain the attributes as encapsulated instance variables, an alternate solution is to create a new class that, for all intents and purposes, is a C struct. It will contain only instance variables representing the essential data.

You will not need accessor methods in the PARAMETER OBJECT, because you will be accessing its instance variables directly. This is one of the few cases where directly accessing instance variables externally is OK. I know, I said *never* do this. Lesson learned — never say never.

Define an inner class that stores the parameters. **Listing 1.22** demonstrates this for the payroll example from METHOD OBJECT.

Listing 1.22 *PARAMETER OBJECT Example*

```
public class Payroll
{
    // ... other methods 'n' stuff ...

    private void calculatePay(Employee employee,
                             int payPeriod)
    {
        // ...original method code here ...
    }
```

(3)
```
    class CalculatePayParms
    {
        int payPeriod;
        Employee employee;
        List taxItemizations;
        List preTaxDeductions;
```

```
         List postTaxDeductions;
      }

      //  ... other methods 'n' stuff ...
}
```

Note that the definition of the inner class CalculatePayParms goes right after `calculatePay()` (line [3]). Also note that the class is named by appending "Parms" to the method name.

Once the inner class has been declared, create an instance of it in `calculatePay()` and directly set its instance variables. This modification of `calculatePay()` is shown in **Listing 1.23**.

Listing 1.23 *Using the PARAMETER OBJECT*

```
private void calculatePay(Employee employee,
                          int payPeriod)
{
   ComputeParms parms = new ComputeParms();
   parms.taxItemizations = new ArrayList();
   parms.preTaxDeductions = new ArrayList();
   parms.postTaxDeductions = new ArrayList();
   parms.payPeriod = payPeriod;
   parms.employee = employee;
   //  ... rest of method code ...
}
```

Now you can apply COMPOSED METHOD to `calculatePay()`. For each method invoked, simply pass it the instance of ComputeParms. Within the composed methods, directly access the instance variables of ComputeParms. **Listing 1.24** shows `calculatePay()` and some associated method implementations after COMPOSED METHOD has been applied.

Listing 1.24 *After Applying COMPOSED METHOD*

```
public calculatePay()
{
   ComputeParms parms = new ComputeParms();
   parms.taxItemizations = new ArrayList();
   parms.preTaxDeductions = new ArrayList();
   parms.postTaxDeductions = new ArrayList();
   parms.payPeriod = payPeriod;
   parms.employee = employee;

   double basePay = calculateBasePay(parms);
   calculateFICA(parms, basePay);
   if (isInTaxDistrict(parms))
      calculateLocalTax(parms, basePay);
   calculateStateTax(parms, basePay);
   calculateOutOfStateAdjustments(parms, basePay);
```

(continued)

Listing 1.24 (cont.)   *After Applying* COMPOSED METHOD

```
      calculateFederalIncomeTax(parms, basePay);
      calculateMedicareTax(parms, basePay);
      calculatePreTaxDeductions(parms);
      calculatePostTaxDeductions(parms);
}


private double calculateBasePay(ComputeParms parms)
{
   int contractedRate =
          parms.employee.getContractedRate();
   boolean isContracted = contractedRate > 0;
   if (isContracted)
      return
         contractedRate *
         parms.employee.getHoursWorked(
             parms.payPeriod);
   else
      return parms.employee.getBaseSalary() / 26.0;
}


private void calculateFICA(ComputeParms parms,
                            double basePay)
{
   double baseFICA = basePay * .0751;
   double ytdFICA = parms.employee.getYtdFICA();
   double maxFICA = Payroll.getMaxFICA();
   if (ytdFICA > maxFICA)
      ficaTax = 0.0;
   else
      if (ytdFICA + baseFICA > maxFICA())
         ficaTax = maxFICA() - ytdFICA();
      else
         ficaTax = baseFICA;
   parms.taxItemizations.add(
      new LineItem("FICA Tax", ficaTax));
}
```

When should you prefer METHOD OBJECT over PARAMETER OBJECT? Use METHOD OBJECT when the number of methods resulting from applying COMPOSED METHOD becomes excessive and clutters the original class definition. Otherwise, PARAMETER OBJECT should suffice.

DEBUG PRINTING METHOD

Answers the Question	How do you provide a printable representation of an object for debugging purposes?
Solution	Override `toString()` and have it return a concise string that uniquely describes the object.
Category	Behavioral
Related Patterns	None

Java provides the method `toString()` in Object. According to the JDK documentation, the purpose of this method is to return a string that "textually represents" this object.

The behavior that Object provides is to return a string with the class name followed by a hex representation of the object's hash code, for example, "Employee@fc825d21." This sort of information will not often be very useful, so `toString()` is one of the methods that you should override in your classes.

It is ill-advised to use `toString()` for purposes of representing objects within a user interface. The implementation of the method in the class Object should be a hint that this is not something your application users want to see. There is no guarantee that `toString()` will consistently provide a user-consumable representation.

In java.io.PrintWriter and java.io.PrintStream, the `toString()` method is indirectly called by the `print(Object)` method. The `print(Object)` method first calls `String.valueOf(Object)`, which in turn sends the message `toString()` to your object to get its printable representation. System.out, the standard output stream used often for debugging purposes,[5] is a PrintStream object.

Some IDEs, such as IBM's VisualAge for Java, use `toString()` as an integral part of the development environment. Instance inspectors send the message `toString()` to objects being inspected. This gives the developer an immediate, concise description of the object. The developer can avoid digging into the object to individually inspect its instance variables, which can mean lots of mouse clicks. Having appropriate debug print representations of objects is especially valuable when inspecting collections.

---

5 What year is this? A large number of developers I have come across who are doing enterprise or other large-scale Java development do not use one of the off-the-shelf IDE packages. Instead, it's usually a home-grown environment centered around a very customizable editor of choice. Debugging hearkens back to the days of inserting DISPLAY statements in COBOL code. Java is still a very immature development platform, and has a long way to evolve.

Use `toString()` to provide a short, concise debugging string. **Listing 1.25** shows an example `toString()` method for Employee.

Listing 1.25 *A toString() Method for Employee*

```
public String toString()
{
    return getName() + " (" + getSSN() + ")";
}
```

Example output from the `toString()` method in **Listing 1.25**:

```
Joseph Schmo (999-31-9999)
```

In addition, you may wish to provide the class information, especially if the debugging string is ambiguous within the context of a collection. For example, suppose you have an inheritance hierarchy with classes Management and Grunt inheriting from the superclass Employee. If you create a list of Employee objects, you will have no effective way to determine what type of employees are contained in the collection when you are debugging. **Listing 1.26** provides a more useful `toString()` method for your Employee class by also returning the object's class name.

Listing 1.26 *A toString() Method That Prints the Class Name*

```
public String toString()
{
    return
        getClass().getName() + " [" +
        getName() + " (" + getSSN() + ")]";
}
```

which would print something like:

```
Grunt [Joseph Schmo (999-31-9999)]
```

This is one possible convention. The important thing is to decide upon a standard and stick with it. In fact, the repetitive code in **Listing 1.26** cries out for COMPOSED METHOD. Factor out the common code to support whatever convention you choose. This will also help ensure consistency of presentation. For example, you might provide a method called `classTaggedString()` and pass it both the object (so the class name can be retrieved) and the string representing the object. A possible implementation is provided in **Listing 1.27**.

Listing 1.27 *classTaggedString() Example*

```
public String classTaggedString(Object object,
                                String string)
{
    return object.getClass().getName() +
           " [" + string + "]";
}
```

The only question is where to put `classTaggedString()`. Many systems have a Debug class for managing debugging facilities; this method would probably work best as a class (static) method there.

With the above solution, your `toString()` method should look like the code in **Listing 1.28**.

Listing 1.28 *A toString() Method for Consistent Presentation*

```
public String toString()
{
    return
        Debug.classTaggedString(this,
                                getName() +
                                " (" + getSSN() +
                                ")");
}
```

METHOD COMMENT

Answers the Question	How do you comment methods?
Solution	Provide a developer-oriented comment, apart from the javadoc comment, at the beginning of a method, *only if necessary*. This comment should only communicate important information that is not obvious from the code. Refactor unclear code using other patterns, including COMPOSED METHOD.
Category	Behavioral
Related Patterns	Composed Method

Few things are more painful for the typical programmer than commenting code. More often than not, this exercise is performed well after the programming is complete, a practice generally looked upon with great disdain. But the reality is: Commenting after coding is complete requires that the programmer undergo the sometimes embarrassing task of having to understand his or her own code.

Sometimes the programmer is methodical enough to ensure that comments are inserted while he or she is coding. What this usually means is that the programmer is aware of the inscrutable nature of the code just written and figures that a comment would be prudent (in the off chance that the section of code in question has to be maintained).

Then there is the obligatory "commentator." This is either someone who is following departmental dogma to the letter or someone who perhaps should engage in a career as a legal copywriter. Virtually every line is commented, and every getter/setter method contains a comment. The volume of comments is almost always greater than the amount of code, as demonstrated in **Listing 1.29**.

Listing 1.29 *Too Many Comments!*

```
/**
 * Copies one file, byte by byte, to another.
 * Quick & dirty but costly performance-wise
 * since IO operations are not buffered.
 * @param  from  String representing the filename
 *               to copy from
 * @param  to    String representing the filename
 *               to copy to
 * @exception    IOException if opening either
 *               input or output files fails
 */
```

```
public void fileCopy(String from, // copy-from file
                     String to)    // copy-to file
    throws IOException    // exception thrown if
                          // file ops. fail
{
    DataInputStream input =    // create input stream
        new DataInputStream(new FileInputStream(from));
    DataOutputStream output = // create output stream
        new DataOutputStream(new FileOutputStream(to));
    //   attempt to loop through the input file,
    //   writing byte-by-byte to the output file for
    //   each byte read from the input file.
    //   If an IO operation against either file
    //   fails, an IO exception is thrown.  But when
    //   the end of file is reached, an EOF exception
    //   is thrown.  This EOF exception is trapped
    //   and accepted as part of normal operation --
    //   no error handling is done.  The files are
    //   subsequently closed.
    try  // trap read/write operation exceptions
    {
        while (true)  // loop infinitely
            output.writeByte(
            input.readByte()); // read & write
                               // the same byte
    }
    catch (EOFException e) {} // trap the inevitable
                             //   EOF exception
                             //   but do nothing
    finally     // regardless of result
    {
        input.close();   //  close input file
        output.close();  // close output file
    }
}
```

Not only are most of the comments in code like **Listing 1.29** useless, they tend to clutter to the code, making it more difficult to read. The worst aspect of comments is that they are just that, plain English comments — one person's interpretation of what they think is going on. There is no way to completely enforce the accuracy of comments versus code. The result is that inaccurate comments are inserted into code, and accurate comments rapidly become outdated when code is modified.

Some automation tools exist. VisualWorks Smalltalk, for example, includes a class comment checker. This tool notes the class type for all instance variables declared in the class comment. Then the class comment checker ensures that the actual messages being sent to these instance variable objects match the declared type.

The Java solution is to provide a level of automation that can expose code information to people who do not necessarily read code. Javadoc stipulates a specific format for code commenting. If the developer correctly follows this specification, javadoc can be run against the code to produce a nicely formatted, highly hypertext-oriented, indexed Web reference. Javasoft's JDK API specifications on the Web are themselves generated by javadoc.

Javadoc does some minor consistency checking, but for the most part, it just takes what it finds and spits it out in HTML format. If you forget to add an @param comment for a method parameter, javadoc doesn't complain at all. There are other problems with javadoc; in short, do not trust that javadoc will catch all documentation problems.

The real problem with javadoc, however, is that it is intended to be a tool for providing a published API specification. Yet many programmers also use it as the end-all for what comments a program should have. "If it isn't something javadoc can parse out, why bother including the comment?" But the premise of javadoc is to enhance user (client) understanding of a package, not to provide detailed documentation so a developer can maintain the contents of a package. Proper Javadoc comments will impart some information to a developer modifying the class, but only as a side effect of what they provide to a client *using* the class.

Javadoc standards *should* always be followed by the developer, but only as far as they document a package's public interface. Javadoc comments for private methods are unnecessary and only help bolster the misguided idea that they solve the code documentation problem.

So what is the solution to the documentation problem? Should every method contain a comment? Every block?

By adding an obligatory comment to every method, you have significantly increased maintenance time with possibly no gain. Programmers tend to be lazy about adding comments in the first place; why would they be any better at maintaining them? Far worse than no comment is an inaccurate comment.

Adding a comment to a getting method like the one in **Listing 1.30** is not only wasted effort, it is insulting.

Listing 1.30 *Useless Accessor Comment*

```
public String getCustomerSSN()
{
    // return the customer's SSN
    return customerSSN;
}
```

Also, if the code needs to be changed to retrieve a generic ID instead of an SSN, I warrant that you will see code like that in **Listing 1.31** fairly often.

Listing 1.31 *Useless* and *Incorrect Accessor Comment*

```
public String getCustomerID()
{
    // return the customer's SSN
    return customerID;
}
```

(4)

Now, the comment [4] implies something that is not necessarily true. What are valid things to comment?

- Confusing code: Code that is not obvious.

- Dependencies: A method requires that another method be executed first.

- To do: Code that is not complete.

- Change reason: Why code was changed in a method.

If you find yourself writing a large amount of the first type of comment — for confusing code — you need to apply more of the patterns in this book to clean it up. If you refactor your code appropriately, the amount of code that requires commenting should dwindle to well below 10%. **Listing 1.32** provides a very simple example of where a comment is necessary to explain what is being tested.

Listing 1.32 *Code That Requires a Comment*

```
if (ftpResponse.charAt(0) == '2')
    // ftp result in 200s = success
```

If this test is executed in multiple places throughout the code, the same comment will end up in all places as well. And of course, if the FTP result codes were to change, the code would have to change in all those places.

Using COMPOSED METHOD, create the new method in **Listing 1.33**.

Listing 1.33 *Factoring into a Method*

```
public boolean wasSuccessful(String ftpResponse)
{
    return ftpResponse.charAt(0) == '2';
}
```

The client (calling) code is simplified to what is shown in **Listing 1.34**.

Listing 1.34 *Look, Mom, No More Comment*

```
if (wasSuccessful(ftpResponse))
```

The end result is that the client code no longer needs a comment. Nor does the code in the wasSuccessful() method.

INTENTION-REVEALING METHOD NAME

Answers the Question	What should a method be named?
Solution	Name a method after what it does, not how it does it.
Category	Behavioral
Related Patterns	Composed Method Getting Method Setting Method Query Method

Method naming is one of the most critical parts of class design. Without appropriate public method names, clients will have no clue as to how to use the class. Without appropriate private method names, maintenance developers will spend much more time trying to understand a class.

If you use COMPOSED METHOD, you will have very short methods, each of which performs a single task that can be precisely defined in a few words. Usually the most appropriate method name will be fairly obvious. Generally it is a verb that describes the action being completed by the method — transmit(), encode(), and the like. But if your method does many different tasks, coming up with a good method name that declares what the method is doing can be rather difficult. You will find yourself with methods called processData() and doLotsOfWork().

The bulk of your methods can be categorized as action methods, testing methods, and accessor methods. Action methods, as mentioned, should be verbs. Naming conventions for accessor (getting and setting) methods are described in GETTING METHOD and SETTING METHOD. For testing methods, use the naming convention described in QUERY METHOD.

Spell out the names of your methods. Avoid abbreviations, unless they are common in the business domain of your application. Instead of getFld(), call your method getField(). Instead of fsetpos(), use setPosition(). You will type your code once (you hope); it may be read hundreds of times. The seconds you save typing are not worth it. Strive for readability.

Simple Implementations

Providing reusable methods for a class is an exercise in determining how you think the class might be used. Often the class evolves as new uses are determined, and sometimes the methods do not reflect what they are accomplishing. For some extremely simple operations, you might not even provide methods to accomplish them directly.

If you are the developer of an object, looking at how client code uses your objects can be revealing. Let's say your Employee object is in heavy use. Looking at the client code, you find the following expression scattered throughout:

```
if (employee.getTerminationDate() != null)
```

The code determines whether or not an employee is terminated.

Even in this small amount of code, there are a few problems. First, it does not read well. "Not" logic is frowned upon by many (perhaps a bit more than is necessary) and generally forces you to think more about what is really going on. Thus a comment would be prudent for the code:

```
if (employee.getTerminationDate() != null)
    // employee is terminated
```

But by now you should know that the need for a comment often cries out for you to apply COMPOSED METHOD. Except in this case, the method should be factored out of client code and into your Employee class. If your class's client developers have read this book, it's to be hoped that they have come to you by now and insisted that you make the change.

Second, even though this code represents a very simple test, it depends on a specific implementation — the fact that a termination date is null if the employee is still on the payroll. What if the Employee class changes its implementation so that open dates are represented by any date in the year 9999?

Using INTENTION-REVEALING METHOD NAME, your method on Employee should be what is shown in **Listing 1.35**.

Listing 1.35 *INTENTION-REVEALING METHOD NAME Example 1*

```
public boolean isTerminated()
{
    return getTerminationDate() != null;
}
```

This is also a QUERY METHOD.

A similar reason to apply INTENTION-REVEALING METHOD NAME is when you are exposing an implementation detail via the method name. A Stack implementation needs to provide a method to return the top element. If the Stack is implemented with a Vector, lastElement() provides this functionality. This does not reveal intent, it reveals implementation. It also breaks encapsulation — What if I change my Stack to use a data structure where returning the first element is more efficient?

Use INTENTION-REVEALING METHOD NAME to remap the implementation to a more meaningful message. **Listing 1.36** provides the top() method for the stack example.

Listing 1.36 INTENTION-REVEALING METHOD NAME *Example 2*

```
public Object top()
{
    return lastElement();
}
```

One interesting use of INTENTION-REVEALING METHOD NAME in the JDK has been to support deprecated methods. The odd thing is that the methods to be ultimately phased out are the ones that have the actual implementation. For example, the java.awt.List component has deprecated the clear() method in favor of removeAll(). But if you look at the code, removeAll() ends up delegating to clear(), which is where the real work ends up getting done.

You would think things would be the other way around — that the deprecated method should be the one incurring the performance penalty of a second message send. The decision to delegate from the newer method to the older one was done for backward-compatibility reasons.

Chapter 2   *BEHAVIOR — MESSAGES*

Most objects communicate with other objects in order to be useful. Even if
you have an object that sits there and quietly processes, it is probably communicating with other objects. Maybe it is working with Strings or manipulating a file — these are still objects that your object is talking to.

Objects also communicate with themselves to invoke their own behavior.
Your body is an example of an object whose systems communicate with each
other. Your brain sends messages to your muscle systems to get them to do
work. If you have followed the patterns in this book, particularly COMPOSED
METHOD, your objects may have even more internal communication than
they have external communication.

The mechanism by which your object communicates, either with itself or
with other objects, is the message. To get an object to do something, you
send it a message. It is entirely up to the object that receives the message to
determine what will happen. The implementation in Java when an object
receives a message is to invoke a method with the appropriate signature. In
C++, the implementation is for a member function to be called.

There is a fine line between a method pattern and a message pattern.
Methods are more about specific implementation and organization of code
within your class. The message patterns within this chapter are about how
your methods communicate with each other. They are intended to help you
coordinate the flow of messages through your objects.

MESSAGE

Answers the Question	How do you invoke computation?
Solution	Send a message in the form of a function call to an object or class; let the receiver decide which method to invoke.
Category	Behavioral
Related Patterns	Choosing Message Decomposing Message

Subroutines have been around, at least conceptually, since long before modern computing. Charles Babbage had the idea of creating a library of routines for his Analytical Engine in the 1800s. Grace Hopper wrote the first modern computer function to calculate the sine of a number in the 1940s.[1] COBOL evolved the ability to execute subroutines; C has always provided functions.

Up until object-oriented languages, the scope of functions has been more or less at a global or module level. As long as a function's declaration is available to you, you can execute it in any context. Object-oriented languages introduced the concept of scoping method execution to a logical class definition.

Java and Smalltalk go one step further and require *all* methods to be implemented within a class, which means they can only be invoked in that context. Unlike C++, they do not have a global function. Thus, all messages being sent to invoke functionality must be sent to an object (or a class, which is an object in Smalltalk anyway).

The concept of polymorphism in object-oriented languages allows for dynamic determination of which subroutine is executed as the result of a message send. Send a message to an object in Java and the class of the object determines which method is invoked. The correct method will be executed whether the method is implemented in the class of the receiving object or in one of its superclasses. A method with the same name might be implemented in one of several classes; the class of the receiving object is what makes the determination. The receiving object may also have implemented several methods with the same name but different parameter types. Determination of the parameter type passed in the message send will lead to the correct method being executed.

CHOOSING MESSAGE

Answers the Question	How do you execute one of several alternatives?
Solution	Send a message to an object; let the class of the object determine its behavior (polymorphism).
Category	Behavioral
Related Patterns	None

Languages always provide good ways to abuse them. Despite the hype, Java is no different. Some constructs available in Java give you a world of possibilities, but it's like giving a china doll to a child: you must tell them to look but not touch because of the potential for disaster.

In Java, `instanceof` is one of these fragile toys. In certain cases, there are valid uses for `instanceof`. The common implementation of the `equals()` method, for example, requires that you test the parameter being passed to your object to ensure that it is of the same class. But in most cases, use of `instanceof` points out that your objects could perhaps be better organized. **Listing 2.1** provides an example of how `instanceof` is often abused:

Listing 2.1 *Not a Good Use of `instanceof`*

```
double annualCompensation = 0;
if (employee instanceof Contractor)
    annualCompensation =
        (Contractor)employee.getHourlyRate * 2000;
else
    if (employee instanceof Grunt)
        annualCompensation =
            (Grunt)employee.getMonthlySalary() * 12;
    else
        if (employee instanceof Manager)
            annualCompensation =
                (Manager)employee.getContractRate() *
                (Manager)employee.getContractPeriod();
```

The use of `instanceof` here is akin to a switch statement; you can imagine the multiple cascading `if` statements if new classifications of employees are added. There are several drawbacks to this approach:

- When a new class is added, all methods that use this `instanceof` construct must be modified.

- `instanceof` is an expensive operation.

- The code quickly becomes difficult to follow, especially if a large number of conditionals must be tested.

CHOOSING MESSAGE takes advantage of one of the three main precepts of object orientation, polymorphism: "one interface, many methods." Polymorphism as implemented in Java allows for a message to be sent to an instance variable; the class of the object referenced by the instance variable determines which actual method is invoked. The method `size()` is a polymorphic method prevalent in the Java class library.

For the example shown in **Listing 2.1**, the result of applying CHOOSING MESSAGE is that each employee subclass contains its own method to return the annual compensation. The result is shown in **Listing 2.2**.

Listing 2.2   *Using CHOOSING MESSAGE*

```java
public class Contractor
{
    // ...
    public double getAnnualCompensation()
    {
        return getHourlyRate() * 2000;
    }
}

public class Grunt
{
    // ...
    public double getAnnualCompensation()
    {
        return getMonthlySalary() * 12;
    }
}

public class Manager
{
    // ...
    public double getAnnualCompensation()
    {
        return getContractRate() *
                getContractPeriod();
    }
}
```

After adding `getAnnualCompensation()` to the superclass Employee as an abstract method, your client code becomes:

```java
employee.getAnnualCompensation();
```

Advantages? You no longer need to do any casting. The `if` statements go away. `instanceof` no longer needs to be used. Best of all, you end up with one-line methods that need no comments.

To avoid embedding compensation calculations into Employee objects, where they probably do not belong, you could have used the Visitor pattern as described in *Design Patterns*.

DECOMPOSING MESSAGE

Answers the Question	How do you invoke parts of a computation?
Solution	Send several messages (implicitly) to `this`.
Category	Behavioral
Related Patterns	Composed Method

Good old functional decomposition never goes away. Once you have used a good OO design process to come up with a subsystem of objects and public methods, COMPOSED METHOD requires that your objects be broken up into small, comprehensible chunks. Ideally these chunks should only be doing one thing, but that is not always possible. Some methods are controller or driver methods, responsible for coordinating a sequence of complex events.

The VLVU method `calculatePay()` in the METHOD OBJECT pattern is an example of a driver method. It must sequence a number of very complex actions.

After you have applied COMPOSED METHOD, you will end up with a series of method calls to accomplish the subtasks in `calculatePay()`. Each of these methods is invoked by a series of messages to `this`. **Listing 2.3** clearly shows the steps that must occur in `calculatePay()`.

Listing 2.3   *Decomposing Message Example*

```
private void calculatePay(Employee employee,
                          int payPeriod)
{
   calculateBiWeeklyPayAmount();
   calculateFICATax();
   calculateLocalTax();
   calculateStateTax();
   addOutOfStateAdjustments();
   calculateFederalIncomeTax();
   calculateMedicareTax();
   subtractPreTaxDeductions();
   subtractPostTaxDeductions();
}
```

If you look at the original VLVU code in METHOD OBJECT, you will note that I have taken the comments intended to break the code up into sections and converted them almost verbatim into method names.

DISPATCHED INTERPRETATION

Answers the Question	How can two objects cooperate when one wishes to conceal its representation?
Solution	Encapsulate the representation within the responsible object. Create an interface that client objects must implement. Client objects dispatch back to the responsible object a request for one of its interface methods to be executed.
Category	Behavioral
Related Patterns	Mediating Protocol

Like frequent use of the `instanceof` operator, use of switch statements[2] can often point out the need for better code organization. In an ideal object world, each object has its own responsibilities. If your object is shirking its responsibilities, then every client of your object will have to do the work that your object was too lazy to do. If a client object must code a switch statement on one of your object's attributes, then other clients will no doubt need to code the same switch statement. This would mean code duplication, an enemy of good object-oriented programming.

Also, by depending on a client developer to properly code the switch statement, you run the risk of getting runtime errors. This can occur if the domain of your object changes and client code has not been properly updated.

You really want to code the switch statement once and only once, which means putting it where it belongs — in your object. DISPATCHED INTERPRETATION provides a pattern that allows your object to reclaim its proper responsibilities.

Suppose you are an order entry developer responsible for the Order object. An order can be a new order, a cancellation, or modification of specific services attached to the order, including deletion or addition of services. **Listing 2.4** is a small portion of the Order class, which allows access to an order's type (an ENUMERATED CONSTANT).

Listing 2.4 *Order Class Allowing for Type Specification*

```
package order;

public class Order
{
    private OrderType type;
```

2 I use the term *switch statements* also to refer to cascading of constructs where you are testing a single instance variable against multiple values. Yet another deficiency of Java — Why include switch statements if they are only going to support native ints?

```
    public Order(OrderType _type)
    {
        type = _type;
    }
    public OrderType getType()
    {
        return type;
    }
}
```

Orders can be processed by a number of other systems, including fulfillment, pricing, and billing systems. The BillingSystem class in **Listing 2.5** demonstrates typical client code before the use of DISPATCHED INTERPRETATION. **Listing 2.5** shows how the billing system must determine the type of order to be able to bill it.

Listing 2.5 *Switch Statement External to Object*

```
public class BillingSystem
{
    public void bill(Order order)
    {
        OrderType type = order.getType();
        if (type.equals(OrderType.NEW))
            System.out.println("new");
        else
            if (type.equals(OrderType.CANCEL))
                System.out.println("cancel");
        else
            if (type.equals(OrderType.ADD_SERVICE))
                System.out.println("add service");
        else
            if (type.equals(OrderType.REMOVE_SERVICE))
                System.out.println("rmv service");
        else
            if (type.equals(OrderType.MODIFY_SERVICE))
                System.out.println("mod service");
    }
}
```

Let's get this switch logic into the Order object where it belongs. You must first define a Java interface. Create one method in the interface for each possible order type. The interface will force all interested clients to implement each of the possible order action methods. The action represented in each method name should be generic. This allows other interested parties (such as the pricing system) to use the methods in any context without the names being misleading. However, you must also ensure that client objects will have no naming conflicts with the methods in the interface. For this example, implement the interface shown in **Listing 2.6**.

Listing 2.6   *OrderProcessor Interface*

```
public interface OrderProcessor
{
    public void
        processOrderNew(Order order);
    public void     -
        processOrderCancel(Order order);
    public void
        processOrderAddService(Order order);
    public void
        processOrderRemoveService(Order order);
    public void
        processOrderModifyService(Order order);
}
```

Use the generic action verb "process" along with the class name "Order" to help create a unique method name. Next, the Order object must broadcast these operations based on its type, as in **Listing 2.7**.

Listing 2.7   *Switch Statement Internal to Object*

```
public void
    processBy(OrderProcessor processor)
{
    if (type.equals(OrderType.NEW))
        processor.processOrderNew(this);
    else
        if (type.equals(OrderType.CANCEL))
            processor.processOrderCancel(this);
    else
        if (type.equals(OrderType.ADD_SERVICE))
            processor.processOrderAddService(this);
    else
        if (type.equals(OrderType.REMOVE_SERVICE))
            processor.processOrderRemoveService(this);
    else
        if (type.equals(OrderType.MODIFY_SERVICE))
            processor.processOrderModifyService(this);
}
```

So now you have the switch statement in the Order object where it belongs. Note that this method is named `processBy()` and takes an OrderProcessor as its parameter. This should be a hint to you that an interested client object will be calling back to the Order object via `processBy()` and will be passing itself back as the parameter. Sure enough, the `bill()` method in the billing system now has only the single line of code:

```
order.processBy(this);
```

It no longer has a switch statement. Instead, the Billing System class must be modified so that it implements the OrderProcessor interface and provides the required methods. **Listing 2.8** provides the modified BillingSystem object.

Listing 2.8 *The Modified BillingSystem Client*

```
public class BillingSystem
   implements OrderProcessor
{
   public void bill(Order order)
   {
      order.processBy(this);
   }
   public void
      processOrderNew(Order order)
   {
      System.out.println("new");
   }
   public void
      processOrderCancel(Order order)
   {
      System.out.println("cancel");
   }
   public void
      processOrderAddService(Order order)
   {
      System.out.println("add service");
   }
   public void
      processOrderRemoveService(Order order)
   {
      System.out.println("remove service");
   }
   public void
      processOrderModifyService(Order order)
   {
      System.out.println("modifying service");
   }
}
```

This looks like more code, doesn't it? Indeed, there may be additional lines of code, but you now have the guarantee that your client objects will be able to properly manage your object's attribute states without having to code a switch statement. You have also eliminated any client knowledge of how Order encoded its types, which frees you to change the encoding without any external impacts. Not to mention that your code is a lot cleaner, making it easier to read and maintain.

DOUBLE DISPATCH

Answers the Question	How do you delegate responsibility based on the classes of two receiving objects?
Solution	Send a message to the argument; append the name of this class to the message name, and pass `this` as a parameter to the message.
Category	Behavioral
Related Patterns	None

Most OO languages available today, including Java, Smalltalk, and C++, support a concept called single dispatch. This is a fancy term; all it means is that when a message is sent, two pieces of information are used to determine which method is invoked: the receiving object and the message name. The class of the receiving object determines where the method corresponding to the message name is implemented. Double dispatch (twice as fancy a term, I suppose) is supported directly by a few languages, including CLOS. It means that the method being invoked depends on the message name and *two* receiving objects.

Java does not directly support DOUBLE DISPATCH. This pattern describes how to implement it in your methods.

The classic place where DOUBLE DISPATCH is used is in mathematical operations involving various types. But because you can't modify the definition of numeric objects in Java (e.g., Integer, Double) and because native types (e.g., ints, floats) are not first-class objects,[3] the example would not be very useful. DOUBLE DISPATCH requires the ability to modify all classes involved as well as the ability to send messages to all operands involved.

An example of DOUBLE DISPATCH that you would actually be able to implement is in the context of the Visitor Pattern described in *Design Patterns*. A Visitor object provides an operation that is to be performed on one or more objects in a collection. It allows you to add functionality without changing the classes of the objects on which it operates.

The following (abbreviated) example demonstrates calculating scores for a fantasy football-league application. The application contains a football

---

3 This is another problem I have with Java. Wrapper objects (such as Integer and Boolean) in Java are a hack to allow the primitive types (int, double, for example) to coexist in a real-object world. You cannot send a message to a native type, nor can you store it in a collection other than an array, so you must first wrap it in a first-class object. Unfortunately, the wrappers do not support much except printing and simple comparisons. So you spend half your time shuttling native types back and forth between wrapper objects. This is something I have resented since I first worked with Java. For more information and a legitimate proposal for a solution, refer to Alpert, Sherman R. "Primitive Types Considered Harmful." *Java Report*. New York, NY: SIGS Publications, November 1998, pp. 49–65.

player hierarchy, with Quarterback, Kicker, RunningBack, and so forth, all inheriting from Player. The Visitor pattern is used to remove the calculation of scores from the player classes. This promotes optimal flexibility and reuse: The player classes can be used in any context without the extraneous clutter of score calculations, and the score calculations can be replaced without impacting the player classes.

First things first — players must be objects that can be visited. An interface called Visitable is declared (see **Listing 2.9**). The interface simply says that an object will accept a Visitor.

Listing 2.9 *The Visitable Interface*

```
public interface Visitable
{
    public void accept(Visitor visitor);
}
```

The Player superclass implements the interface and provides the `accept()` method. This is where DOUBLE DISPATCH comes into play. The whole point of Visitor is to avoid implementing functionality that doesn't belong in the Player subclasses. With DOUBLE DISPATCH, the responsibility for calculating scores is delegated back out to the Visitor subclasses. To implement DOUBLE DISPATCH:

1. Send a message to the argument (`visitor` in this example).

2. Pass `this` as a parameter to the message.

Listing 2.10 demonstrates how the Player class is modified.

Listing 2.10 *Player Implementation of Visitable*

```
public class Player
    implements Visitable
{
    // ... constructor & other methods here ...

    public void accept(Visitor visitor)
    {
        visitor.visit(this);
    }
}
```

The second part of the solution is to implement the Visitor hierarchy. Define a Visitor superclass (**Listing 2.11**) with the abstract method `visit(Visitable)`. This abstract method is the one that will be dispatched from the `accept()` method in the player classes.

Listing 2.11 *The Visitor Superclass*

```
public abstract class Visitor
{
    public abstract void
        visit(Visitable visitable);
}
```

The real work is done in the Visitor subclasses. The concrete visitor example in **Listing 2.12** calculates the Quarterback scores.

Listing 2.12 *Concrete Visitor Example*

```
public class QuarterbackVisitor
   extends Visitor
{
   int totalScore = 0;
   public void
      visit(Visitable visitable)
   {
      Quarterback qb = (Quarterback)visitable;
      totalScore += qb.getNumberOfTDs() * 6 +
                    qb.getNumberOfCompletions();
   }
   public int getTotalScore()
   {
      return totalScore;
   }
}
```

You will have a Visitor subclass for every Player subclass.

So how is the Visitor used? The following example (**Listing 2.13**) loops through a list of quarterbacks (qbs) and uses a QuarterbackVisitor object to calculate the total score for all quarterbacks.

Listing 2.13 *Example of Visitor Use*

```
public int totalQBScore(List qbs)
{
   QuarterbackVisitor qbVisitor =
      new QuarterbackVisitor();

   Iterator iterator = qbs.iterator();
   while (iterator.hasNext())
   {
      Quarterback qb =
         (Quarterback)iterator.next();
      qb.accept(qbVisitor);
   }

   return qbVisitor.getTotalScore();
}
```

The Visitor pattern demonstrates some key features of good object-oriented design. Most importantly, it demonstrates how to delegate responsibilities where they belong via the use of DOUBLE DISPATCH as a consistent pattern for implementing the delegation.

MEDIATING PROTOCOL

Answers the Question	How do you code the interaction between two objects that need to remain independent?
Solution	Refine the protocol between the objects so that the words used are consistent.
Category	Behavioral
Related Patterns	Dispatched Interpretation Double Dispatch

Tight object coupling is avoided in object development. Once you have messages going back and forth between two or more objects, they must coexist — one cannot be used without the other. Worse, it is difficult to maintain any of the objects involved in this web of objects. Tracing the messages going back and forth between the objects can be extremely difficult. Maintaining any one of the objects runs the risk of breaking another object.

Like all rules, the rule of keeping objects loosely coupled must sometimes be broken. And anytime you do break a rule, it behooves you to explain yourself — not so much to make an excuse, as to document just what is going on.

Tight coupling requires you to document just which messages end up flowing between the objects involved. The best way to document things is in code itself. For the order entry/billing system example in DISPATCHED INTERPRETATION, the messages sent by the Order that must be implemented by the billing system are documented in the OrderProcessor interface shown in **Listing 2.14**.

Listing 2.14   *The OrderProcessor Interface*

```
public interface OrderProcessor
{
   public void
      processOrderNew(Order order);
   public void
      processOrderCancel(Order order);
   public void
      processOrderAddService(Order order);
   public void
      processOrderRemoveService(Order order);
   public void
      processOrderModifyService(Order order);
}
```

The billing system couples back to the order in its `bill()` method (shown in **Listing 2.15**).

Listing 2.15 *Tight Coupling*

```
public void bill(Order order)
{
    order.processBy(this);
}
```

MEDIATING PROTOCOL has you ensure that messages going back and forth between coupled objects are consistent. Thus the `bill()` method sends the `processBy()` message to its order parameter. In turn, the order sends a message whose name starts with `processOrder` from its `processBy()` method (see **Listing 2.16**).

Listing 2.16 *Consistent Messages Used for Coupled Objects*

```
public void
    processBy(OrderProcessor processor)
{
    if (type.equals(OrderType.NEW))
        processor.processOrderNew(this);
    // ...
}
```

I liken interfaces to contracts that a client must follow. For tightly coupled objects, interfaces allow you to predefine just how your object will communicate with its clients and vice versa. The MEDIATING PROTOCOL pattern becomes almost automatically enforced with interfaces.

SUPER

Answers the Question	How do you invoke superclass behavior?
Solution	Explicitly send a message to `super` as the receiving object.
Category	Behavioral
Related Patterns	Extending Super Modifying Super

The ability to use `super` to explicitly call superclass methods is one of those Java features that needs to be used carefully. You generally want to be sending messages to `this` and assume that if there is no corresponding method implemented directly in `this` object, it will be found somewhere up the inheritance hierarchy. By directly referring to `super`, you are tightly coupling your subclass to your superclass.

The only time you want to use `super` is to invoke the method with the same name in the superclass. There are two legitimate reasons for doing this, described in EXTENDING SUPER and MODIFYING SUPER. There is never a legitimate reason for one method to invoke super on a method with a different name.

In most cases, your subclasses will be overriding superclass behavior. When building a class, part of the reason for using COMPOSED METHOD is to refactor behavior into small methods that can be overridden if necessary. Java has an unfortunate catch-22, however, that often prevents successful inheritance: the `final` keyword.

By definition, the `final` keyword allows you to finalize a method, which means it cannot be overridden in a subclass. For strict object-design purposes, normally there is little good reason to prohibit subclassing. You rarely know that no one will ever want to subclass off your object.

The reason that use of `final` is so prevalent is that it has the side effect of increasing performance.[4] This is because if Java can know in which class a specific method is defined (i.e., that a subclass cannot override a method definition), it can inline the code. Because Java is so miserably slow, developers tend to squeeze every bit of execution time out. Using `final` is an easy way to do this. Remember, only make sacrifices for performance when there is a performance problem.

---

4 The `final` keyword does have legitimate uses, of course. The Template Method pattern in *Design Patterns* allows for definition of an incomplete or skeleton algorithm. Subclasses override pieces of the algorithm in the form of methods called from the Template Method. In this context, `final` is used to ensure that the template algorithm cannot be compromised in a subclass. Another use for final is in creating immutable instances. The JDK String class produces String objects that cannot be changed. If String was not defined as final and was subclassed, subclass methods could conceivably alter the String contents.

EXTENDING SUPER

Answers the Question	How do you add to the implementation of a superclass method?
Solution	Override the superclass method. Call the superclass method from within the overriding method using `super`.
Category	Behavioral
Related Patterns	Super Modifying Super

The main reason you would want to extend behavior in a superclass method is to avoid duplication of code, which is always a noble goal.

You will see valid uses of EXTENDING SUPER most often in constructor code. Subclass constructors need to take on all parameters necessary to create valid instances of the class. Instead of redundantly executing the same code as in the superclass to set the constructor parameters, you invoke the superclass constructor and pass along parameters representing all instance variables not defined in the subclass.

Listing 2.17 *EXTENDING SUPER Example*

```
public class Manager extends Employee
{
    private int contractedRate;
    private boolean hasGoldenParachute;
    public Manager(String name,
                   String ssn,
                   int _contractedRate,
                   boolean _hasGoldenParachute)
    {
        super(name, ssn);
        contractedRate = _contractedRate;
        hasGoldenParachute = _hasGoldenParachute;
    }
}
```

(1)

In **Listing 2.17,** `name` and `ssn` are set (at line [1]) using the constructor within the Employee superclass because Manager does not define them.

Apart from extending constructor initializations, EXTENDING SUPER is used frequently in the Decorator design pattern. The example in **Listing 2.18** shows how auditing can be added to a transaction facility through a subclass extension:

Listing 2.18 *Decorator Use of EXTENDING SUPER*

```
public void execute(Transaction xn)
{
    log.add(xn);
    super.execute(xn);
}
```

MODIFYING SUPER

Answers the Question	How do you change superclass behavior when you do not have the ability to directly modify the superclass?
Solution	Override the superclass method. Invoke it using `super`. Execute code that modifies the results.
Category	Behavioral
Related Patterns	Composed Method

MODIFYING SUPER is one of those last-resort patterns. The only excuse for using this pattern is if you are unable to fix the superclass that is forcing you down this less-than-happy path. The need for MODIFYING SUPER points out that the superclass could use some refactoring.

If you are fortunate, the developer of the superclass is at hand. If that is the case, your job is to seek out that developer and make your case for code modifications. Take a copy of this book to support your argument. If you cannot sway the developer, or if the superclass has been developed by a third party, you must use MODIFYING SUPER.

A contrived example follows. Someone else has built a superclass to provide a panel containing an OK button (see **Listing 2.19**).

Listing 2.19 *Unfactored Superclass Method*

```
public Component createButtonPanel()
{
    JButton button = new JButton("OK");
    button.setBackground(Color.yellow);
    JPanel pane = new JPanel();
    pane.add(button);
    return pane;
}
```

You need this panel, but unfortunately your button has to be blue. You do not want to rewrite the code in your subclass (perhaps there is a lot more going on in the method than these five lines of code). Using MODIFYING SUPER, the overridden method is shown in **Listing 2.20**.

Listing 2.20 *MODIFYING SUPER Example*

```
       public Component createButtonPanel()
       {
(2)        Component pane = super.createButtonPanel();
(3)        JButton button =
             (JButton)(((Container)pane).getComponent(0));
(4)        button.setBackground(Color.blue);
           return pane;
       }
```

The ugliness of the MODIFYING SUPER pattern reveals itself in just the three lines of code in **Listing 2.20**. You first explicitly call the superclass `createButtonPanel()` method and grab its return value (line [2]), the panel to be returned. In this case, you know that the panel contains only one component — the JButton — so you can use `getComponent()` with an index value to access it directly (line [3]). Finally, you execute `setBackground()` against the JButton with your preferred color (line [4]).

If the superclass method had put more components in the container, your subclass hack to modify one of those components would definitely be more complex. In any case, you run a considerable risk that your method will break if the superclass implementation of `createButtonPanel()` changes.

In this example, the superclass developer should have used DEFAULT VALUE METHOD to supply the color for the button. If that was the case, you could simply override that default method in your subclass to provide the preferred color.

DELEGATION

Answers the Question	What is an alternative to inheritance for reusing implementations?
Solution	Delegate work requested of an object to another object.
Category	Behavioral
Related Patterns	Simple Delegation Self-Delegation

Inheritance is my least favorite of the three main object-orientation concepts, well behind encapsulation and polymorphism. A major downside of inheritance is that it can introduce a very tight vertical coupling in your objects. Once you have defined a deep inheritance hierarchy, it becomes very difficult to modify public or even protected behavior up toward the root of the hierarchy.

In C++ development, where multiple inheritance (MI) is possible, the practice of inheriting from multiple classes in order to provide object composition is commonplace. While this may be convenient, it is not good practice — using inheritance implies that your object is one of the things it inherits from. An analogy is an automotive engine, comprised of pistons, valves, a fuel injection system, and so on. The engine is not any one of its parts, however. There are valid reasons for using multiple inheritance, but they are few and far between and object composition is not one of them. I consider the elimination of MI in Java to be one of the wiser decisions in the development of the language.

In most cases, what you truly want is to compose an object of other component objects. When your object receives a request, you may well choose to pass it on, or delegate it, to one of its components. As an analogy: An automotive engine receives the message "accelerate." The engine itself does not do the work; it passes the message on to the fuel injection system to begin accomplishing the task.

Use the SIMPLE DELEGATION pattern when you can simply ask another object to blindly perform an operation. The SELF-DELEGATION pattern is useful when the second object needs the ability to send a message back to the original, delegating object.

SIMPLE DELEGATION

Answers the Question	How do you delegate behavior when the delegate needs no information from the original receiving object?
Solution	Send the message from the original receiving object to the delegate without changing it.
Category	Behavioral
Related Patterns	Delegation Self-Delegation

SIMPLE DELEGATION usually involves loosely coupled objects. A method is invoked in a delegator object; it simply delegates the message to another object without any information from itself. The object delegated to needs to know nothing about the delegator. Return values are passed straight out to the object that originally called the method.

The most common use of SIMPLE DELEGATION is in an instance when you have an object that is implemented using other components. A common mistake is to use inheritance in this situation.

For example, Java provides no stack. The easiest way to provide stack functionality is to inherit from an ArrayList. You could use the List interface, but that would require implementing several operations that are not useful to a stack, such as `asArray()`.

Pushing an object onto the stack is simply `add(object)`; popping from the stack is `remove(stack.size() - 1)`. The only other methods of use are `size()` and `isEmpty()`.

So, you declare the Stack as extending ArrayList. Immediately the Stack class is subject to abuse. Via inheritance, Stack exposes ArrayList's method `remove(int)`, which allows the stack user to remove an element at any position within the stack.

What you are trying to do — inherit the ArrayList but encapsulate its methods — is referred to in C++ as private inheritance.[5] With C++, multiple inheritance is possible, and often subclasses are built from multiple parent classes, using the "has-a" relationship and not the "is a" relationship. An engine has a piston, but to say an engine is a piston is incorrect. In C++, however, this works because inheritance can be treated as private — the engine encapsulates the behaviors of the piston. In Java there is no way to encapsulate methods from an extended class other than to override them.

---

5 Meyers, Scott. *Effective C++*. Reading, MA: Addison-Wesley Publishing Co., p. 146. 1992.

The preferred technique in Java is to implement an interface. In the stack example, List provides a perfect interface to implement. Most destructive methods in List — add, remove, and so forth — are declared as optional, thus Stack would not need to implement them as public methods. The problem, however, is that semantically the Stack is still not a List. List requires implementation of the method d subList(), a view on the List that once more opens the stack up to abuse. All I have to do is code stack.subList(x, x+y).clear() and my unsuspecting stack is in sad shape.

The optimal answer for implementing Stack ends up being object composition. Stack is composed of an ArrayList. It contains an instance variable declared as ArrayList stack. Many of the relevant messages that Stack needs to respond to — isEmpty() and size() — are simply passed on unchanged to the stack object. This is SIMPLE DELEGATION, shown in **Listing 2.21**.

Listing 2.21 *SIMPLE DELEGATION* **Examples**

```
public boolean isEmpty()
{
    return stack.isEmpty();
}
public int size()
{
    return stack.size();
}
```

The irrelevant and potentially harmful messages understood by ArrayList can be ignored. Encapsulation saves the day once again.

SELF-DELEGATION

Answers the Question	How do you delegate behavior to a secondary object when it needs to be able to send messages back to the original receiving object?
Solution	Send along this as a parameter to the message being sent to the delegate.
Category	Behavioral
Related Patterns	Delegation Simple Delegation

SIMPLE DELEGATION works fine if the delegate can do its work without involving the original receiving object. Often, however, the delegate needs the ability to send messages back to the original receiver. SELF-DELEGATION provides the simple technique of passing the original object off to the delegate as a parameter. The less of this the better, as SELF-DELEGATION introduces tight coupling between the original receiver and the delegate.

An example of SELF-DELEGATION from the JDK itself can be found in java.net.URL. A URL object embeds a handler instance variable, which stores an instance of URLStreamHandler. URLStreamHandler is an abstract superclass whose concrete subclasses provide the actual connection logic for various protocols such as http, ftp, and gopher. The toString() method provided in URL defers the job of returning a printable representation to the URLStreamHandler instance.

It turns out that toString() is an implementation of INTENTION-REVEALING METHOD NAME layered on top of the URL method toExternalForm(). The implementation of toString(), in the JDK is as follows:

```
public String toString()
{
    return toExternalForm();
}
```

The method that implements SELF-DELEGATION is toExternalForm():

```
public String toExternalForm()
{
    return handler.toExternalForm(this);
}
```

The actual logic for `toExternalForm()` in URLStreamHandler needs to send quite a few messages back to the URL object in order to provide a printable representation. In **Listing 2.22**, note all the messages being sent to the URL parameter u.

Listing 2.22 *toExternalForm()* *in URLStreamHandler*

```
protected String toExternalForm(URL u)
{
    String result = u.getProtocol() + ":";
    if ((u.getHost() != null) &&
        (u.getHost().length() > 0))
    {
        result = result + "//" + u.getHost();
        if (u.getPort() != -1)
        {
            result += ":" + u.getPort();
        }
    }
    result += u.getFile();
    if (u.getRef() != null)
    {
        result += "#" + u.getRef();
    }
    return result;
}
```

Excessive use of SELF-DELEGATION can indicate a need for moving logic back into the original receiving class.

PLUGGABLE METHOD NAME

Answers the Question	How do you invoke different methods based on another factor?
Solution	Create an instance variable to store the name of the appropriate method to be invoked; append "Message" to the end of this variable name. With Java reflection capabilities, create the corresponding java.lang.reflect.Method object using the message name, and execute it via `invoke()`.
Category	Behavioral
Related Patterns	None

PLUGGABLE METHOD NAME can be used when you need to execute a different method on an instance variable, depending on its class or some other factor.

PLUGGABLE METHOD NAME is a pattern I had to rewrite. The initial example involved a new entry-field class that could store any object, not just a string. Each object would be able to provide its own method name that returned a printable representation of the object. This method name would be passed to the entry constructor. When the entry field needed to display, it would send the stored method name to the object that the entry field was holding and get back the string to be shown in the interface.

Lesson learned from Jerry Jackson: familiar patterns do not always translate well from one language to another. In Smalltalk, PLUGGABLE METHOD NAME is an acceptable solution to a number of problems. Java certainly provides a way to implement PLUGGABLE METHOD NAME via its reflection capabilities. However, there is often a better solution that can be implemented in Java, using interfaces.

For the entry field problem, the better solution would be to force objects interested in using the new widget to implement an interface — UIDisplayable, for example. This interface would define a standard method, `printString()`, for example, that must return a string describing the object. With this interface, an entry field would be able to assume that it could send the `printString()` message to a stored object and receive back an appropriate string.

There are high costs to reflection capabilities, so using an interface-based solution is greatly preferred. With reflections, there is no compile-time-type checking to ensure that all your meta information is correct. Reflection operations also are notoriously slow, and they have the effect of making your code considerably more difficult to understand and debug.

Even in Smalltalk, where there is little compile-time checking, the norm is still to only use reflections when absolutely necessary. In that environment, use of #perform: and similar methods can make image packaging difficult.

Make sure that you have no other course of action before you introduce the negatives associated with reflections into your code. Reflections are most useful in meta-type applications, where you are digging into Java code itself. Debuggers, compilers, object inspectors, test tools, and performance profilers can fall into this category.

Listing 2.23 is a bare-bones method-timing class that demonstrates PLUGGABLE METHOD NAME. It is a nonintrusive means of testing. The class containing the method being tested does not need to be modified to be able to run the test.

Listing 2.23 *MethodTimer.java*

```
import java.lang.reflect.Method;
import java.lang.reflect.InvocationTargetException;
import java.util.Collections;
import java.util.Collection;
import java.util.Date;
public class MethodTimer
{
    private Object instance;
    private Method method;
    private Object[] parameters;

    public MethodTimer(Object _instance,
                        String messageToTime,
                        Class[] parameterTypes,
                        Collection _parameters)
        throws NoSuchMethodException
    {
        instance = _instance;
        parameters = _parameters.toArray();
        Class classToTime = instance.getClass();
        method =
            classToTime.getMethod(messageToTime,
                                    parameterTypes);
    }

    public long run()
        throws IllegalAccessException,
                InvocationTargetException
    {
        long start = new Date().getTime();
        method.invoke(instance, parameters);
        long end = new Date().getTime();
        return end - start;
    }
}
```

(5) (at `public MethodTimer`)

(6) (at `method =`)

(7) (at `method.invoke(instance, parameters);`)

The MethodTimer class takes four parameters in its constructor (line [5]): the object to be profiled, the name of the method to be timed, an array of parameter types, and a collection of actual parameters to be passed to the method. The Class method `getMethod()` is sent to the class of the object being profiled (line [6]). The result is a Method object. Finally, the method is kicked off by sending `invoke()` to the Method object (line [7]).

As an example of use, suppose you have a Payroll class with the method `payAllEmployees()`. The method signature is shown in **Listing 2.24.**

Listing 2.24 *payAllEmployees()*

```
public void payAllEmployees(long payrollRunNumber);
```

To run the MethodTimer against this method, you might provide the code shown in **Listing 2.25**.

Listing 2.25 *Using MethodTimer*

```
long runNumber = 23471015153L;
Class[] types = new Class[1];
types[0] = long.class;
MethodTimer timer =
   new MethodTimer(new Payroll(50000000),
                   "payAllEmployees",
                   types,
                   Collections.singleton(
                      new Long(runNumber)));
System.out.println(timer.run() + " ms");
```

Realistically, you would probably use MethodTimer in the context of a user-interface–based application. The user would select a class name from a list. The Class method `getMethods()` would be called to populate a second list with the Method objects available in the selected class. The Method object selected for performance profiling would provide the method signature parts of information needed to create a MethodTimer object.

PLUGGABLE METHOD NAME is a powerful pattern when used appropriately. It is an undesirable, convoluted intrusion when used inappropriately.

COLLECTING PARAMETER

Answers the Question	How do you return a collection that is the collaborative result of several operations?
Solution	Use COMPOSED METHOD to break each operation into its own method. Return the subcollection from each method and concatenate the results. Optionally, pass a collecting parameter to all of the new methods.
Category	Behavioral
Related Patterns	Composed Method

Often, in preparation for a bulk operation, you will be gathering objects from several sources or based on varying criteria. The bulk operation needs to operate against the collection as a whole, so you need to gather all of the objects into a single List object.

The job of the example method getScoringPlayers() in **Listing 2.26** is to return a list of all football players who have scored.

Listing 2.26 *getScoringPlayers() — Unfactored*

```
public List getScoringPlayers()
{
    List scoringPlayers = new ArrayList();

    // get scoring qbs
    Iterator qbIterator = qbs.iterator();
    while (qbIterator.hasNext())
    {
        Quarterback qb =
            (Quarterback)qbIterator.next();
        if (qb.hasTDs() || qb.hasCompletions())
            scoringPlayers.add(qb);
    }

    // get scoring wrs
    Iterator wrIterator = wrs.iterator();
    while (wrIterator.hasNext())
    {
        WideReceiver wr =
            (WideReceiver)wrIterator.next();
        if (wr.hasTDs() || wr.hasReceptions())
            scoringPlayers.add(wr);
    }
```

(continued)

Listing 2.26 (cont.) *getScoringPlayers() — Unfactored*

```
// ... etc.

// get scoring ks
Iterator kickerIterator = kickers.iterator();
while (kickerIterator.hasNext())
{
   Kicker kicker =
      (Kicker)kickerIterator.next();
   if (kicker.hasFieldGoals() ||
      kicker.hasExtraPoints())
      scoringPlayers.add(kicker);
}

return scoringPlayers;
}
```

Listing 2.26 shows what getScoringPlayers() looks like before applying COMPOSED METHOD. It uses a temporary List to store the players that result from each separate collecting task. Once you start to apply COMPOSED METHOD to break out each task into its own method, you need to determine how to store the subcollections that result from each separate method.

A possible solution is to declare the stack variable as an instance variable. Then your COMPOSED METHODS can simply access and add to the list directly. This representation of temporary variables as object attributes should be avoided. The purpose of instance variables is to represent object state. The List instance in this example would only have a defined state during the execution of the COMPOSED METHODS.

A second solution (**Listing 2.27**) is to have each new method return a partial list. The original method is then responsible for concatenating each of the partial lists.

Listing 2.27 *getScoringPlayers() — Partial List Concatenation*

```
public List getScoringPlayers()
{
   List scoringPlayers = new ArrayList();
   scoringPlayers.addAll(scoringQBs());
   scoringPlayers.addAll(scoringWRs());
   scoringPlayers.addAll(scoringKickers());
   return scoringPlayers;
}

private List scoringQBs()
{
   List list = new ArrayList();
   Iterator iterator = qbs.iterator();
   while (iterator.hasNext())
   {
```

```
        Quarterback each =
            (Quarterback)iterator.next();
        if (each.hasTDs() || each.hasCompletions())
            list.add(each);
    }
    return list;
}

private List scoringWRs()
{
    List list = new ArrayList();
    Iterator iterator = wrs.iterator();
    while (iterator.hasNext())
    {
        WideReceiver each =
            (WideReceiver)iterator.next();
        if (each.hasTDs() || each.hasReceptions())
            list.add(each);
    }
     return list;
}

private List scoringKickers()
{
    List list = new ArrayList();
    Iterator iterator = kickers.iterator();
    while (iterator.hasNext())
    {
        Kicker each = (Kicker)iterator.next();
        if (each.hasFieldGoals() ||
            each.hasExtraPoints())
            list.add(each);
    }
    return list;
}
```

While adequate, you may not be able to get away with the solution in
Listing 2.27. Often the operation of collecting objects requires an aware-
ness of what has already been added to the list. The other problem with
using partial-list concatenation as a solution is that it is not optimal. If you
are dealing with larger collections, or if memory is at a premium (and, as
usual, make sure your performance is a problem before taking the less-
clean approach), you will want to maintain only a single collection.

The third solution, then, is to pass the collection into each of the methods and have each method directly append to it. This is the COLLECTING
PARAMETER approach, shown in **Listing 2.28**.

Listing 2.28 *getScoringPlayers()* — COLLECTING PARAMETER

```
public List getScoringPlayers()
{
    List scoringPlayers = new ArrayList();
    addScoringQBsTo(scoringPlayers);
    addScoringWRsTo(scoringPlayers);
    addScoringKickersTo(scoringPlayers);
    return scoringPlayers;
}

private void addScoringQBsTo(List list)
{
    Iterator iterator = qbs.iterator();
    while (iterator.hasNext())
    {
        Quarterback each =
            (Quarterback)iterator.next();
        if (each.hasTDs() || each.hasCompletions())
            list.add(each);
    }
}

private void addScoringWRsTo(List list)
{
    Iterator iterator = wrs.iterator();
    while (iterator.hasNext())
    {
        WideReceiver each =
            (WideReceiver)iterator.next();
        if (each.hasTDs() || each.hasReceptions())
            list.add(each);
    }
}

private void addScoringKickersTo(List list)
{
    Iterator iterator = kickers.iterator();
    while (iterator.hasNext())
    {
        Kicker each = (Kicker)iterator.next();
        if (each.hasFieldGoals() ||
            each.hasExtraPoints())
            list.add(each);
    }
}
```

List is most often the appropriate class for your COLLECTING PARAMETER. In some cases a Stream, Set, or other collection class might be more appropriate or more efficient.

Chapter 3   *STATE PATTERNS*

By the time you get around to actually implementing your classes, you should already have defined what their attributes are. These object attributes, represented by instance variables in Java objects, define the *state* of the object. The definition of state is a critical part of object design. And because this book is about implementation and not object design, it does not contain many state patterns.

The first half of this chapter contains patterns specific to instance variables. They are geared toward specific coding techniques for manipulating object state rather than specifically modeling state. Included are patterns for accessing, initializing, modifying, and describing state. The second half of the chapter includes a set of patterns that describes how temporary variables are used.

Instance Variables

Instance variables should be directly traceable back to attributes defined during the analysis-and-design phase. If you find yourself introducing instance variables during your implementation phase, you may be corrupting the intent of instance variables. Your instance variables exist to help provide you with a snapshot of your object's state at any given point in time. By introducing temporary storage in the form of instance variables, you take away the ability to deterministically ensure just what your object's state is.

There are a few basic categories of instance variables. First are those that directly represent attributes in your object model, such as `employeeName` and `dateOfBirth`. You will also have instance variables to represent object relationships such as composition and aggregation. Some instance variables will exist to uniquely identify objects in the context of persistence, such as a `customerID` used to map a customer to its corresponding record in a database. Finally, you may design instance variables into your class to improve performance by caching calculated values. If you cannot place an instance variable in one of these categories, make it a temporary variable.

The instance variable patterns within this chapter are not so much about *what* instance variables are used for; rather they are about *how* the instance variables are used. The patterns reflect more of the behavior of your state — how your object interacts with its state. While the implementation phase should not result in changes to your instance variables, it still requires significant decisions as to how the instance variables will be accessed and manipulated.

The instance variable patterns begin with COMMON STATE and VARIABLE STATE to provide a basis for how state can be implemented within your objects.

Temporary Variables

This chapter ends with six patterns for temporary variables, starting with TEMPORARY VARIABLE itself. These patterns are the furthest removed from actual object design, since temporary variables are purely implementation tools. The patterns COLLECTING TEMPORARY VARIABLE, CACHING TEMPORARY VARIABLE, REUSING TEMPORARY VARIABLE, and EXPLAINING TEMPORARY VARIABLE represent the complete set of uses for temporary variables within a method. ROLE SUGGESTING TEMPORARY VARIABLE NAME describes how temporary variables should be named.

These temporary variable patterns apply equally well to just about any language that allows for the definition of locally scoped variables.

COMMON STATE

Answers the Question	How do you represent state?
Solution	Provide an instance variable within your class definition.
Category	State
Related Patterns	Variable State

The snapshot of an object's attributes at any point in time is its state. Without any attributes to represent its state, an object is otherwise just a collection of functions. While you may frequently use general-purpose algorithms from stateless classes (java.lang.Math, java.util.Collections), the bulk of the objects you use and build will contain attributes. You may have static objects whose attributes do not change; you may have very dynamic objects whose attributes are constantly being updated.

Java provides instance variables as its default implementation of attributes. Instance variables can be defined throughout your class file. They are globally available to all methods within a class instance.

From a design standpoint, attributes are often how many classes come about. I mentally divide my classes between data-based objects and behavior-based objects. The Employee class used for examples in this book is very data-based. Often the initial definition of these data classes will have come from taking a relational table somewhere and mapping it into an object structure. A behavior-based class, such as the Payroll class used in the Behavior chapters (Chapters 1 and 2), will usually have state, but its origin comes out of the need to manage other objects and produce some sort of output.

State is also how objects are tested. Any operation on an object that is invoked via a message send has two outputs that must be tested: the return value from the method invoked and the resultant state of the object afterward. To determine whether the results are correct, the resultant state must be compared to the state of the object *prior* to the message send.

As a simple example of state, an Employee object maintains its own copy of a `socialSecurityNumber`, `hireDate`, `dateOfBirth`, `terminationDate`, and so on. These are all instance variables that represent the attributes in Employee. The state of these attributes will vary over the lifetime of the object. Some of the attributes (`terminationDate`, for example) may not even be defined at some or all times during the object's lifetime.

VARIABLE STATE

Answers the Question	How do you represent state that can vary between instances of a single class?
Solution	Use a HashMap to store the attributes as key-value pairs. Allow access to the attributes via a getProperty() method; allow updates to the attributes via a setProperty() method.
Category	State
Related Patterns	Common State

VARIABLE STATE is an infrequently needed pattern used to represent classes whose attributes may change from instance to instance — not the value of the attributes, but the attributes themselves. From an object-design standpoint, this is a fairly rare need. If you find yourself wanting to implement VARIABLE STATE, think again — perhaps your objects are crying out for a classification scheme implemented through inheritance.

Implementation-wise, the java.util.Properties class is an example of VARIABLE STATE. Each properties instance can contain a separate set of keys and their values. Conceptually, however, Properties is a class with one attribute — a lookup table that contains key-value pairs. The values are just Strings. (Technically, because Properties subclasses Hashtable, you can put any sort of object into it. You are not supposed to, according to the JDK reference.)

If you must model VARIABLE STATE, you should pattern it so that it is similar to the Properties class itself. Declare an instance variable called properties to store a HashMap. If you are still using JDK 1.1, Hashtable is a poor substitute however, because it does not allow for null values.

Using the same method names as in Properties, the state of your VARIABLE STATE object is accessed and updated via getProperty(String key) and setProperty(String key, String value).

I find that VARIABLE STATE is very difficult to test and debug. If you have to use VARIABLE STATE as the basis for critical objects, you will want to create a small toolset to aid your coding, debugging, and testing efforts.

EXPLICIT INITIALIZATION

Answers the Question	How do you initialize instance variables to their default value?
Solution	Assign an initial value to the instance variable when it is declared in the class.
Category	State
Related Patterns	Lazy Initialization

There are a few ways to treat the subject of initial values in Java. The easiest is to do nothing — declare your instance variables and assume that they will be set correctly. Numeric primitives initialize to 0 as you might expect, `boolean` to `false`, and `char` to "\0". Instances of classes are set to the null object, represented by the keyword `null`.

Depending on implicit initialization by type is acceptable, but not necessarily a good idea, for a few reasons. First, it is one of those "forgettable" language rules, much like operator precedence. While the default rules are small in number, the default initialization value for a specific type may not be apparent for someone coming to Java from a different language such as C++, C, or Smalltalk. The fact that primitives are initialized to a useful value, but object references are not, only adds to the confusion.

More importantly, if you do not initialize your variables, the initial state of your class is not clear — your code no longer speaks its intent. Finally, program maintenance and debugging are more difficult when you have to determine just how an instance variable is initialized. If you declare an instance variable without initializing it, a developer often has to follow streams of logic through multiple methods in order to confirm whether the default initialization was used.

Unless you are using LAZY INITIALIZATION, all variables should be explicitly initialized, even if the initial value is the same as the default initialization value. EXPLICIT INITIALIZATION should be done where the instance variables are declared in your class, as in **Listing 3.1**.

Listing 3.1 *EXPLICIT INITIALIZATION*

```
public class Employee
{
    int hoursPerWeek = 40;
    boolean isPartTime = false;
    // ...
}
```

If an instance variable is not modified by a constructor (or a CON-STRUCTOR PARAMETER METHOD) but instead in some other method after the instance has been created, you should explicitly initialize the instance variable to `null` for clarification purposes. **Listing 3.2** demonstrates this.

Listing 3.2 *EXPLICIT INITIALIZATION to `null`*

```
public class Employee
{
    private Beneficiary beneficiary = null;
    public Employee()
    {
    }
    public void setBeneficiary(String name)
    {
        beneficiary = new Beneficiary(name);
    }
}
```

This example declares to a developer that a legitimate initial object state is for a employee's beneficiary to be null.

For any initialization value that is unclear, you should use DEFAULT VALUE CONSTANT or DEFAULT VALUE METHOD to avoid the need to comment the instance variable declaration.

LAZY INITIALIZATION

Answers the Question	How do you initialize instance variables to their default value?
Solution	Test the value of the instance variable each time it is accessed in its GETTING METHOD. If it is uninitialized, set the variable to its initial value.
Category	State
Related Patterns	Explicit Initialization

Ideal object design often sacrifices performance for purity. LAZY INITIALIZATION, the opposite of EXPLICIT INITIALIZATION, is an implementation example of the same principle. The "lazy" in the pattern name means that the initialization of instance variables is deferred until the variable is accessed the first time.

LAZY INITIALIZATION is done in your SETTING METHODS. **Listing 3.3** provides an example. In the example, the `title` instance variable is tested and initialized to the default string `"Grunt Level I"` if it is null.

Listing 3.3 LAZY INITIALIZATION

```
public String getTitle()
{
    if (title == null)
        title = "Grunt Level I";
    return title;
}
```

The initialization to a default value can be accomplished via a DEFAULT VALUE METHOD. LAZY INITIALIZATION is a bit more "pure" in the object sense because it encapsulates the state initialization for an attribute in the same place that it is accessed. The main benefit is that if someone decides to subclass your object, they can override this initialization if necessary.

On the downside, it should be apparent that LAZY INITIALIZATION is a potential source of performance problems. Every access to the instance variable includes a conditional test as to whether the variable has been initialized yet.

The real value of LAZY INITIALIZATION is when it is costly to prematurely initialize object state. This is especially true if an attribute is infrequently accessed, or if it might never be accessed for a given object. For example, your system might store scanned photographs for all your Employee objects. Retrieving these images to process a payroll run would be an unnecessarily expensive operation, both in terms of retrieval time and memory requirements.

If you use LAZY INITIALIZATION, you *must* also use INDIRECT VARIABLE ACCESS. The benefit of LAZY INITIALIZATION is that it guarantees a valid value for an instance variable. Client code internal to the object no longer needs to test for the null condition. But you lose that guarantee if you directly access the variable. Habitually, once I begin using LAZY INITIALIZATION, I use INDIRECT VARIABLE ACCESS for accessing all attributes within a given object.

Object development choices are usually tradeoffs between cleanliness (extensibility, clarity, flexibility, and so forth) and performance. The debate of LAZY INITIALIZATION versus EXPLICIT INITIALIZATION is a good example. In many situations it will be clear which one is more appropriate. The rest of the time you will just have to adhere to an agreed-upon standard.

DEFAULT VALUE CONSTANT

Answers the Question	How do you represent the default value of a variable?
Solution	Provide a CONSTANT that specifies the default value; initialize the variable to this CONSTANT.
Category	State
Related Patterns	Default Value Method Explicit Initialization Lazy Initialization

When you initialize a variable, it often needs to be given a meaningful initial value. The initial value for the variable represents either a state that the variable must be in before its first use, or the most useful default value for the attribute, or both.

For example, the number of hours an employee will work per week must be predesignated. Each firm will specify a customary amount of hours, usually somewhere around 40. For the employee to be in a valid state and to be useful to other objects such as a payroll processor, the number of hours attribute in the employee must be populated. Because most employees will work the 40 hours, the number of hours should be defaulted to that value.

Default values can be set on instance creation, or they can be used in LAZY INITIALIZATION. If it is possible to supply a default value at instance creation, the most succinct way to specify it is to just provide the value as part of EXPLICIT INITIALIZATION:

```
private int hoursPerWeek = 40;
```

A small problem with this is that the initial default is not available to anything else. If a method needs to reset the value to the default, it cannot do so. It is also possible that the initial value is provided by another object. And finally, the default value may need some explanation.

A better way to represent the default value of a variable is to use the DEFAULT VALUE METHOD pattern, presented right after this one. The more commonly accepted solution, though, is DEFAULT VALUE CONSTANT. I will patiently explain DEFAULT VALUE CONSTANT with the forewarning that I do not recommend it.

The DEFAULT VALUE CONSTANT solution is to initialize the variable to a CONSTANT that represents the default value, as shown in **Listing 3.4**.

Listing 3.4 *Default Value Constant with Explicit Initialization*

```
private static final int
   defaultFullTimeHoursPerWeek = 40;
private int hoursPerWeek =
   defaultFullTimeHoursPerWeek;
```

The use of Default Value Constant in Lazy Initialization is demonstrated in **Listing 3.5**.

Listing 3.5 *Default Value Constant with Lazy Initialization*

```
public int getHoursPerWeek()
{
   if (hoursPerWeek == 0)
      hoursPerWeek = defaultFullTimeHoursPerWeek;
   return hoursPerWeek;
}
```

Default Value Constant cannot be overridden in a subclass, since its declaration is `final`. Default Value Method solves this problem.

DEFAULT VALUE METHOD

Answers the Question	How do you represent the default value of a variable?
Solution	Provide a method that returns the default value.
Category	State
Related Patterns	Default Value Constant Constant

Again, there are two solutions to providing a default value. While DEFAULT VALUE CONSTANT tells you to define a final instance variable, DEFAULT VALUE METHOD says to provide a method that returns the default value. That's all there is to it. **Listing 3.6** shows how.

Listing 3.6 DEFAULT VALUE METHOD

```
public int getDefaultHoursPerWeek()
{
    return 40;
}
```

You can go one step further and use a CONSTANT to specify the return value (**Listing 3.6**)

Listing 3.6 DEFAULT VALUE METHOD Using CONSTANT

```
public int getDefaultHoursPerWeek()
{
    return defaultFullTimeHoursPerWeek;
}
```

By providing a DEFAULT VALUE METHOD as opposed to a DEFAULT VALUE CONSTANT, subclasses may now override the default value. The other nice thing is that DEFAULT VALUE METHOD can still be used with either LAZY INITIALIZATION or EXPLICIT INITIALIZATION, shown in **Listings 3.7** and **3.8**.

Listing 3.7 DEFAULT VALUE CONSTANT with EXPLICIT INITIALIZATION

```
private int hoursPerWeek =
    getDefaultHoursPerWeek();
```

Listing 3.8 DEFAULT VALUE CONSTANT with LAZY INITIALIZATION

```
public int getHoursPerWeek()
{
    if (hoursPerWeek == 0)
        hoursPerWeek = getDefaultHoursPerWeek();
    return hoursPerWeek;
}
```

CONSTANT

Answers the Question	How do you represent a constant value?
Solution	Declare a final class variable and assign it the constant value.
Category	State
Related Patterns	Constant Method

CONSTANT is one of those patterns I have a hard time promoting. The reality is that the standard was more or less set by JavaSoft, and most code out there adheres to it.

There is no `const` modifier in Java as there is in C++ (but note that `const` is a reserved word!). The `final` keyword is used instead to indicate that a variable cannot be changed.

Java `switch` statements, which is where CONSTANTS can be most useful, are a disappointing language construct. Perhaps it is just as well that they are lame, because they often point out poor object design. They are disappointing for two reasons: Each case expression must be a constant expression, and only `int`s or smaller native types (including `char`s) are supported. I would like to have a switch statement that supports objects, expressions, longs, whatever, for its cases. I realize there is some compilation magic that differentiates `if...else...` constructs from `switch` statements, but frankly I don't care. Java could have made a break for the better by moving away from the C/C++ definition of `switch`, but the designers chose not to.

Regardless of my whining about switch statements, when you need one, you need one. They can certainly help clarify code. And if you want to use meaningful constants in a switch statement, the CONSTANT pattern is the only way to do it. My preferred pattern for representing constant values, CONSTANT METHOD, will not work for switch statements.

To implement a constant, you declare a new instance variable, make it final, and assign it an initial value. As far as naming is concerned, this is another convention established by JavaSoft: Constants are named with all uppercase letters; words are usually separated with underscores[1] (yet another leftover convention from C programming). A better, easier solution would have been to adopt the mathematical notation of prefixing the variable name with the letter k. (Oh well.) **Listing 3.9** demonstrates the declaration of a few constants using the de facto standard.

---

1 This is a miserable convention if ever I saw one, especially after suffering years of it in C programming. The underscore character is difficult to type, and even the word "underscore" is annoyingly obscure.

Listing 3.9   CONSTANTS

```
public static final char SPACE = ' ';
public static final double PI =
    3.141592653589793d;
public static final String OPEN_FILE =
    "Open File";
public static final java.awt.Point ENDPOINT =
    new java.awt.Point(100, 120);
```

(1)

Take note of line [1] in **Listing 3.9**, which declares a CONSTANT called
ENDPOINT. This brings up another point about the final keyword:
ENDPOINT is a constant pointer in the C++ sense, but the data is not constant. The *reference*, not its object contents, is constant. For native types
this does not matter – you cannot change the value of an int, char, double,
and so forth. For objects, the fact that the object contents are not constant
does matter. Unless an object is immutable itself (via its class definition),
making it final does not guarantee that no one will change its contents.
String is the most famous class to produce immutable objects.

As an example of how the object pointed to by ENDPOINT above can
be changed, even though ENDPOINT is declared as final, you can code:

```
ENDPOINT.y = 222;
```

and the y value of ENDPOINT will be updated. But if you code:

```
ENDPOINT = new Point(2, 3);   // error!
```

you will receive the error message, "Can't assign a value to a final variable."

While you can design an object to be immutable (like String), you cannot individually specify instance variables to act as references to constant
objects. A possible solution would be to provide an immutable flag in the
constructors of the object.

Also note the additional convention of making CONSTANTS static. The
benefit is that you save space in your object, because each object does not
need to contain a separate copy of the instance variable. You do not sacrifice anything in terms of additional coding from within your object to
access the static variable: unlike C++, you do not have to scope the static
variable with the class name.

CONSTANT METHOD

Answers the Question	How do you represent the default value of a variable?
Solution	Provide an accessor method that returns the value of the constant.
Category	State
Related Patterns	Constant

The interesting thing about constants is that they rarely are — constant, that is. Obviously there are those mathematical constants such as pi and Avogadro's number that will never change. But constants as used by applications often need to change without warning.

Consider a constant used to represent the number of states in the United States. It wasn't always 50. And the number will likely change within the next 100 years. Or consider a constant used to represent the number of grade levels within your company. As soon as you have coded the value, the edict will come down that there will be new grade levels due to the merger of the week.

But even if your constant changes on a whim to a new value, the CONSTANT pattern should suffice for most of your needs. The risky proposition that you take on, though, is that a constant may someday no longer be a static number. Today your company may have a 40-hour work week. What if tomorrow the standard work week becomes unique for each class of employee, derived as a computed value?

If your constant becomes a calculation and you have used the CONSTANT pattern, code that refers directly to the class variable holding the constant value is dead. All client code will need to change to use message sends instead of static variable references.

CONSTANT METHOD proposes providing a simple method whose sole job is to return the value of the constant, as demonstrated in the examples in **Listing 3.10**.

Listing 3.10 CONSTANT METHOD

```
public int hoursPerWeek()
{
    return 40;
}
public String disclaimer()
{
    return
"Systems Systems, Inc. claims no liability " +
"for injuries sustained while using this product.";
}
```

The other advantage of CONSTANT METHOD over CONSTANT is that it allows subclasses to override the constant value. With the CONSTANT pattern, you must declare all constants as `final`, lest you risk a client changing the value of the constant.[2] The side effect of doing so is that your constant cannot be overridden in a subclass.

As far as naming the CONSTANT METHOD, you have one of two options. First is to name it using the convention for GETTING METHOD. Second is to omit the "get" part of the method name. I prefer to name it just like a GETTING METHOD. That way, if the constant does become a calculated value or even an instance variable, there is no need to change the method name.

Yet another side effect (a glorious one, from my standpoint) of using CONSTANT METHOD instead of CONSTANT is that you no longer need to make your constants UNDERSCORED_AND_UPPERCASED. Go ahead, mix that case!

---

2 Not to mention that you cannot use the CONSTANT in a switch statement unless it is final.

Constant Pool

Answers the Question	How do you share a pool of common constants that are needed by multiple classes?
Solution	Define an interface. Declare the pool constants within the interface. Implement the interface in classes that need the constants.
Category	State
Related Patterns	Indirect Variable Access Lazy Initialization

Often, you will have a group of constants that are needed by several classes. Initially they will derive out of a single class. After a while, you will see references to the constants everywhere. It may become apparent that they really do not "belong" to the single class they came from.

The Constant Pool pattern provides a means of isolating and grouping logically related constants. It is to be used with care — just as you should never lump things haphazardly into a single class for convenience, you should not use Constant Pool as a catch-all for random constants that happen to be floating around.

To implement Constant Pool, declare an interface and drop in the constants. An example, PayrollConstants, is shown in **Listing 3.11**.

Listing 3.11 *Constant Pool*

```
public interface PayrollConstants
{
    final int HOURS_PER_WEEK = 40;
    final int HOURS_PER_YEAR = 2000;
    final double OVERTIME_RATE = 1.5;
    final int WEEKS_IN_PAY_PERIOD = 2;
}
```

To use the pool, declare your class as implementing the PayrollConstants interface. The constants can then be used without the need for dereferencing them with a class name. **Listing 3.12** provides a stand-alone class that demonstrates this.

Listing 3.12 *Using Constant Pool*

```
public class ConstantPool
    implements PayrollConstants
{
    public static void main(String[] args)
    {
        new ConstantPool();
    }

    public ConstantPool()
    {
        double hourlyRate = 30.0;
        System.out.println("Pay for rate of " +
                hourlyRate + " = " +
                calculatePay(hourlyRate));
    }

    public double calculatePay(double baseRate)
    {
        return baseRate *
                WEEKS_IN_PAY_PERIOD *
                HOURS_PER_WEEK;
    }
}
```

To get the most effective use out of Constant Pool, combine this pattern with Enumerated Constants to ensure type safety.

DIRECT VARIABLE ACCESS

Answers the Question	How do you get and set an instance variable's value?
Solution	Access and set the instance variable directly.
Category	State
Related Patterns	Indirect Variable Access Lazy Initialization

The term "variable access" in the name of this pattern refers to internal access of object state, not external access from client objects. Your class's methods will need to access the instance variables defined within the object. You must choose whether the instance variables will be accessed directly in method code or indirectly via an internal method call to a GETTING METHOD.

Either solution is valid, and you will find plenty of arguments both ways. The main benefit of DIRECT VARIABLE ACCESS over INDIRECT VARIABLE ACCESS is that your code is greatly simplified. No method calls are required to access attributes.

On the downside, you cannot safely use DIRECT VARIABLE ACCESS for an attribute if it is initialized via LAZY INITIALIZATION. If your object's attributes vary between EXPLICIT INITIALIZATION and LAZY INITIALIZATION, the chance that you will mistakenly use DIRECT VARIABLE ACCESS on a lazy-initialized instance variable will increase.

Another drawback to using DIRECT VARIABLE ACCESS is that it violates encapsulation. Sure, it's your object; you have the capability to access and manipulate its internal representation as you wish. But by directly accessing instance variables, you run the risk of considerable code changes. This can happen, for instance, if the attribute represented by the instance variable becomes a calculated value or if it is modified to obtain its value from another object via DELEGATION. Additionally, if someone subclasses your object, they may wish to provide a different source for an attribute. Use of DIRECT VARIABLE ACCESS prevents this.

Subclassing is also made difficult or impossible by the use of DIRECT VARIABLE ACCESS. Suppose you have a computational method that refers to an instance variable directly. If a subclass wants to change what is populated in the instance variable, the only way to do it is to completely recode the method in the subclass.

If I am not using LAZY INITIALIZATION, my preference is to directly access instance variables. It is much quicker to code (if I wanted to type more parentheses I would be doing Lisp) and is also considerably easier to read. If I am hacking out an object that will not be subclassed or accessed from other packages, I use DIRECT VARIABLE ACCESS. For application-level user-interface objects, you can safely do the same, since you usually do not need to worry about subclasses or attributes changing from instance variables to calculated values (even if they do, it's not as big a deal). But for any object that could be subclassed — just about any other kind of object — or for any object that may undergo heavy internal changes, INDIRECT VARIABLE ACCESS is preferable. Even user interface components may need to be subclassed from time to time.

To implement DIRECT VARIABLE ACCESS, simply use the object's instance variables directly within the code expressions that make up your object's methods. An example is presented in **Listing 3.13**.

Listing 3.13 *DIRECT VARIABLE ACCESS*

```
class Employee
{
    private String lastName;
    private String firstName;
    private int hoursWorkedPerWeek;

    // ...
    public void setHoursWorkedPerWeek(int hours)
    {
      hoursWorkedPerWeek = hours;
    }
    public int getAnnualHours()
    {
      return hoursWorkedPerWeek * 50;
    }
    public String toString()
    {
      return lastName + ", " + firstName;
    }
}
```

(2) appears beside `hoursWorkedPerWeek = hours;`
(3) appears beside `return hoursWorkedPerWeek * 50;`
(4) appears beside `return lastName + ", " + firstName;`

Lines [2], [3], and [4] demonstrate DIRECT VARIABLE ACCESS. Note that a SETTING METHOD (line [2]) will have to directly set its value.

INDIRECT VARIABLE ACCESS

Answers the Question	How do you get and set an instance variable's value?
Solution	Use GETTING METHODS and SETTING METHODS to access and update the value of the instance variable.
Category	State
Related Patterns	Direct Variable Access Lazy Initialization

INDIRECT VARIABLE ACCESS is simply using the GETTING METHOD for an object attribute for all internal access and the SETTING METHOD for all internal updates to the instance variable.

Read the DIRECT VARIABLE ACCESS pattern first. The problems involved with DIRECT VARIABLE ACCESS — risk if LAZY INITIALIZATION is used, risk of attribute changes, risk to successful inheritance — are solved by using INDIRECT VARIABLE ACCESS. Of course, the things that are good about DIRECT VARIABLE ACCESS become bad here. For example, your code will look a bit more cluttered.

Another advantage of INDIRECT VARIABLE ACCESS is that there is no chance of confusing an instance variable with a temporary variable. One of the things that Java allows you to do is to declare a temporary variable with the same name as an instance variable.[3] This effectively hides the instance variable for the scope of existence of the temporary. Hiding instance variables is not something you want to do, but it can happen by accident. With longer methods, it is easy enough to mistake a temporary for an instance variable, which can lead to some surprising results. By using INDIRECT VARIABLE ACCESS only, you know precisely what your temporaries are.

Listing 3.14 shows some examples of INDIRECT VARIABLE ACCESS.

---

3 Oddly, Java does not allow redeclaration of temporary variables that appear within an embedded block. The ability to quickly add a block of code that is to be removed later is very useful; the inability to redefine a variable within the scope of this temporary block can be a nuisance.

Listing 3.14 *INDIRECT VARIABLE ACCESS*

```
class Employee
{
    private String lastName;
    private String firstName;
    private int hoursWorkedPerWeek;

    // …
    public int getHoursWorkedPerWeek()
    {
        return hoursWorkedPerWeek;
    }
    public int getAnnualHours()
    {
        return getHoursWorkedPerWeek() * 50;
    }
    public String toString()
    {
        return getLastName() +
            ", " + getFirstName();
    }
}
```

(5)

(6)

(7)

Lines [6] and [7] demonstrate INDIRECT VARIABLE ACCESS. Note that your GETTING METHODS (line [5]) will have to directly access their values.

Getting Method

Answers the Question	How do you provide access to an instance variable?
Solution	Provide a method that returns the instance variable. Name it using the pattern `getInstanceVariable()`.
Category	State
Related Patterns	Setting Method

The question of whether or not to declare instance variables as public has hopefully been answered by introductory Java books. Just in case it is unclear: *never* declare instance variables as public. I will avoid the lengthy diatribe on encapsulation and simply state that your job is to protect your instance variables from prying clients, whose actions can adversely affect the state of your object. You must provide a GETTING METHOD for any instance variable that needs to be accessible from client objects.

As part of your class design, you must determine just which of your object's attributes should be publicly available. The best tactic to take when providing public access to instance variables is to determine what your class is publishing in terms of behavior at the outset of your class design. Do not blindly declare all getting methods as public.

If you choose to use INDIRECT VARIABLE ACCESS, you will be providing a GETTING METHOD for each of your instance variables. By Java convention, always name one of these methods by capitalizing the first letter of the instance variable being accessed and then prefixing it with `get`. For example:

Instance Variable	Getting Method Name
`newEmployees`	`getNewEmployees()`
`ytdAmount`	`getYtdAmount()`

SETTING METHOD

Answers the Question	How do you change the value of an instance variable?
Solution	Provide a method to set the value of the variable. Name the method using the pattern `setInstanceVariable(Object)`.
Category	State
Related Patterns	Getting Method

SETTING METHODS allow clients to change the state of your object. Providing this capability to clients is not something you should treat lightly. You do not want just anyone messing with your class's data. Declare your instance variables as private.

Reality intervenes, however, and you will sometimes have to trust client objects to properly modify your object's attributes. For each attribute that you must expose, provide a SETTING METHOD. *Do not* provide public SETTING METHODS for every attribute defined in your class! While this may seem pretty obvious, I have encountered many developers whose first task after declaring instance variables is to create public setters for each attribute. Why risk your object's state? To build a solid, reusable object, you must have complete control over external forces wanting to compromise the integrity of your object. Each SETTING METHOD is yet another chink in the armor that must be fully tested.

If you are using INDIRECT VARIABLE ACCESS, you will be declaring SETTING METHODS for all of your attributes. Just make sure that these methods are declared as private or protected.

I usually refer to SETTING METHODS as "setters" or "accessors." The term accessor is sometimes used to only specifically refer to GETTING METHODS, in which case setters are then called "mutators." But in the general sense, an accessor is a method that has access to an object's attribute, to either get or set it.

As in GETTING METHOD, the naming convention for these accessor methods should be consistent. Capitalize the first letter of the instance variable and then use the prefix `set`. For example:

Instance Variable	SETTING METHOD Name
`newEmployees`	`setNewEmployees()`
`ytdAmount`	`setYtdAmount()`

COLLECTION ACCESSOR METHOD

Answers the Question	How do you provide access to an instance variable that holds a collection?
Solution	JDK 1.1: Allow access to the collection only through delegated messages. JDK 1.2: Use the unmodifiable wrappers provided by the Collections class.
Category	State
Related Patterns	Getting Method

JDK 1.1

Before JDK 1.2, the rule was that collections are private. If you make your collection public, you run the risk that someone else will modify the collection without informing your object. If you are maintaining an internal computed value that changes when new objects are added to or deleted from the collection, the value of your computation value can become invalid if a client developer directly changes the collection.

As an example, you have a petty cash system and need to be able to retrieve the total cash amount disbursed so far on each day. Rather than recalculate the amount with each withdrawal, the petty cash object uses a CACHING INSTANCE VARIABLE to add to a running total. If the application goes down and must restart, the total can be easily be recalculated from the stored transactions.

In **Listing 3.15,** the main() method (line [8]) of the PettyCash class withdraws three amounts from the petty cash office and then deletes the first recorded withdrawal by directly accessing the withdrawals Vector. The actual computed balance no longer matches the incorrect cached balance.

Listing 3.15 *PettyCash.java*

```
import java.util.Vector;
import java.util.Enumeration;

public class PettyCash
{
    private Currency cashWithdrawnToday;
    private Vector withdrawals = new Vector();

    public static void main(String[] args)
    {
        PettyCash cashOffice = new PettyCash();
        System.out.println("balance now = " +
```

(8)

```
        cashOffice.getCashWithdrawnToday());
    cashOffice.withdraw(new Currency(12));
    cashOffice.withdraw(new Currency(20));
    cashOffice.withdraw(new Currency(9, 99));
    System.out.println("computed balance = " +
        cashOffice.computeCashWithdrawnToday());
    cashOffice.getWithdrawals().remove(0);
    System.out.println(
        "removed 1st xn; balance = " +
        cashOffice.getCashWithdrawnToday());
    System.out.println(
        "but the real computed balance = " +
        cashOffice.computeCashWithdrawnToday());
}

public PettyCash()
{
    cashWithdrawnToday = new Currency(0);
}
public Vector getWithdrawals()
{
    return withdrawals;
}
public void withdraw(Currency amount)
{
    System.out.println("withdrawing " + amount);
    withdrawals.addElement(amount);
    cashWithdrawnToday.add(amount);
    System.out.println("total withdrawn = " +
                        getCashWithdrawnToday());
}
public Currency getCashWithdrawnToday()
{
    if (cashWithdrawnToday == null)
        cashWithdrawnToday =
            computeCashWithdrawnToday();
    return cashWithdrawnToday;
}
public Currency computeCashWithdrawnToday()
{
    Currency total = new Currency(0);
    Enumeration iterator =
        withdrawals.elements();
    while (iterator.hasMoreElements())
        total.add(
            (Currency)iterator.nextElement());
    return total;
}
}
```

Listing 3.16 provides the Currency domain class used in the example.

Listing 3.16 *Currency.java*

```java
public class Currency
{
    private long whole;
    private long fraction;
    public Currency(long _whole)
    {
        whole = _whole;
        fraction = 0;
    }
    public Currency(long _whole, long _fraction)
    {
        whole = _whole;
        fraction = _fraction;
    }
    public double asDouble()
    {
        return whole + fraction * 0.01;
    }
    public Currency add(Currency currency)
    {
        whole += currency.whole;
        fraction += currency.fraction;
        if (fraction > 99)
        {
            fraction -= 100;
            whole++;
        }
        return this;
    }
    public String toString()
    {
        return whole + "." +
            (fraction < 10 ? "0" : "") + fraction;
    }
}
```

If you run the example `main()` method, line [8] in **Listing 3.15**, the output in **Listing 3.17** shows how the cached balance becomes incorrect.

Listing 3.17 *Output from PettyCash*

```
balance now = 0.00
withdrawing 12.00
total withdrawn = 12.00
withdrawing 20.00
total withdrawn = 32.00
withdrawing 9.99
total withdrawn = 41.99
computed balance = 41.99
removed 1st xn; balance = 41.99
but the real computed balance = 29.99
```

Unfortunately, returning the naked collection is a very common practice. The problem is easily solved by eliminating direct access to the withdrawals collection. You will need to provide a method for each possible operation against withdrawals: remove(), add(), and so on. Most of these methods will be a variant of the SIMPLE DELEGATION pattern. The difference is that you will want the name of each method to reflect the specific collection being modified. This is critical if you have more than one embedded collection.

For iterating over the collection, modify the getWithdrawals() method to return the collection's Enumeration object instead:

```
public Enumeration getWithdrawals()
{
    return withdrawals.elements();
}
```

Since Enumerations do not support the size() method, you will likely want to provide a method that returns this value:

```
public int getNumberOfWithdrawals()
{
    return withdrawals.size();
}
```

JDK 1.2

The Collections Framework in Java 2 requires a different solution. The Iterator object returned from a List provides a remove() method, which allows for elements to be removed from the collection as it is iterated over. So you cannot trust giving out your collection's iterator, either.

Fortunately, the Collections Framework provides a set of unmodifiable wrappers. The wrappers are returned by static methods on the class Collections. Each of these methods acts as a factory method to produce a reference to an original collection. A wrapper prohibits any modifications to the collection. It simply throws an exception (UnsupportedOperationException) for any messages sent to the wrapper that would result in the collection being modified.

There are specific unmodifiable wrappers for each of the six core collection interfaces — Collection, Set, List, Map, SortedSet, and SortedMap. The Java 2 implementation for the example PettyCash class is shown in **Listing 3.18**. The method getWithdrawals() (line [9]) has been modified to demonstrate the use of the Collections.unmodifiableList() factory method.

Listing 3.18   *PettyCash.java*

```java
import java.util.List;
import java.util.Iterator;
import java.util.Collections;

public class PettyCash
{
    private Currency cashWithdrawnToday;
    private List withdrawals =
        new java.util.ArrayList();

    public static void main(String[] args)
    {
        PettyCash cashOffice = new PettyCash();
        System.out.println("balance now = " +
            cashOffice.getCashWithdrawnToday());
        cashOffice.withdraw(new Currency(12));
        cashOffice.withdraw(new Currency(20));
        cashOffice.withdraw(new Currency(9, 99));
        System.out.println("computed balance = " +
            cashOffice.computeCashWithdrawnToday());
        cashOffice.getWithdrawals().remove(0);
        System.out.println(
            "removed 1st xn; balance = " +
            cashOffice.getCashWithdrawnToday());
        System.out.println(
            "but the real computed balance = " +
            cashOffice.computeCashWithdrawnToday());
    }

    public PettyCash()
    {
        cashWithdrawnToday = new Currency(0);
    }
    public List getWithdrawals()
    {
        return
            Collections.unmodifiableList(withdrawals);
    }
    public void withdraw(Currency amount)
    {
        System.out.println("withdrawing " + amount);
        withdrawals.add(amount);
        cashWithdrawnToday.add(amount);
        System.out.println("total withdrawn = " +
                           getCashWithdrawnToday());
    }
```

(9)

```
    public Currency getCashWithdrawnToday()
    {
       if (cashWithdrawnToday == null)
          cashWithdrawnToday =
             computeCashWithdrawnToday();
       return cashWithdrawnToday;
    }
    public Currency computeCashWithdrawnToday()
    {
       Currency total = new Currency(0);
       Iterator iterator = withdrawals.iterator();
       while (iterator.hasNext())
          total.add((Currency)iterator.next());
       return total;
    }
}
```

Executing the `main()` method produces the output shown in **Listing 3.19**.

Listing 3.19   *Output*

```
balance now = 0.00
withdrawing 12.00
total withdrawn = 12.00
withdrawing 20.00
total withdrawn = 32.00
withdrawing 9.99
total withdrawn = 41.99
computed balance = 41.99
Exception in thread "main"
 java.lang.UnsupportedOperationException
 at java.util.Collections$UnmodifiableList.remove
    (Collections.java:704)
 at PettyCash.main(PettyCash.java:20)
```

The huge benefit of returning an unmodifiable collection is that your work is done. You no longer need to provide methods to delegate to the underlying collection.

Because this is a runtime solution, you must indicate in your javadoc comment when a COLLECTION ACCESSOR METHOD returns a nonmodifiable collection.

ENUMERATION METHOD

Answers the Question	How do you provide safe, general access to collection elements?
Solution	Provide a method that takes a closure as a parameter. Iterate through the collection and send a message to the closure for each element of the collection.
Category	State
Related Patterns	Collection Accessor Method

You may want to prohibit clients from modifying your collection completely but still allow them to perform an operation on each element in the collection. To accomplish this, you could pass out an Enumeration under JDK 1.1 or return an unmodifiable collection under JDK 1.2. Each client must then loop through the enumeration of the collection and perform the desired operation on each extracted element.

A cleaner way, which encapsulates the iteration of the collection within the source object, uses closures. A closure is a function plus the environment in effect when the function is defined.[4] This allows for functions to be dynamically created. Smalltalk implements closures via blocks or BlockClosure objects. Java's implementation of closures is via anonymous inner classes.

An ENUMERATION METHOD provides a function that iterates through an object's internal collection. For each object, the ENUMERATION METHOD sends a message back to the closure to execute an operation, passing the extracted object as a parameter.

Listing 3.20 defines an appropriate Closure interface.

Listing 3.20   *Closure.java*

```
public class Closure
{
    public void exec(Object item) {}
}
```

---

4 Jackson, J., and McClellan, A. *Java by Example,* 3rd ed. Palo Alto, CA: Sun Microsystems Press, 1999, pp. 192–193..

Within the object containing the collection to be protected, you create a method to operate on the collection. Let's say that an Employee object embeds an ArrayList of Dependent objects (children, spouses, and so forth). **Listing 3.21** provides a method in the Employee class called dependentsDo(). This method takes a closure as a parameter (line [10]), iterates through the dependents list (line [11]), and for each dependent sends the exec() message to closure, passing the dependent as a parameter (line [12]).

Listing 3.21 ENUMERATION METHOD

(10)
(11)
(12)

```
public void dependentsDo(Closure closure)
{
    Iterator iterator = dependents.iterator();
    while (iterator.hasNext())
    {
        Dependent dependent =
            (Dependent)iterator.next();
        closure.exec(dependent);
    }
}
```

Client code can now use the Closure interface to dynamically define a closure to be passed to dependentsDo(). An example is provided in **Listing 3.22**, which prints the name and age of each dependent object contained within an employee object, employee.

Listing 3.22 *Using the* ENUMERATION METHOD

```
employee.dependentsDo(
    new Closure()
    {
        public void exec(Object item)
        {
            Dependent dependent = (Dependent)item;
            System.out.println(dependent.getName() +
                            " is " +
                            dependent.getAge() +
                            " years old.");
        }
    });
```

To name the ENUMERATION METHOD, append the word "Do" to the name of the collection.

ENUMERATED CONSTANTS

Answers the Question	How do you provide a safe, C-like enum capability?
Solution	Create a special class to represent the enumeration.
Category	State
Related Patterns	Constant

Suppose you have a status attribute in your Employee class representing whether an employee is full-time or part-time. It gets its value from a CHAR field in a DB2 DB sitting on mainframe DASD miles away in IA.[5] This status field stores the number 0 for part-time employees and 1 for full-time employees. So naturally you provide an accessor method called `getStatus()` that returns the status attribute. And you are even nice enough to provide some class constants:

```
public static final int FULL_TIME = 1;
public static final int PART_TIME = 0;
```

Code in client methods ends up reading like this:

```
if (employee.getEmployeeStatus()
    == Employee.FULL_TIME)
```

What a handful of typing. But OK, it works, and at least it reads fairly straightforward.

Next day, the mainframe programmers decide to change this to a PIC X field (they are using COBOL of course). Full-time is now an "F" and part-time is a "P," and they have added flex time, represented by an "X." No problem. You change the type of your status attribute, the return value of your `getEmployeeStatus()` method, and the type of your class constants to char. You also tell your client developers to recompile, "but everything should still be OK."

The following day, all heck breaks loose as the payroll application starts cutting bonus checks for $240,000 and more. Fingers point at you as the owner of the Employee class. After several late hours of sweating, you discover that some genius out there has coded the following:

```
double bonus = employee.getEmployeeStatus() *
               (employee.getBaseSalary() * .1);
```

---

5 That's "Iowa." Sorry, the excitement of the mainframe got me carried away with the abbreviations.

What the heck? After staring at it for a second, you realize that this code took advantage of the fact that part-timers, who as it turns out get no bonus, had the integer 0 as their status. Now they have character value "P" as their status. And part of the beauty of Java is that chars cast automatically to ints, which is why the client recompile worked just fine. The bad reality is that the character value "P" equates to the int value 80. The good news for the very fortunate part-time employees is that this means they will get a bonus of eight times their salary. The bad news for you is that it will probably come out of your paycheck.

Your mistake was to violate the principle of encapsulation, by exposing implementation details. There was no guarantee that a client developer would even use your thoughtful class constants.

Another problem that can possibly stem from this arrangement is failure directly within your Employee class. If this happens, you will *definitely* get blamed. You must test that incoming parameters to the mutator method setEmployeeStatus() fall within an acceptable range. Otherwise, you run the risk that an int passed in as the new employee status puts your employee object into an invalid state. You can imagine the kind of havoc this bad state can wreak.

The direct solution is to code a GUARD CLAUSE in each method, throwing an exception if the parameter is outside the expected range. This adds a lot of code to your classes — more code that needs to be tested and maintained. It still does not solve the problem that client developers can misinterpret your class constants.

You would much rather catch the problem at compile time. Too bad Java does not provide an enum type as do C or C++. However, you can create one easily with a new class. The code in **Listing 3.23** provides a reusable superclass for implementing ENUMERATED CONSTANTS.

Listing 3.23   *Enum.java*

```
package enum;
import java.util.List;
import java.util.ArrayList;

public class Enum
{
    protected static int numberOfEnums = 0;
    protected static List list = new ArrayList();

    private int ordinal;
    private String name;
    protected Enum(String _name)
    {
        name = _name;
        ordinal = numberOfEnums++;
        list.add(this);
    }
```

(continued)

Listing 3.23 (cont.) *Enum.java*

```
   public String toString()
   {
      return name;
   }
   public int getOrdinal()
   {
      return ordinal;
   }

   public static Enum get(int ordinal)
   {
      return (Enum)list.get(ordinal);
   }
   public static int size()
   {
      return numberOfEnums;
   }
}
```

You will need to create this Enum superclass only once. Once it exists, you can create any number of enum subclasses. An example providing various marital status constants is shown in **Listing 3.24**.

Listing 3.24 *MaritalStatus.java*

```
package member;
public class MaritalStatus
   extends enum.Enum
{
   private MaritalStatus(String maritalStatus)
   {
      super(maritalStatus);
   }
   public static final MaritalStatus SINGLE =
      new MaritalStatus("Single");
   public static final MaritalStatus MARRIED =
      new MaritalStatus("Married");
   public static final MaritalStatus DIVORCED =
      new MaritalStatus("Divorced");
   public static final MaritalStatus SEPARATED =
      new MaritalStatus("Separated");
   public static final MaritalStatus WIDOWED =
      new MaritalStatus("Widowed");
}
```

The code in **Listing 3.25** demonstrates how the MaritalStatus enum is used. Note that if you uncomment the attempt to create a new MaritalStatus enum value (line [13]), the compilation will fail — the constructor to MaritalStatus is private.

Listing 3.25 *Member.java*

```
package member;
import enum.*;
import java.util.*;

public class Member
{
    String name;
    MaritalStatus status;

    public static void main(String[] args)
    {
        Member m1 =
            new Member("Jeff Langr",
                        MaritalStatus.MARRIED);
        Member m2 =
            new Member("Joe Blow",
                        MaritalStatus.WIDOWED);
        Member m3 =
            new Member("José Canusi",
                        MaritalStatus.DIVORCED);
```
(13)
```
        // m1.setStatus(new MaritalStatus("HOPELESS"));

        if (m3.getStatus() == MaritalStatus.DIVORCED)
            System.out.println(m3);
    }

    public Member(String _name,
                    MaritalStatus _status)
    {
        name = _name;
        status = _status;
    }
    public void setStatus(MaritalStatus _status)
    {
        status = _status;
    }
    public MaritalStatus getStatus()
    {
        return status;
    }
    public String toString()
    {
        return getClass() +
                " [" + name + ", " +
                status + "]";
    }
}
```

This is a good amount of work to just do enums, a simple construct in C or C++.

BOOLEAN PROPERTY-SETTING METHOD

Answers the Question	How do you set a boolean property?
Solution	Create two methods: one to set the property on and another to set the property off. Neither method takes a parameter.
Category	State
Related Patterns	Setting Method

By sheer force of habit, developers often treat their boolean attributes just like any other attribute. They blindly declare a SETTING METHOD, naming it using the pattern setBoolValue(boolean). While technically this will work just fine, it is perhaps not the best solution.

The number of possible values for a boolean attribute is exactly two — true and false. Yet as simple as the implementation of a boolean attribute is, there is always the possibility that it can change. The most likely situation is when the boolean changes from being an attribute to being a calculated quantity.

BOOLEAN PROPERTY SETTING METHOD uses encapsulation to isolate any such change impacts to the object itself.

Because there are two possible values for a boolean, to set it to all possible states you will need to define two methods instead of a single SETTING METHOD. One method sets the property on (true), and one method sets it off (false).

As with most method names, BOOLEAN PROPERTY SETTING METHOD names should start with a verb. The convention for regular SETTING METHODS — "set" — sounds just fine in most situations, as it reads better. In some cases, another verb may sound better, but the consistency of using "set" will help make the pattern more recognizable.

For the method that turns on the attribute, the second part of the method name should be the name of the attribute. For the method that turns off the attribute, the second part of the method name should be an appropriate opposite of the attribute name.

Two examples are provided in **Listing 3.26**. The fullTime attribute is set on and off by the methods setFullTime() and setPartTime(), respectively. The locked attribute is set using the methods setLocked() and setUnlocked().

Listing 3.26 BOOLEAN PROPERTY SETTING METHODS

```
public void setFullTime()
{
    fullTime = true;
}

public void setPartTime()
{
    fullTime = false;
}

public void setLocked()
{
    locked = true;
}

public void setUnlocked()
{
    locked = false;
}
```

An additional benefit of BOOLEAN PROPERTY SETTING METHOD is the clarification of client code. The message send employee.setPartTime() is considerably more expressive than employee.setFullTime(false).

ROLE-SUGGESTING INSTANCE VARIABLE NAME

Answers the Question	What do you name an instance variable?
Solution	Name the instance variable after the role it plays as an attribute of an object, not after how it is implemented.
Category	State
Related Patterns	Role-Suggesting Temporary Variable Name

Good naming, whether it be naming of classes, instance variables, temporary variables, or methods, is one of the most important parts of developing maintainable software. Even COMPOSED METHOD would do you little good if your method names made no sense.

One of the very first things I do when tasked to maintain code is to make sure I understand what it is doing. Before touching any of the logic, the first thing I often need to do is change instance-variable names to something more meaningful. I then execute a global search and replace each occurrence one by one, using more appropriate instance variable names. This also gives me the opportunity to see how and where an instance variable is used in the class.

Because instance variables are supposed to be tied to your object modeling, it is important that their names be implementation-neutral. An example in Java is how you name an instance variable that stores a collection. Suppose you have a Catalog that stores Product objects. If you implemented it using a java.util.List, you might be tempted to call the instance variable `productsList`. What if you change your implementation to use a HashMap for efficiency reasons? Your instance variable name must be changed, otherwise your class code becomes misleading. The solution is to just call the collection `products`.

To use ROLE-SUGGESTING INSTANCE VARIABLE NAME, name your instance variables after what they do or are, not how they do it or how they are implemented. Instead of `idNumber`, use `id`. Instead of `filenameString`, use `filename`.

TEMPORARY VARIABLE

Answers the Question	How do you store a value for later use in a method?
Solution	Declare a locally scoped variable and assign it a value.
Category	State
Related Patterns	Collecting Temporary Variable Caching Temporary Variable Reusing Temporary Variable Explaining Temporary Variable

TEMPORARY VARIABLES, or "stack" variables, are variables whose scope of existence is either a method or an enclosing block. From an object-oriented design perspective, temporary variables are irrelevant, as they do not represent any modeling constructs. TEMPORARY VARIABLES instead provide solutions for specific implementation challenges.

The C language forced your TEMPORARY VARIABLE declarations to be the very first things in a function. C++ came along and allowed them to be declared virtually anywhere within a method or function. The accepted convention became to declare TEMPORARY VARIABLES as close as possible to where they would be used. The intent was to make code more understandable.

With Java, the rule is still valid — you probably still want to declare your temps where they are first used in a method. But if you have adhered to these patterns, particularly COMPOSED METHOD, your methods should be small enough so that it is no longer such a big deal. Within the scope of an ideal 1- to 12-line COMPOSED METHOD, locating a declaration is not a problem. The only pattern here is that you must declare the TEMPORARY VARIABLE before it is used, something the compiler enforces anyway.

More important than where the declaration appears in a method is at which time the TEMPORARY VARIABLE is initially assigned a value. In many cases, you can immediately assign an initial value. In some cases, Java will force you to assign a value. If you use a temp in an expression and the compiler cannot determine whether it has been initialized, you will get the error "Variable x may not have been initialized."

You may not necessarily want to create an object instance immediately upon declaration of a temp. It could be costly, or the instantiation could differ, based on a condition appearing later. In this case, the best solution is to explicitly assign the initial value of null to the variable.

The following four patterns describe the reasons why a TEMPORARY VARIABLE is used. COLLECTING TEMPORARY VARIABLE gathers information to be used later in a method. CACHING TEMPORARY VARIABLE stores the result of an expensive operation. EXPLAINING TEMPORARY VARIABLE is used to reduce complexity and declare intent. REUSING TEMPORARY VARIABLE ensures a consistent value for an expression throughout a method.

COLLECTING TEMPORARY VARIABLE

Answers the Question	How do you collect values that will be used later in a method?
Solution	Use a TEMPORARY VARIABLE to hold the values that are collected.
Category	State
Related Patterns	Temporary Variable

Most frequently, the COLLECTING TEMPORARY VARIABLE pattern is used in conjunction with a collection, such as a List or Vector object. Objects resulting from one or more expressions are added to a collection. The method may later iterate through the contents of this COLLECTING TEMPORARY VARIABLE, return the collection as the result of the method, access elements from it dynamically, and so on. The collection could be an aggregating object, such as a PARAMETER OBJECT.

If you apply COMPOSED METHOD like you are supposed to (have I driven this point home yet?), you will need to use this pattern less frequently. The example shown in **Listing 3.27** demonstrates a simple use for COLLECTING TEMPORARY VARIABLE.

Listing 3.27 COLLECTING TEMPORARY VARIABLE

```
protected void writeRequiredFieldsFunction(
PrintWriter toClient)
{
    toClient.println("function validate(form)");
    toClient.println("{");

    Vector fields = new Vector();          (14)
    fields.addElement("userId");           (15)
    fields.addElement("password");
    writeRequiredFieldCode(toClient,
                           "form",
                           fields);        (16)
    toClient.println("    return true");
    toClient.println("}");
}
```

The writeRequiredFieldFunction() method is part of a servlet. It drives writing a JavaScript function that requires field inputs to the HTML output stream. Line [14] in **Listing 3.27** creates the Vector fields that acts as a COLLECTING TEMPORARY VARIABLE. It gathers the list of HTML input fields that are required and gets passed (line [16]) to another method that writes out the specific JavaScript code for each field.

To be honest, writeRequiredFieldFunction() could have been factored a bit better. Most of the code can be reused for anyone who needs to set up a number of required fields. The only specific code is the two lines starting at line [15]. A preferred solution would be to create the vector externally in client code and have writeRequiredFieldFunction() accept it as a parameter.

Streams can also act as useful COLLECTING TEMPORARY VARIABLES. StringBuffers act as COLLECTING TEMPORARY VARIABLES for collections of strings and/or characters.

CACHING TEMPORARY VARIABLE

Answers the Question	How do you improve the performance of a method?
Solution	Assign the value of a costly expression to a TEMPORARY VARIABLE that will act as a cache. Use the variable in the remainder of the method.
Category	State
Related Patterns	Temporary Variable

Yes, I know I said that you should not consider performance unless performance is a problem. CACHING TEMPORARY VARIABLE is a possible solution to speeding up a method, but it can usually be used without detriment to the understanding of a method. In fact, even if a CACHING TEMPORARY VARIABLE is ineffective in terms of helping improve performance, it still acts as a useful EXPLAINING TEMPORARY VARIABLE that makes your code more readable.

Certain operations in Java are expensive. If you happen to know what they are or if you discover an operation during a performance evaluation that is causing a bottleneck, use a CACHING TEMPORARY VARIABLE. The basic idea is to take the performance hit once by assigning the results of a slow computation to a temporary variable.

One such costly operation in Java is the format() method in SimpleDateFormat. The code in **Listing 3.28**, which paints the time and also writes it in the titlebar, demonstrates an inefficient use of format() to repetitively produce a formatted time string (lines [17] and [18]). While running this example would by no means result in poor performance, it is used as a simple demonstration of how to apply CACHING TEMPORARY VARIABLE.

Listing 3.28 *Could Use CACHING TEMPORARY VARIABLE*

```
public void paint(Graphics g)
{
    Date currentTime = new Date();
    frame.setTitle("Time = " +
        formatter.format(currentTime));
    g.drawString(formatter.format(currentTime),
                 20, 20);
}
```
(17)
(18)

Listing 3.29 shows the `paint()` method after the pattern has been applied. Using CACHING TEMPORARY VARIABLE, the `format()` operation is executed only once. The resultant string is stored in `currentTimeString` (line [19]).

Listing 3.29 CACHING TEMPORARY VARIABLE

```
public void paint(Graphics g)
{
    Date currentTime = new Date();
    String currentTimeString =
        formatter.format(currentTime);
    frame.setTitle("Time = " +
                    currentTimeString);
    g.drawString(currentTimeString, 20, 20);
}
```

(19)

As an aside, most people are surprised by the fact that SimpleDateFormat is a performance hog. I discovered that the corresponding operation in Smalltalk was slow via performance profiling. I was, hence, suspicious of SimpleDateFormat upon coming to Java. Sure enough, it turned out to provide similarly poor performance. Remember, though, that I only determined this by a series of performance tests.

EXPLAINING TEMPORARY VARIABLE

Answers the Question	How do you simplify a complex expression within a method?
Solution	Break subexpressions out of the complex expression. Assign the result of each subexpression to a Temporary Variable that has a Role-Suggesting Temporary Variable Name.
Category	State
Related Patterns	Temporary Variable Role-Suggesting Temporary Variable Name

An important goal in writing code is to make it understandable. Appropriate application of the COMPOSED METHOD pattern can help clarify the intent of a complex method. Factoring out a single expression into its own method is usually overkill, however. Reuse is the deciding factor here: if an expression will never be called more than once, then it should not be made into its own method.

An EXPLAINING TEMPORARY VARIABLE can take the place of COMPOSED METHOD. Given a complex expression, factor out a conceptually understandable chunk — a subexpression — and assign its value to a temporary variable. Then use the temporary variable in place of the original subexpression.

For example, consider the simple expression in **Listing 3.30** that returns the difference in days between two dates.

Listing 3.30 *Without EXPLAINING TEMPORARY VARIABLES*

```
int days = (int)((laterDate.getTime() -
                  earlierDate.getTime()) /
                 (60 * 60 * 24 * 1000));
```

While it should only take a few seconds to determine how this code works, a couple of EXPLAINING TEMPORARY VARIABLES can make understanding almost instantaneous, as demonstrated in **Listing 3.31**.

Listing 3.31 *With Explaining Temporary Variables*

```
long msDifference =
   laterDate.getTime() - earlierDate.getTime();
long msInADay = 60 * 60 * 24 * 1000;
int days = (int)(msDifference / msInADay);
```

The number of milliseconds in a day, `msInADay`, should really be a constant, anyway.

Use of temporary variables is not without cost. They can make it difficult or impossible for a compiler to optimize code. Normally the additional cost is negligible. As usual, strive for clarity first.

REUSING TEMPORARY VARIABLE

Answers the Question	How do you use the results of an expression several times in a method when its value may change?
Solution	Assign the results of the expression to a TEMPORARY VARIABLE. The variable may be reused throughout the remainder of the method.
Category	State
Related Patterns	Temporary Variable

There are many expressions that will not return the same value if executed more than once. If you need to get the current date and time, you simply create a new Date instance with no parameters. Execute the same new Date() expression later in the method, and the time will likely have changed. Similarly, each time you execute the next() method on an Iterator or the nextToken() method on a StringTokenizer, you get the next object in succession.

You need to save the resultant expression value in a REUSING TEMPORARY VARIABLE. **Listing 3.32** demonstrates an example using StringTokenizer.

Listing 3.32 *REUSING TEMPORARY VARIABLE*

```
       StringTokenizer tk =
          new StringTokenizer(
             "This is a test of the EBS.");
       while (tk.hasMoreElements())
       {
(20)      String token = tk.nextToken();
          System.out.println("token = \"" +
(21)                          token +
                             "\"; length = " +
(22)                          token.length());
       }
```

A StringTokenizer is basically an Enumeration with a few extra utility methods, including two INTENTION-REVEALING METHOD NAMES, hasMoreTokens() and nextToken().[6] Each call to nextToken() (line [20]) changes the state of the tokenizer. The next available token is extracted from the source string, and a pointer internal to StringTokenizer is moved to the next element. If you wish to use a token in more than one expression (lines [21] and [22]), you must assign it to a REUSING TEMPORARY VARIABLE (line [20]).

---

6 The benefit of using nextToken() over nextElement() is that you do not need to cast the result of nextToken() to a String.

ROLE-SUGGESTING TEMPORARY VARIABLE NAME

Answers the Question	What do you name a TEMPORARY VARIABLE?
Solution	Name it after the role it performs in the computation.
Category	State
Related Patterns	Role-Suggesting Instance Variable Name

There is little difference between this pattern and ROLE-SUGGESTING INSTANCE VARIABLE NAME. While TEMPORARY VARIABLES are tactical and implementation-specific, there is still no need to require them to expose type information. Expressions using temps generally become more clear if the temporary variable name is meaningful. If your methods are short like they are supposed to be, determining the type of a TEMPORARY VARIABLE is visually instantaneous.

As with instance variables, spell things out. I have seen patterns that suggest using shortcut references to help reduce your typing time. One such example would have you assign System.out to a single-character temporary variable:

```
private static final PrintStream o = System.out;
```

This allows you to write code like:

```
o.println("output text");
```

In order to save a few seconds of typing, you have now cost all future maintenance efforts considerably more time. A developer now has to keep eyeballing back to the declaration of "o" to understand what it represents in an expression.

Most modern editors have rapid expansion capabilities or comparable macro facilities. Even without the advantages of a good editor, it's to be hoped that you will type the code only once. But your code might be looked at hundreds of times thereafter.

The use of cryptic variables can make successful searches nearly impossible. If the identifier c refers to a customer object, how will you easily find all uses of the identifier c? Remember that you may have to find references to your customer object in the context of parameter lists (add(c)), instance creation (new c()), method execution (c.getName()), and assignment (c = new Customer()). Searches will be considerably easier if you use a meaningful identifier such as customer.

Chapter 4   *COLLECTIONS*

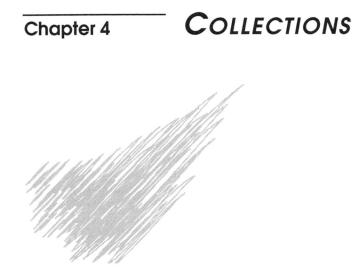

Building robust, scalable applications with JDK 1.1 is a questionable effort at best. In order to work with collections of data, you either have to grow your own data structures, use a third-party product such as the JGL,[1] or deal with the one-size-fits-all workhorses, Vector and Hashtable. While not terrible, Vector and Hashtable have their limitations, and being forced to use them in every situation is like the old analogy of the carpenter with just a hammer: Everything becomes a nail to get banged around.

Thankfully, JDK 1.2 introduces the *collections framework*. It is just what its name suggests, plus a bit more. It provides classes for representing aggregations, or *collections*, of objects. It is not just a series of class definitions for data structures, however. While JDK 1.2 provides a set of concrete collection implementations, its real focus is to provide a set of interfaces for defining a coordinated infrastructure, or *framework*, for consistent implementations of collection classes.

Additionally, the collections framework contains a set of wrappers for additional functionality, including synchronization and the capability to define collections as unmodifiable. A set of useful algorithms for sorting,

---

1 Java Generic Library, a collections and algorithm library available from ObjectSpace.

searching, and more is also provided. Finally, the collections framework ensures compatibility with the older JDK collections such as Vector by providing a series of conversion methods. Vector and Hashtable have also been retrofitted to implement the collections framework interfaces, so methods like addAll() and putAll() are now supported.

This chapter on collection patterns is geared toward the collections framework in Java 2. Many but not all of the patterns can be implemented in JDK 1.1 and earlier. Where there are significant differences, I will point out specifics in implementation between the two sets of versions. Otherwise the remainder of the chapter will use the collection classes from JDK 1.2. In general, you should be able to replace an ArrayList with a Vector. Similarly, a HashMap can be replaced with a Hashtable.

Many of the basic collection "patterns" within this chapter may not seem like patterns at all. The goal of a pattern such as ARRAY is to educate you about how to use one of the data structures available in Java. The pattern answers the question of how to most appropriately use a certain kind of collection to solve a problem.

The pattern language in *Essential Java Style* derives from a Smalltalk pattern language for implementation. Thus some of the patterns within may seem a bit alien to the seasoned programmer with a C/C++/Java–oriented background. The DO, SELECT/REJECT, DETECT, COLLECT, and INJECT INTO patterns are provided as basic constructs in Smalltalk. Their addition to Java development can provide a rich expressiveness to working with collections of data. Within each of these patterns, I provide both the classic procedural solution and the alternate, more object-oriented solution.

COLLECTION

Answers the Question	How do you represent aggregations of objects?
Solution	Use a collection.
Category	Collections
Related Patterns	List Array Map Set

Programming without collection classes is almost unthinkable. You need a place to put all your objects. The ability to hold collections of objects (aggregations) is an essential and pervasive need in application development. Examples include: (1) opening a cursor from a relational database query and fetching all its entries results in a set of elements; (2) users save documents and later access them from a list, or collection, of file names; (3) a window in a user interface contains a collection of widgets such as buttons and entry fields.

Java 1.1 only provides three classes[2] to hold collections of objects:

- Array, which holds a fixed-size list of elements;

- Vector, which manages a variable-sized list of elements;

- Hashtable, which contains a set of elements that are each accessed by a specific key value.

Each of these collection classes is distinct from the other. All of them directly extend Object, thus there is little common inheritance. The available public methods (and their names) are inconsistent between the classes. While Vectors are implemented in terms of Arrays, the two classes cannot be interchanged. The only means of directly converting between Arrays and Vectors is the `copyInto(Object[])` method (which populates an Array object using the Vector's contents). Finally, Hashtables have little in common with Vectors or Arrays.

Enter Java 2, which provides a somewhat unified collections framework. Java 2 defines two main hierarchies: one for collections of discrete objects, and one for collections based on mappings between objects. There is little overlap between how you work with the two types of collections, hence the decision was made to keep the hierarchies separate. For clarity I will refer to the hash-based collections by the Java 2 term *maps*. For the "regular" collections of objects, I will use the generic term *collections*.

---

2 Technically BitSet is a collection class, but it can only contain bits.

Collection Interfaces

Figure 4.1 shows the inheritance relationship for the interfaces on the collections side of the fence. Note that this hierarchy, as well as the Map hierarchy, is made up of interfaces and not class implementations.

Figure 4.1 *Collection Interface Hierarchy*

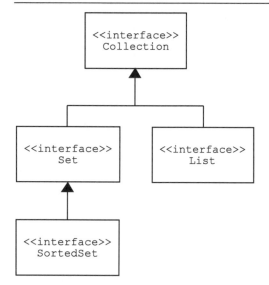

The Collection interface, at the root of the hierarchy, specifies the messages that all implementing classes must provide. Some of the methods include `add(Object)`, `addAll(Collection)`, `clear()`, `isEmpty()`, `remove(Object)`, `toArray()`, `iterator()`, and `contains(Object)`. A total of 15 methods must be implemented.

The JDK documentation also states that implementing classes should provide two constructors. The first constructor takes no arguments and creates an empty collection of a default size. The second constructor takes another Collection as its parameter.[3] Elements from this source collection are mapped one-for-one into the new collection.

Some of the methods in the Collection interface (and in the Set and List interfaces) are designated as *optional*. A concrete class implementing the interface can choose to not provide any real behavior for an optional method. The method must instead throw an UnsupportedOperationException, since Java requires that implementing classes provide definitions for all methods.

---

3 Interfaces cannot contain definitions for constructors, so this ends up being a request that must be specified in the documentation.

The List interface, which extends the Collection interface, is the definition for LISTS. A LIST is an ordered sequence of objects that can grow and shrink in size. ArrayList and Vector are concrete classes available in Java 2 which implement the List interface. This implementation is indirect: It turns out that Java 2 provides a hierarchy of abstract classes to make the implementation of the concrete classes considerably easier. There is an AbstractCollection that implements some of the Collection interface methods, and similarly there is an AbstractList class that extends AbstractCollection and implements some of the List interface methods.

On the other side of the Collection tree, there is a similar hierarchy of set collections. A SET is an unordered collection of objects that does not contain duplicate elements. A SortedSet interface is also provided to allow for sets to maintain a specific order.

Map Interfaces

Maps in Java 2 are considered different enough to warrant their own separate hierarchy. **Figure 4.2** shows the Map interface hierarchy.

Figure 4.2 *Map Interface Hierarchy*

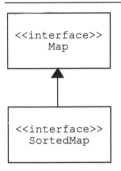

A MAP is an object that maps keys to values. The best analogy is a dictionary, where a word — a key — can be quickly looked up to return a definition — a value. A MAP can only have one entry per lookup key. In Java 2, the concrete implementations of the Map interface are Hashtable, HashMap, and TreeMap. Hashtable is left over from JDK 1.1; HashMap is the general-purpose implementation; and TreeMap provides a MAP whose keys remain in sorted order.

Suppose you emulate a dictionary in an application. To create and add a new mapping to this dictionary, you might code the following:

```
Map dictionary = new HashMap();
dictionary.put("smelt", "a small salmonoid fish");
```

The string "smelt" is the key and the string "a small salmonoid fish" is the value. To retrieve the definition stored at the word "smelt", you would code the following:

```
(String)dictionary.get("smelt");
```

The Collections Framework

Three things comprise the collections framework:

1 The set of **interfaces** that provide commonality between the various collection implementations;
2 Concrete **implementations**, the actual classes that will be instantiated and used as data structures;
3 A set of **algorithms**, to provide various code solutions that can be used on any collection.

You should get immediate gratification from the implementations and algorithms part of the framework. It certainly is nice not to have to create your own tree structure or code a sort routine.

More importantly, the interfaces ultimately provide flexibility in your application development. You may initially code your application so that employees are loaded into an ArrayList and later change the implementation to a LinkedList when you need different performance characteristics. This ends up being a one-line change, since both LinkedList and ArrayList respond to the same messages.

Your methods should be coded to take interfaces as parameters (Collection, List, Set, and so on) and not the concrete collection implementations (ArrayList, LinkedList, HashSet, and so on). This will allow you to pass into the method any other collection that implements the appropriate interface.

The collection interfaces support the notion of encapsulation: a collection can be represented by any structure, but clients sending messages to the collection need no understanding of the actual implementation.

ARRAY

Answers the Question	How do you store a fixed-size ordered collection of elements?
Solution	Use an Array object.
Category	Collections
Related Patterns	Collection List

ARRAY is implemented in just about every procedural language. Most languages depend on the concept of an array, a linear allocation of data in memory space. Accessing elements within an ARRAY is simply a matter of adding an offset to the base address of the memory allocation.

The problem with arrays, however, is that their size must be static. Once an array has been created, you cannot increase it's memory allocation, because contiguous available space at the end of the initial allocation cannot be guaranteed. Arrays depend on existing in contiguous memory space, to allow elements to be extracted by adding an offset to the base address. If the need for additional array space arises, a new array must be allocated and all of the elements from the original array must be copied into it.

ARRAYS still exist in Java as a somewhat special case. They appear at first glance to be implemented solely using Java language syntax. But arrays in Java are really instances of a class, Array, that is initialized and accessed using special syntax. Array is implemented using native methods and as a result provides optimal speed. Java Array objects still have the limitation of being fixed in size.

Arrays in Java are defined using the class name of objects that can be contained within. The [ ] operator is appended to the end of the class name. The size of the array is specified as part of the array instantiation. The following line of code initializes an array of seasons to four slots, each of which can hold a string object:

```
String[] seasons = new String[4];
```

If you want your array to hold any kind of object, you can declare an array of Object. Native types are also supported:

```
int[] sizes = new int[100];
```

A plus in Java is that there is special syntax for Array initialization. When creating an Array instance, you can assign it an initial list of values. This also has the effect of defining the fixed size of the Array. A few examples of Array initialization are shown in **Listing 4.1**. Note that the initializer list can contain either literals (line [1]), references to objects (line [2]), or object instantiations (line [3]).

Listing 4.1 *Array Initialization*

```
       String[] seasons =
(1)        {"Spring", "Summer", "Autumn", "Winter"};
       Customer firstCustomer =
          new Customer("Smelt Industries");
       Customer[] customers =
(2)        {firstCustomer,
(3)          new Customer("ABC Systems"),
             new Customer("DKING Tech")};
```

If you absolutely know that your collection will never vary in size, and if you need the performance, use an ARRAY. ARRAYS will give you the fastest possible performance at the cost of flexibility. But most of the time, you will either need the flexibility now or somewhere down the road. Most collections have a tendency to grow, so use a LIST, LINKED LIST, or some other more dynamic collection instead.

JDK 1.2 provides a set of static methods for manipulating arrays in the Arrays class. These methods provide sort, fill, search, and equality methods. Additionally, an `asList()` method is provided to convert an Array into a List object.

LIST

Answers the Question	How do you store a collection where elements can be added and removed?
Solution	Use a List object.
Category	Collections
Related Patterns	Collection Array

It would be nice if all your collections were fixed in size and did not need to grow or shrink in your application. Unfortunately most sets of data do not adhere to this ideal. Someone is always wanting to hire a new employee or remove a line item from a bill. Data is continually added, deleted, or moved from one place to another, often in increments of one.

A LIST is a series of data elements, represented in a specific order. As with an ARRAY, elements are accessed on the basis of an index, or offset, into the series of data. But a LIST differs from an ARRAY in that the collection size can grow or shrink as elements are added to and removed from the series.

With the classic array, your best bet is to allocate space for what you hope are enough elements. You can then choose to not worry about things, assuming that they will stay the same for now. Some poor future developer will have to update the code when a fifty-first state is added to the United States. Or you can be a nice developer and write the code to manage dynamically growing the array.

The beauty of objects is that you can take the flexible, second alternative to dynamically size the array. The encapsulated solution, unwieldy as it is, has to be written only once. In the classic world, your application has to deal with sizing each array on an individual basis. In the object world, each collection is an object that can manage its own sizing.

The Vector class, the first attempt at a LIST workhorse in the JDK, manages dynamic growth. All it really does is encapsulate an Array object and maintain the number of elements contained within (`elementCount`). The `addElement()` method, for example, puts the object to be added at the end of the array and bumps up the value of `elementCount` by one. Before doing so, though, it checks to see if the array will need to grow in size first. If so, a new array is allocated and `System.arrayCopy()` is used to quickly dump the contents of the old array into the new one.

As you can imagine, Vector has some performance drawbacks. First, searches for a specific element must traverse all elements contained within to locate a match. Second, if the initial allocation is not optimal, the expensive operation of reallocating the array must be performed. And finally, inserting elements into or deleting elements from the middle of the array requires an array copy to shift the remainder of elements to the right or left, respectively, by one position. The closer the element to be added is to the beginning of the list, the more expensive the insertion operation.

You can create a Vector object without any parameters. Performance can be improved, however, if you take care to specify appropriate sizing information on construction. Vector provides two additional constructors to help control sizing. The first additional constructor takes an initial capacity as its sole parameter, which represents the number of elements initially allocated for the internal array. The default allocation is for 10 elements. If you know you will need more space than that, you should always provide an initial capacity.

The second Vector constructor takes both an initial capacity and a capacity increment. This capacity increment specifies how the array will grow if reallocation is necessary. If you do not specify an increment, the array doubles each time; otherwise your increment is added to the current array size to produce the new allocation size.

In JDK 1.2, ArrayList is the workhorse concrete implementation of a LIST. It implements the List interface. There is not a lot of difference between the implementation of ArrayList and Vector. They both use an Array for the underlying collection. ArrayList contains slightly modified growth algorithms. Interestingly, the capacity increment can no longer be specified in JDK 1.2. ArrayLists under JDK 1.2 grow using the formula `newCapacity = (oldCapacity * 3) / 2 + 1`. The new ArrayList thus increases by 50% in size, as opposed to 100% in size for Vectors.

ArrayList also provides a CONVERTER CONSTRUCTOR METHOD, which allows for creation of the collection using another collection. The source collection must implement the Collection interface. The JDK 1.2 implementation of Vector has been retrofitted to support this CONVERTER CONSTRUCTOR METHOD as well. Vector under JDK 1.2 implements List, which in turn implements Collection. This allows Vector to work seamlessly within the JDK 1.2 collections framework.

A significant difference between ArrayList and Vector is that Vector is synchronized; you cannot change that fact. Most accesses to the collection are single-threaded. If you do not require synchronization, this is expensive overhead. In contrast, the JDK 2 collections framework provides unsynchronized collections as the default. It allows you to wrap the collections in synchronization wrappers if you need that functionality.

What is a LIST good for? Most user-driven applications provide lists of data to be manipulated by the user. In an object model, these data elements are the "many" in a one-to-many relationship from one domain object to another. For instance, an Employee may have many Dependent objects; a

Bill may contain several LineItem objects. In a user interface, you might have an employee window that sports a list box of dependents. The list box points off to an underlying Dependent collection. Dependents can be added or removed from the collection via Add and Delete button controls.

Typically these lists are reasonably manageable in size. An employee usually has only a handful of dependents; a bill might contain up to a few hundred line items. With small collections of this nature, where either the list is manipulated as a whole or individual elements are accessed one at a time by a user, the need for high-speed access is generally unnecessary. Collections of up to a few hundred elements can be scanned rapidly. A LIST provides the simplest, most straightforward means of implementing the collection.

If you must frequently insert elements into the middle or at the beginning of the collection order, consider using a LINKED LIST. A LINKED LIST dynamically allocates entries in the collection on an individual basis, as opposed to making an initial contiguous allocation to store a predefined number of elements.

If it is possible to specify a unique key for each object in a collection and high-speed or repetitive access is required, a HASH MAP might be more appropriate.

LINKED LIST

Answers the Question	What do you use when elements are frequently added to/removed from the middle or beginning of a collection?
Solution	Use a LinkedList object.
Category	Collections
Related Patterns	List

A LINKED LIST eliminates the need to worry about how many elements a collection needs to contain over its lifetime. As opposed to preallocating a block of space for an ARRAY, space in a LINKED LIST is allocated on an element-by-element basis. An element is *linked* to another by use of a pointer, or reference. A series of these linked elements forms the list.

The simplest form is a singly linked list. The first element contains a reference to the next element in the list, which in turn contains a pointer to the next element, and so on. The reference variable in each element is often named next. The next reference in the last element in the list points to null. A separate reference must be maintained to the first element in the list, referred to as the header.

To maintain reusability, a list element is implemented as an object with minimally two variables. The first is the next reference; the second is an Object reference to the data itself. A possible list element implementation is shown in **Listing 4.2**. This class would typically be an inner class, private to the LINKED LIST class.

Listing 4.2 *LINKED LIST Element Implementation Example*

```
private class Element
{
    Object data;
    Element next;

    Element(Object _data, Element _next)
    {
        data = _data;
        next = _next;
    }
}
```

Traversal of a LINKED LIST is done using another reference. This traversal reference, often named `current`, is initially set to point to the header (by copying the existing header reference). This reference is moved along the links of the list by dereferencing the `next` pointer in each element. Adding an element to the list requires traversing the list to determine the appropriate location. Once the location is determined, it is a constant operation to modify `next` pointers to include the new element.

LINKED LISTS can also be doubly linked. A second pointer, typically called `previous`, must be added to each Element object. As a new Element is added, its `next` reference is set to point to the following object in the list and its `previous` reference is set to point to the preceding object in the list. This double linking allows for traversal of the list in both ways and can speed up access.

The LinkedList class in JDK 1.2 is doubly-linked. Additionally, it is *circular* in that the last element's `next` points to the first element and the first element's `previous` reference points to the last element.

A LINKED LIST is ideal as the basis for implementing a QUEUE, where insertions and deletions take place at both ends of the list. It can also be used effectively as a STACK (but so can an ArrayList). Insertions and deletions at the front or in the middle of a list are most costly in an ArrayList implementation, since the remainder of the elements must be shifted right or left. If you must manage a collection that must constantly be in sorted order, and elements are frequently added, a LINKED LIST is a good choice.

EQUALITY METHOD

Answers the Question	How do you provide a method to test whether or not two objects are equal?
Solution	Code an equals(Object) method to return true if the Object parameter is equal to this object.
Category	Collections
Related Patterns	None

One of the great things about inheritance hierarchies is that you get a lot of behavior by default. In Java, Object is the root of all hierarchies. Every method implemented in Object belongs to your subclassing object as well. You owe it to yourself to fully understand what the designers of Java felt was behavior important enough to belong in every class. Take some time, look at the source for java.lang.Object, and learn just what it is that you are always inheriting.

The equals() method is one of about a dozen methods provided in Object. The default implementation of equals() — the behavior that you get unless you override it — is shown in **Listing 4.3**.

Listing 4.3   *Object's equals() Method*[4]

```
public boolean equals(Object obj)
{
    return this == obj;
}
```

Pretty simple! If you do not provide a new definition for equals(), it does the same thing as ==. And just in case you are not clear, the equality operator (==) returns true if both object references (this and obj in **Listing 4.3**) point to the same object in memory. This is known as *object equivalence*.

You must determine if this default behavior is what you need. But if you know that your object comparisons absolutely must be based on object identity, you should forgo use of the equals() method entirely. Using == instead will clarify your intent to other readers of your code, that you are using object equivalence to compare objects.

---

4 This method has been reformatted from what Sun Microsystems provided for readability purposes.

More often, though, you will want to use the `equals()` method for object comparisons. Comparing two objects this way is known as testing for *object equality*. It is up to you to define what the tests are that result in two objects being equal. For example, a common way to compare employees is to test whether their Social Security numbers are the same. Two points are equal if their x and y coordinates are the same. Yet these equal points could be two separate objects in memory space. One point object might have been created by a user clicking on a specific window location, while the other point instance may have been created directly within code.

Listing 4.4 provides a complete test program, Point.java, to demonstrate the distinction between object equivalence and object equality.

Listing 4.4   *Point.java*

```
public class Point
{
    int x;
    int y;
    public static void main(String[] args)
    {
(4)     Point p1 = new Point(4, 3);
        Point p2 = new Point(4, 4);
(5)     Point p3 = new Point(4, 3);
        System.out.println("p1.equals(p2) ? " +
            p1.equals(p2));
        System.out.println("p1.equals(p3) ? " +
            p1.equals(p3));
        System.out.println("p1 == p3 ? " +
            (p1 == p3));
    }
    public Point(int _x, int _y)
    {
        x = _x;
        y = _y;
    }
(6) public boolean equals(Object point)
    {
(7)     if (!(point instanceof Point))
            return false;
        return ((Point)point).x == x &&
                ((Point)point).y == y;
    }
}
```

The output produced by running the `main()` method in **Listing 4.4** is:

```
p1.equals(p2) ? false
p1.equals(p3) ? true
p1 == p3 ? false
```

The first two tests are for object equality; the final test is for object equivalence. Note that `p1` is equal to `p3` but not equivalent, since each of the two points was created as a separate object via the `new` operator (lines [4] and [5]).

Pay close attention to the `equals()` method in **Listing 4.4** (line [6]). The first thing it does is ensure that the parameter passed, `point`, is a Point object (line [7]). If it is not, the comparison immediately returns false.[5] This is necessary because the parameter is defined to be of class Object.

So why declare the parameter as a generic Object? Rarely will you be trying to compare apples and oranges. Most of the time you will be trying to compare one employee to another, not employees to managers. In fact, it is almost always a mistake when objects of different classes are compared.

With this knowledge in mind, you could code a much simpler method, as demonstrated in **Listing 4.5**.

Listing 4.5   A Cleaner `equals()` Method?

```
public boolean equals(Point point)
{
    return
        point.x == x &&
        point.y == y;
}
```

Listing 4.5 looks much nicer, especially since the casts are gone. It is also much faster, since the use of the costly `instanceof` operator was removed.

All that improvement on aesthetics and performance is for naught, however. Just as you will rarely compare apples and oranges, you won't often compare two objects pointed to by discrete instance or temporary variables. Your code will probably do few direct comparisons of objects using the `equals()` method. Instead, it turns out that most object comparisons are done behind the scenes with collections.[6]

If you use the method `indexOf(Object)` to determine where an object is in an ArrayList, the code in ArrayList scans the list and returns the index of the first occurrence of the argument. It tests each element in turn

---

5 See the GUARD CLAUSE pattern in Chapter 6, "Formatting," for an explanation of why the method is formatted this way.

6 A-HA! Now you know why this pattern appears in the chapter on collections.

by sending the equals() method to the argument, with the element as a parameter. Ignoring the special case where the elem argument is null, the actual JDK code is provided in **Listing 4.6**.

Listing 4.6   *java.util.ArrayList indexOf() Method*

```
public int indexOf(Object elem)
{
    for (int i = 0; i < size; i++)
        if (elem.equals(elementData[i]))
            return i;
    return -1;
}
```

ArrayList only knows the argument object and each element contained within as generic Objects. This means it must call an equals() method with the signature equals(Object). So if you provide a method in Point with the signature equals(Point), it will never get called by indexOf().

Comparing the individual instance variables in order to get a boolean result from equals() can be expensive. If it is frequently the case that two objects are equivalent (that they are the same object), you can speed up the equals() method by testing equivalence before you test equality. The equals() method in java.lang.String does just that, as shown in **Listing 4.7**. The GUARD CLAUSE at line [8] causes an early exit from the method, with a true value, if the parameter anObject is the same as this.

Listing 4.7   *Testing Equivalence Before Equality*

```
public boolean equals(Object anObject)
{
    if (this == anObject)
        return true;
    if ((anObject != null) &&
        (anObject instanceof String))
    {
        String anotherString = (String)anObject;
        int n = count;
        if (n == anotherString.count)
        {
            char v1[] = value;
            char v2[] = anotherString.value;
            int i = offset;
            int j = anotherString.offset;
            while (n- != 0))
                if (v1[i++] != v2[j++])
                    return false;
            return true;
        }
    }
    return false;
}
```

(8)

The use of instanceof, otherwise generally frowned on, is pretty much required in the equals(Object) method to ensure that you are comparing an Apple to an Apple. Otherwise you run the risk of trying to compare an Apple to an Orange, which will usually throw an exception. There is an alternate solution that I will briefly discuss, but do not recommend.

The theory behind the alternate solution is that because you rarely compare apples and oranges, attempts to do so are exception conditions. For our Point example, you just cast the Object argument to a Point and trap any ClassCastException that is thrown. The benefit of using try/catch blocks to handle the special case is that they create less overhead than instanceof if the exception is never thrown. But once again, it takes quite a few (million) equals() comparisons before a smidgen of speed difference is even noticed. The alternate solution is provided in **Listing 4.8**, just in case you are compelled to use it.

Listing 4.8   *A Sometimes-Faster equals() Method*

```
public boolean equals(Object object)
{
    if (object == null) return false;
    try
    {
        Point point = (Point)object;
        return
            point.x == x &&
            point.y == y;
    }
    catch (ClassCastException e)
    {
        return false;
    }
}
```

(9)

Note that this technique requires a GUARD CLAUSE (line [9]) that returns false if the argument is null.

MAP

Answers the Question	How do you map keys to values?
Solution	Use a data structure that implements the Map interface.
Category	Collections
Related Patterns	Hashing Method

A MAP is an object that maps keys to values and cannot contain duplicate keys. Their ideal use is for rapid lookups based on a unique key value, such as retrieving the string value for a system property name.

Common MAP behavior is provided in Java by the Map interface in java.util. This interface replaces the Dictionary abstract superclass in JDK 1.1 and earlier. Concrete Map implementations provided in JDK 1.2 include HashMap, Hashtable (to provide backward compatibility with earlier JDK versions), WeakHashMap, and TreeMap.

The chief methods provided by the Map interface are put() and get(). The put() method takes two Object parameters, key and value. When invoked, put() stores a value at the location specified by the key. It can be later retrieved by sending the get() message to the Map object with the same key. A simple use of a MAP would be to map a set of error strings to their corresponding error codes. **Listing 4.9** demonstrates this example.

Listing 4.9   MAP Example

```
(10)   Map errorStrings = new HashMap();

(11)   errorStrings.put("001",
          "You shouldn't have done that.");
(12)   errorStrings.put("002",
          "I wish I could understand you better.");
(13)   errorStrings.put("003",
          "Please don't click your mouse so rapidly.");

(14)   System.out.println(errorStrings.get("002"));
```

Each message send of put() in the example (lines [11], [12], and [13]) adds a new error string at the location derived for the key error code value. The get() message send in line [14] results in the string "I wish I could understand you better" being returned.

If you are using JDK 1.1, you can simply replace line [10], which creates the HashMap object, with an instantiation of Hashtable:

```
Hashtable errorStrings = new Hashtable();
```

The Map interface provides signature definitions for several methods. remove(Object) deletes a single key/value pair, while clear() removes all such mappings from the Map object. isEmpty() returns true if there are no mappings, or returns false otherwise. The method containsKey(Object) returns a boolean value specifying whether the specified key object was found in the map; containsValue(Object) does the same test against the value objects. putAll(Map) takes a source object that implements the Map interface and adds all of its key/value mappings to this Map.

Three method definitions are provided to facilitate traversal of the mappings within a Map object. The keySet() method returns a Set of the key objects contained within the map. This Set object is a live set of references to the Map. In JDK terms, this means the Set is *backed by* the Map. Changes to the Set are reflected in the Map, and vice versa, with a couple of exceptions. add() and addAll() messages cannot be sent to the Set. Also, if the Map is modified while the set is being iterated over, the iteration results are undefined.

Use of keySet() against the error strings example (**Listing 4.9**) is demonstrated in **Listing 4.10**.

Listing 4.10 *MAP Iteration Using keySet ( )*

```
Set keys = errorStrings.keySet();
Iterator iterator = keys.iterator();
while (iterator.hasNext())
    System.out.println(iterator.next());
```

The output produced by the code in **Listing 4.10** is:

```
003
002
001
```

The second method that can be used to facilitate traversing a Map is values(). Instead of returning the key object from each mapping, it returns the value object. The similar iteration code is shown in **Listing 4.13**.

Listing 4.13   *MAP Iteration Using* `values()`

```
Collection values = errorStrings.values();
Iterator iterator = values.iterator();
while (iterator.hasNext())
    System.out.println(iterator.next());
```

The output produced by the code in **Listing 4.11** is:

```
Please do not click your mouse so rapidly.
I wish I could understand your input better.
You shouldn't have done that.
```

Typically it is not so useful to iterate over only keys or values. More often you will want to loop through all the mappings. You could do this by using keySet(), and then using each key returned to look up its corresponding value via get(). If you are using JDK 1.1, this is unfortunately the only technique that works (note that the method names are different). In JDK 1.2, however, the Map interface specifies a third method, entrySet(), to traverse a Map and return its mappings as a Set. Each element in the set is an instance of Map.Entry, a utility object used to store a key and its corresponding value. GETTING METHODS are provided in Map.Entry to extract these key and value objects. **Listing 4.12** shows how to use entrySet().

Listing 4.12   *MAP Iteration Using* `entrySet()`

```
Set entrySet = errorStrings.entrySet();
Iterator iterator = entrySet.iterator();
while (iterator.hasNext())
{
    Map.Entry mapping = (Map.Entry)iterator.next();
    System.out.println(mapping.getKey() +
                        "->" +
                        mapping.getValue());
}
```

The output produced by the code in **Listing 4.12** is:

```
003->Please do not click your mouse so rapidly.
002->I wish I could understand your input better.
001->You shouldn't have done that.
```

Note that the order for any of these three collections returned is undefined. If you need to insert, access, and remove entries in a MAP as fast as possible but occasionally need to iterate in sorted order against the mappings, use a HASH MAP and sort the results of entrySet() each time. If you need to sort mappings more frequently and can live with slower get() and put() access, use a TREE MAP.

HASH MAP

Answers the Question	How do you provide fast keyed access to a collection of elements?
Solution	Use a HashMap (JDK 1.2) or Hashtable (JDK 1.1) object.
Category	Collections
Related Patterns	Hashing Method

HASH MAPS are one of the most powerful data structures available in Java. They have the astounding capability of bringing lookups, which are typically linear or binary searches, down to a constant-time operation. Lookup time of O(1) is possible with HASH MAPS! HASH MAPS are implemented as Hashtable objects in JDK 1.1 and as Map objects in JDK 1.2.

How Do Hashtables Differ from HashMaps?

First, the HashMap class provided in JDK 1.2 is part of the collections framework and as such implements the Map interface. See the MAP pattern for details on the functionality that HashMap must implement.

Hashtable contains most of the same methods as HashMap, with some significant differences. For example, under JDK 1.1 and earlier, Hashtable does not provide the putAll(Map) method. This method allows for a map object to be dumped wholesale into a HashMap. If you are compelled to use Hashtable under JDK 1.2, it has been modified to implement the Map interface, so all these new methods are now available.

HashMap implements the entrySet() method, declared as part of the Map interface and implemented in HashMap. entrySet() returns a collection view on the Map. Each element in this collection is a special Map.entry object that contains the key and value pair for each element in the original HashMap. This allows for a single-pass iteration to be made over the HashMap as if it were an ordered collection of objects. Without entrySet(), you would need to iterate over the keys and, for each key, use get() to retrieve the corresponding element from the HashMap.

There are a couple of other differences between the two classes. Hashtables do not permit nulls, which HashMaps do, as both values and a key. Also, access to a Hashtable is synchronized, while the default access for a HashMap is unsynchronized. Synchronization may be added to HashMaps by creating a synchronization wrapper.

How Does a HashMap Work?

A HASH MAP is represented by a fixed set of contiguous slots in memory. To put an object in the HASH MAP, an appropriate slot must be found. The determination of just what slot to put the object in is based on an algorithm executed against key data. This algorithm is known as the HASHING METHOD (see the next pattern for information on how to implement it properly). Execution of the HASHING METHOD ideally results in a unique location where the object will be placed within the HASH MAP.

Retrieval of the object depends on the fact that the key generated by the HASHING METHOD remains unchanged as long as the object is contained within the HASH MAP. The same algorithm is executed against the same key data, revealing the appropriate slot where the object was originally stored.

How Should HashMap Objects Be Created?

In conjunction with an appropriate HASHING METHOD, a couple of instance creation parameters can be used to significantly improve the performance of a HashMap. An initial capacity should be specified to set the total number of slots available in the table. This capacity is closely associated with the HASHING METHOD. The capacity should not be too high, otherwise traversal of the HashMap takes a long time in proportion to the number of elements. It should not be too low, otherwise many elements will begin hashing to the same slot, an event known as a *collision*.

There are a couple of solutions to the problem of how to deal with collisions, but the net effect is the same. For each access to an object that was involved in a collision, all the objects that have collided at the same spot must be serially searched in order to find the right one. The more collisions, the slower the average access time.

The second instance creation parameter that can be set is the load factor. This is expressed as a threshold percentage. The number of elements in the HashMap is divided into the capacity of the table; when this ratio goes over the load factor, the table size is roughly doubled. The default load factor is 0.75.

The next pattern, HASHING METHOD, demonstrates in further detail how the capacity interrelates with the hashing algorithm to affect performance.

Hashing Method

Answers the Question	How do you specify where an element will be located within a HashMap?
Solution	Provide a `hashCode()` method to return an integer based on the key values of the object.
Category	Collections
Related Patterns	Hash Map

Your goal in implementing a reusable class is to make it as flexible as possible. For instance, your class should implement Serializable so that it can be streamed out. It should provide an `equals()` method, so that it can be effectively compared to other objects. And, similarly, it should provide a HASHING METHOD. A HASHING METHOD, implemented in Java as `hashCode()`, allows your objects to be used effectively in SETS and HASH MAPS.

Let's go into just a bit more depth toward understanding hashing. A hash table is a set of slots in which objects are placed. The slot, or location, where an object is to be placed is derived from the `hashCode()` method of the key object. The job of `hashCode()` is to produce an integer based on one or more attributes in the key object. The appropriate slot within the hash table is then calculated by dividing the calculated hash code by the table capacity and taking the remainder (modulus). For example, if you have a hash table of size 100, and the hash code for a key is 417, the data is placed in the seventeenth slot of the table.

As long as each key hashes to a different slot, things are OK. But what if, using the above example, the hash codes for two different elements are 317 and 417? The result of the modulus operation is 17 in both cases. This is a *collision* — two objects need to be stored at slot 17. There are a couple of ways of dealing with collisions. The JDK does it by scanning the table until a non-null entry is found. A linked list of collided entries is maintained.

The best case for HASH MAP is that each element hashes to its own unique slot. The worst case is that all elements hash to the same slot. Each collision thus moves the performance of a HASH MAP further away from O(1) and closer to O(n). Keeping performance up to snuff is a matter of understanding your data and how it interrelates with the HASHING METHOD.

The example in **Listing 4.13** creates a HASH MAP with 10 entries, the series of integers from 0 through 180 by twenties.

Listing 4.13   *Hash Example*

```
int initialCapacity = 14;
HashMap table = new HashMap(initialCapacity);
for (int i = 0; i < 200; i += 20)
    table.put(new Integer(i), new Integer(i));
```

The HASHING METHOD for Integer simply returns the Integer object's int value. In this example, then, the more important quantity is the capacity of the table. With a capacity of 14, the slot calculations turn out to be as follows:

Integer	int % 14
0	0
20	6
40	12
60	4
80	10
100	2
120	8
140	0
160	6
180	12

There are already three collisions — at slots 0, 6, and 12. But if the capacity is changed to 17, the hash values end up much better — no collisions:

Integer	int % 17
0	0
20	3
40	6
60	9
80	12
100	15
120	1
140	4
160	7
180	10

Most, but not all, prime numbers tend to provide a good distribution of values when used in modulus operations.

What if you do not provide a hashCode() method? You get the Object implementation, which delegates off to VM-level code. Depending on your needs, this may be acceptable. If you want a HASH MAP that is based on object identity, the slotting will be based on the address of each object.

For most of your domain objects, however, the hashCode() implementation you provide should be some calculation based on unique attributes in the object. For example, an employee object might be uniquely represented by a Social Security number.

So how do you come up with a HASHING METHOD for the unique key?

If a single instance variable represents the unique key for a domain class, things are relatively simple. The unique key is most often a string or integer value. In the event that it is an integer, the integer itself can be used as the hash code. If it is a String — or really, any object — the hash code of that object can be used. **Listing 4.14** shows the hashCode() method for the example Employee Class.

Listing 4.14 *Employee hashCode()*

```
public int hashCode()
{
    return getSSN().hashCode();
}
```

If two or more instance variables are combined to represent a unique key, you must similarly combine hash values to come up with a unique one. The most reliable technique is to combine the values using the bit-wise exclusive-or (xor) operation, represented in Java by the ^ operator. **Listing 4.15** demonstrates this technique.

Listing 4.15 *Employee hashCode() Using xor*

```
public int hashCode()
{
    return
        getFirstName().hashCode() ^
        getMiddleName().hashCode() ^
        getLastName().hashCode();
}
```

The HASHING METHOD must adhere to two rules:

1. It must always return the same value if executed more than once during the lifetime of an application (unless the key values have changed). The value may change with subsequent executions of the application.

2. If two objects are equal, the HASHING METHOD must return the same value for both. Ideally, HASHING METHODS for unequal objects should produce different values, but this is not essential.

TREE MAP

Answers the Question	How do you implement a Map whose keys remain in sorted order?
Solution	Use a TreeMap object.
Category	Collections
Related Patterns	Map

The implementation of TREE MAP in JDK 1.2 shows the true beauty of both encapsulation and Java interfaces. Both TreeMap and HashMap implement the Map interface in Java, thus both are MAP structures. Yet the underlying data structure that HashMap uses to store its elements is a hash table, while TreeMap uses a Red-Black tree. Externally, both TreeMap and HashMap provide the same common MAP functionality, and can be passed to any method that takes a Map object as a parameter. Internally, however, they are implemented completely differently.

A TREE MAP is a MAP that retains its key values in sorted order. It does this by use of a tree structure, which ends up reducing access performance to O(log n).

JDK 1.1 does not provide a TREE MAP. The TreeMap in JDK 1.2 is a subclass of AbstractMap that also implements the SortedMap interface. SortedMap is the contract that ensures that all keys in an implementing MAP will be in ascending key order. The order can be defined by the natural key order of the elements, as specified through their implementation of the Comparable interface. A different order can be specified by passing a Comparator to the TreeMap constructor.

SortedMap defines a total of six method signatures that are implemented in TreeMap:

- `comparator()`, to return the Comparator if one was passed during object construction.
- `firstKey()` and `lastkey()`, which respectively return the lowest and highest keys in the map.
- `subMap(Object fromKey, Object toKey)`, to return a subset view of the map. The subset contains all mappings whose keys are in the range `fromKey` through `toKey`.
- `headMap(Object toKey)` and `tailMap(Object fromKey)`, shortcut methods that provide subset map views for either the head or tail of the map.

For an example that demonstrates TREE MAP, assume you have to map each Department object in a collection to the Manager object that acts as the department head. The Department object must implement the

Comparable interface. The relevant portion of the Department class is presented in **Listing 4.16**.

Listing 4.16 *Department*

```
public class Department
   implements Comparable
{
   private String number;
   private String name;

   public Department(String _number, String _name)
   {
      number = _number;
      name = _name;
   }

   public String getName()
   {
      return name;
   }

   public String getNumber()
   {
      return number;
   }

   public String toString()
   {
      return number + ": " + name;
   }
```

(15)
```
   public int compareTo(Object object)
   {
      Department that = (Department)object;
      return this.number.compareTo(that.number);
   }
```

(16)
```
   public boolean equals(Object object)
   {
      if (!(object instanceof Department))
         return false;
      Department that = (Department)object;
      return this.number.equals(that.number);
   }
}
```

The compareTo() method at line [15] in **Listing 4.16** uses the same basis for comparison — the department number — as the equals() method does (line [16])

Since any Object subclass can be a Map value, the specific implementation of the Manager class is not that important. For this example, assume that a Manager is constructed by passing in a string representing the manager's Social Security number.

Now that Department implements the Comparable interface, it can be used as a key in a TreeMap object. If you forget to implement Comparable, you will get a ClassCastException at runtime. The code in **Listing 4.17** builds a TreeMap and populates it with four mappings between Department objects and Managers.

Listing 4.17   *Creating a Tree Map*

```
Map map = new TreeMap();
map.put(
    new Department("100", "Mailroom"),
    new Manager("994-12-1534"));
map.put(
    new Department("200", "Human Resources"),
    new Manager("993-42-4224"));
map.put(
    new Department("300", "Accounting"),
    new Manager("994-31-5609"));
map.put(
    new Department("400", "Info Technology"),
    new Manager("992-42-0520"));
```

Iterating through the TreeMap works like any other Map iteration. **Listing 4.18** uses the entrySet() iterator to print out each key/value pair.

Listing 4.18   *Iterating Through a Tree Map*

```
Iterator iterator = map.entrySet().iterator();
while (iterator.hasNext())
{
    Map.Entry entry = (Map.Entry)iterator.next();
    System.out.println(entry.getKey() +
                    "->" +
                    entry.getValue());
}
```

The output produced by iterating against the example created in **Listing 4.18** is in department number order:

```
100: Mailroom->Manager [994-12-1534]
200: Human Resources->Manager [993-42-4224]
300: Accounting->Manager [994-31-5609]
400: Info Technology->Manager [992-42-0520]
```

You can also create a TreeMap by specifying a source map to be copied:

```
new TreeMap(map);
```

If you want to specify a different sorting order, the Comparator must be passed in the TreeMap constructor. The `compare()` method for a Comparator that puts the departments in reverse alphabetical order by name is shown in **Listing 4.19**.

Listing 4.19 *compare() Example*

```
public int compare(Object object1, Object object2)
{
    Department dept1 = (Department)object1;
    Department dept2 = (Department)object2;
    return -1 *
        dept1.getName().compareTo(dept2.getName());
}
```

For more information on Comparator methods, refer to COMPARING METHOD in Chapter 1, "Behavior — Methods." In this example, the `compare()` method determines the normal (ascending) relative order of two Department objects and then reverses the sign of the integer compare value in order to flip the order.

The output from the code in **Listing 4.19** using the example data is:

```
100: Mailroom->Manager [994-12-1534]
400: Information Technology->Manager [992-42-0520]
200: Human Resources->Manager [993-42-4224]
300: Accounting->Manager [994-31-5609]
```

SET

Answers the Question	How do you create an unordered collection where there are no duplicate elements?
Solution	Use a Set object.
Category	Collections
Related Patterns	None

The simplest concept of a collection is a bag. You can put objects into a bag and you can take them out. There is no concept of order, and a bag can contain duplicate elements. A SET takes things one step further. It is a bag that cannot contain duplicate elements. If you attempt to add the same element to a SET a second time, it ignores you.[7] Note that the JDK 1.2 implementation of SET allows for a single null element.

The concrete implementation of SET in JDK 1.2 is HashSet. It uses a HashMap object itself to maintain its elements. Since HashSet is so heavily dependent on HashMap, the HASHING METHOD pattern applies equally well to all SETS. Much of the information in the HASH MAP pattern is pertinent to SETS as well, especially the capacity information. The performance of a SET relies on a good capacity and HASHING METHOD.

If you are using JDK 1.1, you can emulate a SET by using a Hashtable. Since you cannot have null values in Hashtables, the easiest solution is to put an element into the Hashtable as both the key and its associated value.

The main operations provided by the HashSet interface in JDK 1.2 are `add(Object)`, `remove(Object)`, and `contains(Object)`. The utility methods you would expect, such as `clear()` and `iterator()`, are all there.

SETS are especially useful in distributed environments, where you have multiple sources of data. Presenting a synchronized view of this data means you must eliminate duplicate information when combining objects from the different sources.

Suppose you are building a client that must hook into several different legacy systems. Your goal is to encapsulate the details of extracting customers from the different systems and present a single list of customers. A SET provides a very straightforward way of accomplishing this. The example in **Listing 4.20** shows how the `addAll()` bulk operation is used to take two source lists of customers and add them to a single set. This results in the elimination of duplicate customers.

---

7 Some implementations maintain a count of how many times each element was added to the SET.

Listing 4.20   *Set Example*

```
Set customers = new HashSet();
customers.addAll(getCustomersFromSource1());
customers.addAll(getCustomersFromSource2());
//...

public List getCustomersFromSource1()
{
    // returns a list of Customer objects
}
public List getCustomersFromSource2()
{
    // returns a list of Customer objects
}
```

Determining whether an object duplicates an element already in a Java Set is done via the EQUALITY METHOD.

TREE SET

Answers the Question	How do you create a sorted collection where there are no duplicate elements?
Solution	Use a TreeSet object.
Category	Collections
Related Patterns	None

A TREE SET is a nice compromise between a SET and a LIST that lets you maintain a sorted collection without duplicates. It only has O(log n) performance instead of the O(1) performance that a SET can provide. A TREE SET is conceptually very similar to a TREE MAP. In fact, the Java 2 implementation of TreeSet uses a TreeMap for its encapsulated collection.

Suppose you need to manage a signed petition and present it in name order. Very important when submitting the petition is that it can not contain duplicate signatures. The solution is to use a TREE SET. **Listing 4.21** shows the implementation of a Petition class that captures a TreeSet of Signature objects.

Listing 4.21 *Petition.java*

```
import java.util.Date;
import java.util.TreeSet;
import java.util.Iterator;
public class Petition
{
    TreeSet signatures = new TreeSet();
    public static void main(String[] args)
    {
        Petition petition = new Petition();
        petition.add(new Signature("Joseph Schmoo",
"1 Tripe Dr", new Date()));
        petition.add(new Signature("Elmer Sklue",
"525 Smelt Ln", new Date()));
        petition.add(new Signature(
"Carmella Coriander", "5 Porkrinds Pl", new Date()));
        petition.add(new Signature(
"Elmer Sklue", "525 Smelt Ln", new Date()));
        petition.add(new Signature(
"Zoey Ziggfeister", "45 Liver St", new Date()));
        petition.add(new Signature("Elmer Sklue",
"525 Sweetbreads Ave", new Date()));
        petition.add(new Signature("Joseph Schmoo",
"1 Tripe Dr", new Date()));
```

(continued)

Listing 4.21 (cont.)   *Petition.java*

```
        petition.print();
    }
    public void add(Signature signature)
    {
        signatures.add(signature);
    }
    public void print()
    {
        System.out.println(
"This petition has been signed by the following:");
        Iterator iterator = signatures.iterator();
        while (iterator.hasNext())
            System.out.println(
                (Signature)iterator.next());
    }
}
```

Signature, shown in **Listing 4.22**, is a fairly straightforward domain class. The important thing is that it implements the Comparable interface in order to provide a natural sort order to the TREE SET. If you need an alternate sort order, pass a Comparator object to the TreeSet constructor.

Listing 4.22   *Signature.java*

```
import java.util.Date;
public class Signature
    implements Comparable
{
    public Signature(String _name, String _address,
Date _dateSigned)
    {
        name = _name;
        address = _address;
        dateSigned = _dateSigned;
    }
    public boolean equals(Object object)
    {
        if (!(object instanceof Signature))
            return false;
        Signature that = (Signature)object;
        return
            name.equals(that.name) &&
            address.equals(that.address);
    }
```

```
    public int compareTo(Object object)
    {
        Signature that = (Signature)object;
        int nameCompare = name.compareTo(that.name);
        if (nameCompare == 0)
            return address.compareTo(that.address);
        return nameCompare;
    }
    public String toString()
    {
        return
            name + "\n\t" +
            address + "\n\t" + dateSigned;
    }
    private String name;
    private String address;
    private Date dateSigned;
}
```

Output from Petition's main() method is shown in **Listing 4.23**.

Listing 4.23 *Petition Output*

```
This petition has been signed by the following:
Carmella Coriander
        5 Porkrinds Pl
        Thu Apr 22 01:09:23 MDT 1999
Elmer Sklue
        525 Smelt Ln
        Thu Apr 22 01:09:23 MDT 1999
Elmer Sklue
        525 Sweetbreads Ave
        Thu Apr 22 01:09:23 MDT 1999
Joseph Schmoo
        1 Tripe Dr
        Thu Apr 22 01:09:23 MDT 1999
Zoey Ziggfeister
        45 Liver St
        Thu Apr 22 01:09:23 MDT 1999
```

STACK

Answers the Question	How do you store a collection of elements so that the last element stored is always the first element removed?
Solution	Use a Stack object.
Category	Collections
Related Patterns	Queue

STACK, a relatively easy structure to implement on your own, is provided in the java.util package of JDK 1.2.

A STACK is a last-in first-out (LIFO) collection of elements. Elements are pushed onto the STACK one by one using the push() method. Sending the pop() method to the STACK returns the last element pushed onto the stack. The JDK 1.2 implementation of STACK also provides the utility methods empty() to determine if there are any elements available, peek() to look at the top object on the STACK without popping it, and search() to determine what position an element is within the STACK.

Interestingly, the JDK 1.2 Stack class still extends Vector, instead of one of the newer concrete collections such as ArrayList. If your stack growth is unpredictable or if you are still using JDK 1.1, you can use a LINKED LIST to emulate the stack. The push() method would delegate to addLast(), and the pop() method would delegate to removeLast().

The simplicity of Java's Stack class could be used to demonstrate a potential pattern called "INTENTION REVEALING CLASS." All behaviors defined directly in the Stack class — push, pop, empty, peek, and search — have an almost one-to-one correspondence with methods in Vector. You could code stack operations just as easily yourself by using ArrayList directly, but the benefit of having methods such as s push() and pop() is that your intent is perfectly clear — you are using a STACK.

Note that the pop(), peek(), and search() methods are synchronized while the push() and empty() methods are not.

Collection Operations

One of the major benefits of having a coordinated collection class framework is the consistency that goes with it. You can send many messages, such as `size()` or `add()`, to a collection without having to worry about whether it is an ArrayList, HashSet, TreeSet, or LinkedList.

This section first provides a handful of patterns to define appropriate uses for some of the methods available in the Collection interface. Patterns for the uninteresting, "obvious" methods are not included. Methods that are either new or demonstrate a certain technique *are* included.

A second set of patterns describes how collections can be iterated over to perform certain common operations. These patterns are Do, SELECT/REJECT, COLLECT, DETECT, and INJECT INTO. They are named after the corresponding constructs available in Smalltalk.

You may be happy enough just using the procedural pattern solution in each of these iterator patterns. But if you want to take a bold step forward, the object-oriented solutions can be very effective. The downside is that you will need to create your own collection class hierarchy to support their use. It is a worthwhile effort, but be forewarned that you will end up with a nonstandard collections framework. If you are intrigued enough by the concept, you may want to consider a third-party collections solution such as JGL, which already has this sort of thing built in.

The unfortunate nature of Java, though, makes these Smalltalk-like iterator patterns less than perfect. The basis for each is using anonymous inner classes, which are syntactically a mess. You need a good understanding of the limitations of inner classes. Also, using inner classes as the solution ends up costing about the same amount of source lines as the classic technique. Finally, the mess of wrapping and unwrapping primitive types is enough to give anyone a headache after a while.

All things considered, the Smalltalk-like iterators demonstrate a powerful feature of Java. They can ultimately make your code more clear and flexible. I recommend you give them a try.

isEmpty()

Answers the Question	How do you determine if a collection does not have any elements?
Solution	Use isEmpty() instead of checking the collection's size.
Category	Collections
Related Patterns	Collection

This pattern is really just a specific example of INTENTION-REVEALING METHOD. It is presented here because it is one of those things that is frequently done incorrectly.

isEmpty() is an abstract method defined in both the Collection and Map interface hierarchies. The java.util.ArrayList implementation is shown in **Listing 4.24**.

Listing 4.24 *isEmpty() Implementation in ArrayList*

```
public boolean isEmpty()
{
    return size == 0;
}
```

Developers will frequently test the size of a collection directly to determine if it is empty:

```
if (list.size() == 0)
```

INTENTION-REVEALING MESSAGE explains why you should prefer the use of isEmpty(). The additional message send represents a small bit of additional overhead, but once again it clarifies your code and also frees you from worrying about the internal implementation of a collection.

To determine if a collection does not contain any elements, use isEmpty():

```
if (list.isEmpty())
```

CONTAINS(OBJECT)/CONTAINSALL(COLLECTION)

Answers the Question	How do you determine if one or more elements are contained within a collection?
Solution	Use the methods contains(Object) or containsAll(Collection).
Category	Collections
Related Patterns	Collection

The classic approach to determining if an element is contained within a collection is to iterate through it and test each element until a match is found. You might use either the DO or DETECT pattern to accomplish this. The contains() method already does the code for you, so save your enumeration efforts. Refer to **Listing 4.25**.

Listing 4.25 *contains() Example*

```
List list = new ArrayList();
list.add(new Department("300", "Accounting"));
list.add(new Department("500", "Billing"));
list.add(new Department("100", "Mailroom"));
list.add(new Department("200", "Human Resources"));
list.add(new Department("400", "Info Technology"));
list.add(new Department("600", "Cryogenics"));
Department locateDepartment =
    new Department("500", "Billing");
System.out.println("contains 500? " +
    list.contains(locateDepartment));
```

Note that for contains() to work, the elements contained within the collection must properly implement the EQUALITY METHOD.

The containsAll(Collection) method takes a subcollection as a parameter. The example in **Listing 4.26** demonstrates how this method can be used to determine if a set of words is contained within a string. The utility method listFrom(String) in the example uses a StringTokenizer to break up a string into its word components. The use of the containsAll(Collection) method at line [17] results in true being returned.

Listing 4.26 *`containsAll(Collection)` Example*

```
// …
    List list = listFrom(
        "Katie, Tim, and Anna went fishing.");
    list.containsAll(listFrom("Katie Tim Anna"));
// …

public List listFrom(String string)
{
    List list = new ArrayList();
    StringTokenizer tokenizer =
        new StringTokenizer(string, ",. ");
    while (tokenizer.hasMoreTokens())
        list.add(tokenizer.nextToken());
    return list;
}
```

(17)

The parameter to `containsAll()` can be any collection. **Listing 4.27** demonstrates the method using a Set as the argument. This time, the result of `containsAll()` is false.

Listing 4.27 *`containsAll()` Example Using a Set*

```
List list = listFrom(
    "Katie, Tim, and Anna went fishing.");
Set words = new HashSet();
words.add("Katie");
words.add("Tim");
words.add("Kathy");
list.containsAll(words);
```

RETAINALL(COLLECTION)

Answers the Question	How do you delete all but a specified list of elements from a collection?
Solution	Use `retainAll(Collection)`.
Category	Collections
Related Patterns	removeAll(Collection)

This pattern is the opposite of REMOVEALL(COLLECTION). It keeps elements in a collection that are contained within the parameter collection.

The simple Swing example in **Listing 4.28** creates a frame window with two controls: a listbox whose model is a list of department objects (line [18]) and a Commit button (line [19]). Upon clicking each department in the list, the corresponding department is deleted from the model (line [20]). When the Commit button is clicked (line [21]), the original list of departments is updated via `retainAll()` (line [22]). Specifically, the model is first converted into an Array object (line [24]) and then is represented as a List (line [23]). The conversions are required because DefaultListModel cannot directly represent its contents as a Collection, which is what `retainAll()` requires. The List view of the array is passed into `retainAll()`, which removes all elements except those specified in the List.

Listing 4.28   *RetainAllApp.java*

```
import javax.swing.*;
import java.awt.*;
import java.awt.event.*;
import java.util.List;
import java.util.Iterator;
import java.util.ArrayList;
import java.util.Arrays;

public class RetainAllApp
{
    public static void main(String[] args)
    {
        JFrame frame =
            new JFrame("Retain All Example");
        RetainAllApp app = new RetainAllApp();
        Component contents = app.createComponents();
        frame.getContentPane().add(
            contents, BorderLayout.CENTER);
        frame.addWindowListener(
            new WindowAdapter()
            {
```

(continued)

Listing 4.28 (cont.)   *RetainAllApp.java*

```
                    public void windowClosing(WindowEvent e)
                    {
                        System.exit(0);
                    }
                });
            frame.pack();
            frame.setVisible(true);
        }

        public Component createComponents()
        {
            departments = loadDepartments();
            initializeModel(departmentsModel,
                            departments);

(18)        keepListBox = new JList(departmentsModel);
            JScrollPane scrollPane =
                new JScrollPane(keepListBox);
            keepListBox.addMouseListener(
                getKeepClickListener());

(19)        JButton button = new JButton("Commit");
            button.addActionListener(
                getCommitListener());

            JPanel pane = new JPanel();
            pane.add(scrollPane);
            pane.add(button);
            return pane;
        }

        public MouseListener getKeepClickListener()
        {
            return
            new MouseAdapter()
            {
(20)            public void mouseClicked(MouseEvent e)
                {
                    int index =
                        keepListBox.locationToIndex(
                            e.getPoint());
                    departmentsModel.remove(index);
                }
            };
        }

        public ActionListener getCommitListener()
        {
            return
            new ActionListener()
            {
```

```
(21)              public void actionPerformed(ActionEvent e)
                  {
(22)                  departments.retainAll(
(23)                      Arrays.asList(
(24)                          departmentsModel.toArray()));
                  }
              };
          }

          public void mouseClicked(MouseEvent e)
          {
              int index =
                  keepListBox.locationToIndex(
                      e.getPoint());
              departmentsModel.remove(index);
          }

          private List loadDepartments()
          {
              List list = new ArrayList();
              list.add(new Department("300",
                          "Accounting"));
              list.add(new Department("500",
                          "Billing"));
              list.add(new Department("100",
                          "Mailroom"));
              list.add(new Department("200",
                          "Human Resources"));
              list.add(new Department("400",
                          "Info Technology"));
              list.add(new Department("600",
                          "Cryogenics"));
              return list;
          }

          private void initializeModel(DefaultListModel model, List
      list)
          {
              Iterator iterator = list.iterator();
              while (iterator.hasNext())
                  model.addElement(iterator.next());
          }

          private JList keepListBox;
          private DefaultListModel departmentsModel =
              new DefaultListModel();
          private List departments;
      }
```

REMOVE*ALL*(C*OLLECTION*)

Answers the Question	How do you remove one collection of elements from another?
Solution	Use `removeAll()` to specify the elements to be removed.
Category	Collections
Related Patterns	retainAll(Collection)

This pattern is the opposite of RETAINALL(COLLECTION). The mechanics for using the `removeAll()` method are fairly straightforward and similar to `retainAll()`. The `removeAll()` method repetitively calls `remove()` to singly delete each element in the parameter collection. Refer to the JDK 1.2 documentation for details.

More interestingly, `removeAll()` can be used for a succinct idiom that removes all instances of an element from a collection. The Collections class provides a class method called `singleton()`. This method takes an Object parameter and returns an immutable Set object, with the parameter as the sole instance. The Set can thus be used in any place where a Collection is expected.

The code:

```
Set set = Collections.singleton(
            new Department("300", "Accounting"));
```

produces a set with a single Department object in it. If you have a List object called `list`, all Department 300 objects can be removed via the line:

```
list.removeAll(set);
```

If you have a collection with undesired null objects, you can similarly remove them in a single line of code:

```
list.removeAll(Collections.singleton(null));
```

CONCATENATION

Answers the Question	How do you append one collection to another?
Solution	Create a list at least large enough to hold both collections. Use addAll() to concatenate each collection to the combined list.
Category	Collections
Related Patterns	Collection

If you are using JDK 1.1, you have to roll your own code to tack one collection to the end of another. Doing so is not difficult, but the lack of a JDK solution is one of those omissions that always strikes me as odd. CONCATENATION is a common enough operation that it should have been available in the JDK class library from its inception.

String is one of those fortunate few classes in Java that is able to overload operators. CONCATENATION is a pattern that would be very succinctly solved via operator overloading. To append one collection to another, you would just use the '+' operator like Strings use:

```
List allEmployees = grunts + managers;
```

Alas, you are stuck with sending a named message. JDK 1.2 provides the addAll(Collection) method in the Collection interface. Unfortunately, it is an in-place operation that returns a boolean and not a new collection, so you cannot code:

```
List allEmployees = grunts.addAll(managers);
```

Instead, you must first create a new collection that contains all the elements of the first and then append the second collection. A first cut at the CONCATENATION implementation is shown in **Listing 4.29**.

Listing 4.29 CONCATENATION — *Not Quite Right*

```
(25)    List allEmployees = new ArrayList(grunts);
(26)    allEmployees.addAll(managers);
```

The solution in **Listing 4.29** is nice and succinct, but it can be improved. CONCATENATION is one of the few areas where performance should be taken into consideration from the outset. In line [25] in **Listing 4.29**, ArrayList allocates new space in allEmployees. A little room for growth is factored in, as the space allocated is 110% of the size of the existing grunts collection. If the size of managers is greater than 10% of allEmployees, space will have to be reallocated in line [26], when managers is appended to allEmployees.

Unfortunately, the constructors for ArrayList do not allow for specification of both a source collection and an initial capacity. To ensure that double allocation will not be required, the ArrayList must be created in a separate step. A preferred solution for CONCATENATION is shown in **Listing 4.30**.

Listing 4.30   CONCATENATION — *Better*

```
int allocationSize =
    (grunts.size() + managers.size()) * 11 / 10;
List allEmployees = new ArrayList(allocationSize);
allEmployees.addAll(grunts);
allEmployees.addAll(managers);
```

You may or may not need growth room. The example in **Listing 4.30** results in 10% additional space being created.

The CONCATENATION solution scales fine for concatenating multiple collections. If you have a considerable number of collections to concatenate, you may wish to automate the process. The method `concatenateLists()` is provided in **Listing 4.31**. It takes an argument, which is a list of lists to be concatenated. An example of client code is shown in **Listing 4.32**.

Listing 4.31   *concatenateLists()*

```
public List concatenateLists(List allLists)
{
    int capacity = 0;
    Iterator iterator = allLists.iterator();
    while (iterator.hasNext())
        capacity += ((List)iterator.next()).size();
    capacity = capacity * 11 / 10;
    List all = new ArrayList(capacity);
    iterator = allLists.iterator();
    while (iterator.hasNext())
        all.addAll((List)iterator.next());
    return all;
}
```

Listing 4.32   *Example Use of concatenateLists()*

```
List alist = new ArrayList();
for (int i = 0; i < 5; i++)
    alist.add("a");
List blist = new ArrayList();
for (int j = 0; j < 7; j++)
    blist.add("b");
List clist = new ArrayList();
for (int z = 0; z < 4; z++)
    clist.add("c");

List allLists = new ArrayList(3);
allLists.add(alist);
allLists.add(blist);
allLists.add(clist);

System.out.println(concatenateLists(allLists));
```

ENUMERATION

Answers the Question	How do you process a collection?
Solution	Use an Enumeration or Iterator object to iterate across its elements.
Category	Collections
Related Patterns	Do Collect Select/Reject Detect Inject Into

If you have even a moderate amount of programming background, you have coded loops thousands of times. "Perform until," "do while," "for," "while," and "repeat until" may all be familiar verb phrases from languages past. The most frequent use of looping is to work through a collection, extracting and doing something with each element in turn. This is known as ENUMERATION.

The classic approach to ENUMERATION is to control looping through the collection externally. The collection itself does not define how the enumeration takes place; the application program must code this functionality. The application typically maintains a counter or pointer that is moved through the collection. Each time the pointer is moved, a message is sent to the collection, requesting it to return the element at that location.

The OO approach is to encapsulate the mechanics of how the pointer is moved through the collection and provide a common interface that all applications can use for enumeration.

The Collection interface in JDK 1.2 defines an `iterator()` method. Each collection must thus provide this method, which returns an Iterator object. An Iterator implements behavior for three methods:

- `hasNext()` returns true if there are more elements in the collection that have not yet been accessed for the current ENUMERATION.

- `next()` returns the next element in the iteration.

- `remove()` deletes the last element retrieved via `next()` from the collection being iterated over. Note that `remove()` is an optional operation. If implementing classes choose not to provide `remove()` behavior, the `remove()` method must throw an UnsupportedOperationException.

The Enumeration interface in JDK 1.1 is comparable to the JDK 1.2 Iterator interface. It defines signatures for `hasMoreElements()` and `nextElement()`, which respectively work the same as Iterator's

hasNext() and next(). Note that no remove() method is provided
— there is no safe way to remove an element from a collection being enumerated in JDK 1.1.

It is entirely up to each collection to determine how the ENUMERATION
will access elements contained within it. For simple collections, such as
List, the Iterator object sets a pointer to the first element in the list. The
next() method returns the object at this current pointer and then bumps it
up to point to the next element in the list.

Why not just have each collection directly implement the Iterator or
Enumeration methods? The reason is that if you have a more complex data
structure, such as a binary tree, one iterator may not suffice. Enumerating
through a binary tree can be done using a preorder, inorder, or postorder
algorithm. By returning objects created using three separate Iterator classes,
the binary tree can successfully support multiple client objects processing
different kinds of iterations.

The most common ENUMERATION technique for Java is discussed in the
Do pattern. It involves iterating forward through a collection using the standard Java Enumeration (JDK 1.1) or Iterator (JDK 1.2) interface and processing each element of the collection in turn. REVERSE ENUMERATION dis-
cusses looping through a collection from the tail-end backwards. Often,
however, there are different goals of iterating through a collection:

- locate a specific element (DETECT)
- produce a subset collection (SELECT/REJECT)
- transform each element (COLLECT)
- use all elements to compute a running total (INJECT INTO)

These specific enumeration techniques are discussed in the next six
patterns.

REVERSE ENUMERATION

Answers the Question	How do you iterate through a list in reverse order?
Solution	JDK 1.1: Code a `for` loop to count down from the size of the collection to 0; access each element of the list directly using the index of the `for` loop.
	JDK 1.2: Use the `hasPrevious()` and `previous()` methods available in the ListIterator interface.
Category	Collections
Related Patterns	Enumeration

One deficiency in JDK 1.1 is the inability of VectorEnumerator to iterate through a Vector in reverse order. The unfortunate solution is to bypass use of the Enumerators and code a `for` loop to directly access each Vector element. An example that prints each element in a Vector is shown in **Listing 4.33**.

Listing 4.33 *REVERSE ENUMERATION in JDK 1.1*

```
for (int i = vector.size() - 1; i >= 0; i-)
    System.out.println(vector.elementAt(i));
```

JDK 1.2 improves things a bit by enhancing the ListIterator returned from a List object. ListIterator adds the methods `previous()` and `hasPrevious()`. The methods are analogous to `next()` and `hasNext()`, respectively.

You have been taught over and over again to use the interface name, and not the name of the implementing class, to declare your iterators and enumerators. That won't work for REVERSE ENUMERATION. To be able to use the `previous()` and `hasPrevious()` methods, you will have to declare a reference to the more specific ListIterator object. Fortunately, the List interface provides the method `listIterator()` to return the appropriate object.

The other problem is that list iterators start by default at the first element in the list. A call to `hasPrevious()` will return false when the iterator is in this state. More luck for you: JDK 1.2 provides the `listIterator(int index)` method, which allows you to specify just where in the collection you want to start iterating. To iterate completely through a list in reverse, first determine the list's size. The constructor of the ListIterator allows for any valid index to be specified as the starting point. Use the list size to initialize the iterator. **Listing 4.34** shows the complete solution for the REVERSE ENUMERATION pattern for JDK 1.2.

Listing 4.34 *REVERSE ENUMERATION in JDK 1.2*

```
ListIterator iterator =
    list.listIterator(list.size());
while (iterator.hasPrevious())
    System.out.println(iterator.previous());
```

Iterating over a collection in reverse is actually faster than forward enumeration. The reason is that the comparison part of the `for` loop is executed for each iteration of the loop. For forward iteration, this comparison must check the index against the size of the collection. The collection's size must be accessed from the collection each time. With REVERSE ENUMERATION, each iteration only has to do a very fast check against 0.

Still, use REVERSE ENUMERATION only when you really need it. Since there is more than one reason why you might be using REVERSE ENUMERATION — speed or algorithm, usually — you will need to document the reason why you are going against the grain (i.e., why you are not using forward enumeration).

Do

Answers the Question	How do you perform an operation using each element in a collection?
Solution	*Procedural:* Iterate through the collection using a `while()` loop, extracting and processing each element within.
	Object-oriented: Create a method called `forEachDo()` in the collection that takes a closure as a parameter. This method encapsulates the iteration over the collection and sends a message back to the closure for each element.
Category	Collections
Related Patterns	Collect Select/Reject Detect Inject Into

Looping through a collection and doing something with each element is code that you will write thousands of times. If you worked in C, you coded `while` loops and `for` loops *ad infinitum*. These same venerable loop constructs are still there in Java. The standard for iterating through a Java collection, as implemented using the classic loop, is depicted in **Listing 4.35**.

Listing 4.35 *Using Do — Procedural*

```
Iterator iterator = list.iterator();
while (iterator.hasNext())
{
    ListObject object =
        (ListObject)iterator.next());
    // … do some processing with the object
}
```

This should be an instantly recognizable idiom. That's a good thing, right? Idioms present things that are not necessarily intuitive. But once learned, the idiom is instantly recognized and comprehended. An idiom presents knowledge that cannot necessarily be gleaned even by dissecting its individual elements.

The solution in **Listing 4.35** is adequate as an idiom. Go ahead, feel free to use it. There really is nothing wrong with the construct. I won't criticize you for doing what most others do.

But is there a better way to do things? I don't mind the above solution, but it leaves a few things to be desired. First, the same few lines that drive the looping are presented over and over again, which means code repetition (duplication) is rampant. Second, it has the disadvantage of being presented in four discrete steps: get the iterator, provide a `while` loop that determines whether or not more elements are available, extract the next available element, and process the element. You can combine the first two steps by using a `for` loop, but that really does not solve the problem, it only confuses the intent.

What is really needed is the ability of the collection itself to take on an operation. That would allow it to control the looping through its own elements and send out a message to process each one. The Do pattern provides such a solution, but it does require that you extend the collection classes to implement it.

Listing 4.36 shows the Block interface. It will be used to create an anonymous inner class that supplies a closure to be passed to the collection.

Listing 4.36 *Block.java*

```
public interface Block
{
    public void exec(Object each);
}
```

To support Do and similar patterns, you must extend the behavior of the Java collections framework. **Listing 4.37** shows how to do this. It creates the class OrderedCollection, which extends ArrayList. OrderedCollection is the name of the Smalltalk class that is similar to Java's ArrayList. Ultimately you will want to create similar subclasses for all kinds of collections.

Listing 4.37 *OrderedCollection*

```
import java.util.ArrayList;
import java.util.Iterator;
public class OrderedCollection
    extends ArrayList
{
    public void forEachDo(Block block)
    {
        Iterator iterator = iterator();
        while (iterator.hasNext())
            block.exec(iterator.next());
    }
}
```

(27)

(28)

The method `forEachDo()` (line [27]) is used to control iteration from within the OrderedCollection itself. In line [28], the message `exec()` is sent to the block object passed in. The argument to `exec()` is the element currently extracted using the iterator. A standalone example that shows two separate Block definitions used in a single method is shown in **Listing 4.38**.

Listing 4.38   Do (Object-Oriented)

```
import java.util.*;
public class TestClosure1
{
    public static void main(String[] args)
    {
        new TestClosure1();
    }

    int total = 0;

    public TestClosure1()
    {
        OrderedCollection list =
            new OrderedCollection();
        list.add("This");
        list.add("Is");
        list.add("Pop");
```
(29)
```
        list.forEachDo(
            new Block() {
                int i = 0;
                public void exec(Object each) {
                    show(each, i++);
            }});

        System.out.println();
```
(30)
```
        list.forEachDo(
            new Block() {
                public void exec(Object each) {
                    total += ((String)each).length();
            }});

        System.out.println("total chars = " + total);
    }

    private void show(Object string, int i)
    {
        if (i > 0)
            System.out.print(" ");
        System.out.print((String)string);
    }
}
```

Lines [29] and [30] show how the Do blocks are created. The message `forEachDo()` is sent to the list. The parameter to the `forEachDo()` message is a new anonymous class definition for the Block interface. In the first example at line [29], the anonymous class defines an instance variable i that is used as a counter in the definition for `exec()`. The output from the `System.out.println()` statement that appears directly after this block is:

```
This Is Pop
```

The second example at line [30] uses the instance variable `total` to store the total count of characters in all the words. The output from the `System.out.println()` statement that appears directly after this block is:

```
total chars = 9
```

Anonymous inner classes are not very aesthetically pleasing constructs. I haven't made a final decision as to how to best organize all the brackets and parentheses to make them look clean. I think the above examples provide a decent presentation. Initially, use of anonymous classes can be disconcerting, but once you recognize it for what it is, the Do pattern is a very effective idiom.

COLLECT

Answers the Question	How do you return a new collection that is a transformation of each object in the original collection?
Solution	*Procedural:* Create an empty list. Iterate through the collection using a `while()` loop, extracting each element within. Transform each element and add it to the new collection.
	Object-oriented: Create a `collect()` method in the list class that takes a closure as a parameter. `collect()` iterates over the collection and sends a message back to the closure for each element. The closure in turn transforms the element and returns an object to be added to a new list in `collect()`. `collect()` returns a new list of transformed elements.
Category	Collections
Related Patterns	Do Select/Reject Detect Inject Into

In preparation for further processing, you will frequently need to process each element in a collection and tack the result onto a new collection. The procedural solution is simple enough (**Listing 4.39**).

Listing 4.39 COLLECT *(Procedural)*

```
List list = new ArrayList();

Employee x = new Employee("Langr", "123-32-2344");
x.setBeneficiary(new Beneficiary("Kathy Langr"));
list.add(x);

Employee y = new Employee("Smith", "999-31-9130");
y.setBeneficiary(new Beneficiary("John Smith"));
list.add(y);

List beneficiaries = new ArrayList();
Iterator iterator = list.iterator();
while (iterator.hasNext())
{
    Employee employee = (Employee)iterator.next();
    beneficiaries.add(employee.getBeneficiary());
}
```

Create a new collection, iterate through the source collection, derive a result using each element, and add this result to the new collection.

If you preferred the closure-oriented Do solution presented in the previous pattern, the same thing will work for COLLECT, with a few minor adjustments (**Listing 4.40**).

Listing 4.40   *COLLECT (Object-Oriented)*

```
OrderedCollection beneficiaries =
    list.collect(
        new Block() {
            public Object exec(Object each) {
                return
                    ((Employee)each).getBeneficiary();
            }});
```

Notice that exec() now needs to return an object to get COLLECT to work. For the Do pattern, we didn't need exec() to return anything, so it was defined in Block as having a void return. Since you cannot overload methods based on return value, something will need to give.

There are a few possible solutions, none of which is perfect. The first would be to call the method that needs to return a value something else, like getExec(). Thus the Block interface would have two methods. But you would then need to provide an implementation for both exec() and getExec() in each closure. As a second solution you could turn the Block interface into a class with empty definitions for exec() and getExec(). This would also be an adequate solution. I chose the third, however, for its simplicity: define a single exec() method that always returns an Object. The new definition for Block is provided in **Listing 4.41**.

Listing 4.41   *All-Purpose Block Definition*

```
public interface Block
{
    public Object exec(Object each);
}
```

Your Do blocks will have to be modified to return a value. Just add a statement to return null at the end of the block.

The implementation of collect() in OrderedCollection is shown in **Listing 4.42**.

Listing 4.42   *OrderedCollection collect() Method*

```
public OrderedCollection collect(Block block)
{
    OrderedCollection list =
        new OrderedCollection();
    Iterator iterator = iterator();
    while (iterator.hasNext())
        list.add(block.exec(iterator.next()));
    return list;
}
```

SELECT/REJECT

Answers the Question	How do you derive a subset of a collection?
Solution	*Procedural:* Create an empty list. Iterate through the collection using a `while()` loop, extracting each element within. Add each element that meets the criteria to the new collection.
	Object-oriented: Create `select()` and `reject()` methods in the list class. Each method takes a closure as a parameter. `select()` and `reject()` iterate over the collection, sending a message to the closure for each element. The closure returns a boolean value indicating whether the object should be added to a new list created in `select()` or `reject()`. The `select()` or `reject()` method returns a new list that is a subset of all elements in the original list.
Category	Collections
Related Patterns	Do Collect Detect Inject Into

SELECT and REJECT are filter patterns. SELECT returns a new collection whose elements are all elements from the source collection that meet certain criteria. REJECT is the opposite; it returns all elements in the original collection that fail the criteria.

Listing 4.43 is the classic solution.

Listing 4.43 *SELECT (Procedural)*

```
List partTimers = new ArrayList();
Iterator iterator = list.iterator();
while (iterator.hasNext())
{
    Employee employee = (Employee)iterator.next();
    if (employee.isPartTime())
        partTimers.add(employee);
}
```

The closure solution is shown in **Listing 4.44**. Due to the pain of working with Boolean wrappers, I chose to add another method signature to the

Block interface, `test(Object)`. This method returns either true or false, instead of an Object containing a Boolean.

Listing 4.44 *Select (Object-Oriented)*

```
OrderedCollection partTimers =
   list.select(
      new Block() {
         public boolean test(Object each) {
            return ((Employee)each).isPartTime();
   }}});
```

The implementation of `select()` in OrderedCollection is shown in **Listing 4.45**.

Listing 4.45 *OrderedCollection `select()` Method*

```
public OrderedCollection select(Block block)
{
   OrderedCollection list =
      new OrderedCollection();
   Iterator iterator = iterator();
   while (iterator.hasNext())
   {
      Object element = iterator.next();
      if (block.test(element))
         list.add(element);
   }
   return list;
}
```

To support the new `test()` method in Block, you will need to change your Block definition from an interface to a class. Otherwise every closure will need to provide a definition for both `exec()` and `test()`. **Listing 4.46** shows the revised definition for Block.

Listing 4.46 *Another Revision to Block*

```
public class Block
{
   public Object exec(Object each)
   { return null; }
   public boolean test(Object each)
   { return false; }
}
```

An alternate solution that would allow Block to remain as an interface requires defining a BlockAdapter class. This class would provide the stub definitions for each method in the interface. This is a cleaner solution, one that is used in the JDK. For example, the MouseListener interface declares five methods that you must implement. MouseAdapter, which implements

MouseListener, provides null definitions for each of these five methods, allowing you to override only those methods you are interested in.

Implementation and use of REJECT is straightforward. **Listings 4.47**, **4.48**, and **4.49**, respectively, show the procedural use, the object-oriented use, and the implementation of the `reject()` method in OrderedCollection.

Listing 4.47 REJECT *(Procedural)*

```
List notPartTimers = new ArrayList();
Iterator iterator = list.iterator();
while (iterator.hasNext())
{
    Employee employee = (Employee)iterator.next();
    if (!employee.isPartTime())
        notPartTimers.add(employee);
}
```

Listing 4.48 REJECT *(Object-Oriented)*

```
OrderedCollection notPartTimers =
    list.reject(
        new Block() {
            public boolean test(Object each) {
                return ((Employee)each).isPartTime();
        }});
```

Listing 4.49 *OrderedCollection* `reject()` *Method*

```
public OrderedCollection reject(Block block)
{
    OrderedCollection list =
        new OrderedCollection();
    Iterator iterator = iterator();
    while (iterator.hasNext())
    {
        Object element = iterator.next();
        if (!block.test(element))
            list.add(element);
    }
    return list;
}
```

The `reject()` and `select()` methods as implemented in OrderedCollection are exactly the same except for the conditional test. It sounds to me like an exercise in properly refactoring out the duplicate code — left to the reader, of course.

DETECT

Answers the Question	How do you extract the first element of a collection that meets a condition?
Solution	*Procedural:* Iterate through the collection using a `while()` loop, extracting each element within. Return the first element that meets the specified criteria.
	Object-oriented: Create a `detect()` method in the list that takes a closure as a parameter. `detect()` iterates over the collection and sends a message back to the closure for each element. The closure returns true if the element meets the specified criteria. Upon receiving the first true result from the closure, `detect()` returns the associated object.
Category	Collections
Related Patterns	Do Collect Select/Reject Inject Into

For DETECT, you want to find the first matching element within a collection. Perhaps you need to locate the first capitalized word in a list, or maybe you want to give a bonus to the first employee who is a part-timer.

For both the procedural solution (example in **Listing 4.50**) and the object-oriented solution (**Listing 4.51**), the result (`firstPartTimer` in the examples) must be tested to determine if it was `null` (i.e., if no matching element was found in the collection).

Listing 4.50 *DETECT (Procedural)*

```
Employee firstPartTimer = null;
iterator = list.iterator();
while (iterator.hasNext())
{
    Employee employee = (Employee)iterator.next();
    if (employee.isPartTime())
    {
        firstPartTimer = employee;
        break;
    }
}
```

Listing 4.51 *DETECT (Object-Oriented)*

```
Employee firstPartTimer = (Employee)
   list.detect(
      new Block() {
         public boolean test(Object each) {
            return ((Employee)each).isPartTime();
      }});
```

The implementation of detect() in OrderedCollection is shown in **Listing 4.52**.

Listing 4.52 *OrderedCollection detect() Method*

```
public Object detect(Block block)
{
   Iterator iterator = iterator();
   while (iterator.hasNext())
   {
      Object element = iterator.next();
      if (block.test(element))
         return element;
   }
   return null;
}
```

Inject Into

Answers the Question	How do you manage a running value as you iterate over a collection?
Solution	*Procedural:* Declare a variable to hold the running value. Iterate through the collection using a `while()` loop, adding to the running value by processing each element within.
	Object-oriented: Create an `injectInto()` method in the list that takes a closure as a parameter. `injectInto()` iterates over the collection and sends a message back to the closure for each element. The closure processes the element and returns a value to be added to a running total stored within `injectInto()`. `injectInto()` returns the final running value after all elements have been processed.
Category	Collections
Related Patterns	Do Collect Select/Reject Detect

In Smalltalk, the `inject:into:` message is one of the more difficult constructs to understand. I suppose part of the reason is that the method name does not properly reveal intention. But it is a powerful idiom, and once you learn how it works, it expresses things quite well.

The INJECT INTO pattern is used to maintain a running value as you iterate over a collection. For example, you may need to generate a sum from a list of numbers or concatenate a list of strings.

Unfortunately, INJECT INTO is one of those patterns that translates poorly into Java, mostly because of Java's messy dichotomy between objects and primitive types. I still include the pattern here, both for completeness and to demonstrate what happens when you try to force-fit things. While design patterns are ideally (but not always) language-neutral, implementation patterns are very much tied to the specifics of a language.

A procedural example is demonstrated in **Listing 4.53**. The example produces the total number of hours worked by all employees.

Listing 4.53 *INJECT INTO* **(Procedural)**

```
int sum = 0;
iterator = list.iterator();
while (iterator.hasNext())
{
    Employee employee = (Employee)iterator.next();
    sum += employee.getHoursPerWeek();
}
```

The closure-based solution appears in **Listing 4.54**.

Listing 4.54 *INJECT INTO* **(Object-Oriented)**

```
        Integer sum = (Integer)
(31)    list.injectInto(
(32)        new Integer(0),
(33)        new Block() {
(34)            public Object execInject(Object inject,
                                         Object each) {
(35)                int previousSum =
                        ((Integer)inject).intValue();
(36)                return new Integer(
(37)                    previousSum +
                        ((Employee)each).getHoursPerWeek());
                }});
```

In **Listing 4.54**, first the message injectInto() is sent to the list
(line [31]), with the initial sum value (line [32]) and the closure to manage
this sum (line [33]) as parameters.

The message execInject() is sent for each element in the list (line
[34]). Its parameters are the current inject value and each element. The
inject value represents the running tally. The job of the execInject()
method is to return the new inject value.

In this example, the current sum (the tally up to but not including this
element) is extracted from the inject parameter (line [35]). The number of
hours per week is added to this current sum (line [37]). Finally, the result
— the new sum — is packaged into an Integer object and returned (line
[36]), to be injected into the next call to execInject().

The execInject() message send represents a new method that our
Block class does not currently implement. **Listing 4.55** gives the new definition for Block.

Listing 4.55   *Block.java with Support for INJECT INTO*

```
public class Block
{
   public Object exec(Object each)
   { return null; }
   public boolean test(Object each)
   { return false; }
   public Object execInject(Object inject,
                             Object each)
   { return null; }
}
```

Listing 4.56 shows the `injectInto()` implementation.

Listing 4.56   *OrderedCollection `injectInto()` Method*

```
public Object injectInto(Object initialValue, Block block)
{
   Object runningValue = initialValue;
   Iterator iterator = iterator();
   while (iterator.hasNext())
   {
      Object element = iterator.next();
      runningValue =
         block.execInject(runningValue, element);
   }
   return runningValue;
}
```

I'm not particularly enamored of using the closure solution for INJECT INTO. Just from looking at **Listing 4.54,** you should be able to see why. First, it just looks horrid. There are several lines more than the procedural solution, and it's really not easy reading.

All the casts and wrappings that are required are worse. A primary use of INJECT INTO is for generating sums or processing other native-type calculations. But to make INJECT INTO generic enough, `injectInto()` has to take Object parameters, otherwise we would have to overload `injectInto()` and `execInject()` for all the different type combinations. In lieu of that, Object parameters have to be used. For native types, such as ints or longs, this means that the wrapper classes (Integer, Long, etc.) must be used. In the example in **Listing 4.54,** the int value has to be extracted from the `inject` parameter so that it can be used in an arithmetic expression. The result of the addition must be wrapped so it can be used as the return value.

The whole thing is one big nuisance. Unless you use INJECT INTO frequently, you will want to keep it out of your Java toolbox.

Collection Idioms

The collection classes provided in Java can be used as the basis for solving certain problems. The remainder of this chapter is devoted to four idioms that demonstrate how collections can be used as part of pattern solutions.

This small number of patterns shows some of the power and relative simplicity of the Java 2 Collections Framework. With careful use of the collections, your programming effort should be reduced, meaning that your code will become simpler. The performance of your code should improve as well. The best part is that you will be able to push many of those CompSci 201 algorithms to the dusty recesses of your brain.

You should grow this part of your implementation patterns toolbox over time. There are countless patterns that can be defined using collections as a basis.

If you have a Smalltalk background, you may wonder why certain implementation patterns do not appear in this section. STACK is already provided as a class in JDK 1.2, so it appears earlier in the collection patterns. SEARCHING LITERAL is an example of one of those patterns that just does not translate well to Java. A Java implementation of SEARCHING LITERAL is easily done, but it does not add any value because of the limitations of Java syntax. Similarly, the implementations of the PARSING STREAM and CONCATENATING STREAM patterns in Java are not very pleasing.

DUPLICATE REMOVING SET

Answers the Question	How do you remove duplicates from a collection?
Solution	Use a temporary set to determine which elements are duplicates.
Category	Collections
Related Patterns	None

The classic algorithm for removing duplicates from a list, while fairly straightforward, results in a good amount of ugly or poorly performing code. The brute-force solution basically compares each object to every other object to determine whether or not it is a duplicate. This involves multiple iterations over subsets of the collection, so that performance[8] approaches $O(n^2)$. Not good. The better performing, more common solution involves using a sort, which in many languages you have to provide on your own. But even then your performance is going to be $O(n \log n)$ at best.

Java 1.1 and earlier versions do not even provide a sort. So much for reuse. Java 2 does provide a good merge, which you might be tempted to use in helping to solve this problem. Don't do it! There is a much simpler and better-performing solution, one that requires no sort.

JDK 1.1

If you are still working with JDK 1.1, the utility method in **Listing 4.57** results in the fastest performance, $O(n)$, at the expense of a bit of temporary memory.

Listing 4.57 *DUPLICATE REMOVING SET Using Hashtable*

```
private Vector removeDuplicates(Vector list)
{
    Vector newList = new Vector(list.size());
    Hashtable set =
        new Hashtable(list.size() * 2 - 1);
    Enumeration enum = list.elements();
    while (enum.hasMoreElements())
    {
        Object element = enum.nextElement();
        if (set.put(element, element) == null)
            newList.addElement(element);
    }
    return newList;
}
```

(38)

---

8 See Appendix A, "Performance," which includes a brief discussion on sort performance.

This idiom essentially uses a Hashtable as a temporary working set to store unique elements from `list`. A set by definition allows no duplicate elements. As the list above is enumerated, the code attempts adding each element to the temporary set (line [38]):

```
set.put(element, element)
```

According to the JDK documentation, Hashtable's `set()` method returns the previous value stored at the specified key or `null` if the key was not previously stored. If `null` is the result, `element` is a nonduplicate and is added to a new list of nonduplicate elements to be returned.

Remember that Hashtable invokes both the `equals()` and `hashCode()` methods against objects contained within. You must implement these methods in the class of objects you wish to store in `list`. Refer to the EQUALITY METHOD and HASHING METHOD patterns for details on the implementation of these methods.

Note that this algorithm retains the original order of the list. Even if you have no requirement to retain the original list order, the above idiom is still the best solution to the problem.

JDK 1.2

If you are using JDK 1.2 and you do not care about retaining the original order of the list, the following idiom is about as succinct as you can get:

```
list = new ArrayList(new HashSet(list));
```

One line, no custom function required! The conversion methods in Java 2 allow the list to be directly converted into a set via the constructor of HashSet. From there, ArrayList's constructor converts the set back into a list.

If you are using Java 2 and you *do* care about retaining the original list order, a variant of the `removeDuplicates()` solution (**Listing 4.57**) for JDK 1.1 is still the way to go. You might consider taking advantage of TreeSet, which can return the elements in sorted order, but to do that you would first have to impart the current order of `list` into each object it contains. You would additionally need to provide a Comparator object if the original list ordering is nonnatural. Seems like too much work to me.

Listing 4.58 shows the JDK 1.2 solution for DUPLICATE REMOVING SET.

Listing 4.58 *DUPLICATE REMOVING SET Using HashSet*

```
public void removeDuplicates(Collection list)
{
    Set set = new HashSet(list.size() * 2 - 1);
    Iterator iterator = list.iterator();
    while (iterator.hasNext())
        if (!set.add(iterator.next()))
            iterator.remove();
}
```

(39)

This pattern takes advantage of two new things to clean up the code somewhat from the Java 1.1 solution. First, Iterator objects allow for elements to be safely removed from the base collection while the collection is being traversed, as shown in line [39]. This is something you cannot do with an Enumeration. Thus we no longer need to create a new collection; list can be modified in place.

The second advantage comes from Java 2's inclusion of a new class, HashSet, in addition to HashMap (which works pretty much the same way as 1.1's Hashtable). The HashMap/Hashtable classes are designed to conceptually store key-value pairs. HashSet is a true set of objects. In the above Java 1.1 solution for DUPLICATE REMOVING SET, we are required to bastardize the Hashtable into acting like a set. This results in the following line of code:

```
set.put(element, element);
```

The second element parameter could have been anything except null, since it is ignored for this idiom. Using a HashSet, the code equates to:

```
set.add(element);
```

This distinction may seem trivial. However, use of the HashSet eliminates the need to provide a comment to explain the (non-)meaning of the second parameter to set.put(). Refer to the COMPOSED METHOD and METHOD COMMENT patterns if you are unsure of why this is important.

TEMPORARILY SORTED COLLECTION

Answers the Question	How do you dynamically demand a collection in sorted order?
Solution	Use the JDK 1.2 collections utility method `Collections.sort(Collection)`.
Category	Collections
Related Patterns	None

More often than not, sorts are temporary things. For a user interface, you might need to see all employees in order by name, but when payroll cuts the checks, the employees need to be in departmental order.

If you have a permanent need for a sorted collection, a TREE MAP is your best bet. However, inserting entries into a sorted collection, or removing entries from one, is a costly process. You will need to balance the tradeoffs between demanding a sort when you need one versus the cost of always keeping a collection in sorted order.

For relatively small collections (up to a few thousand elements) it is often cheaper to use a TEMPORARILY SORTED COLLECTION. A TEMPORARILY SORTED COLLECTION is created by resorting a source collection on demand. You also may have to use a TEMPORARILY SORTED COLLECTION if multiple sort orders are required.

If you are using JDK 1.1, you are out of luck: you will need to code your own sort routines. JDK 1.2 introduced the class Collections, a set of algorithms implemented in class methods. Included in these algorithms is an in-place merge sort. The sort guarantees performance of O(n log n) and also ensures that elements that are already equal will not be reordered (this makes the sort *stable*).

Two methods support invoking this sort:
```
sort(List)
sort(List, Comparator)
```

The first, `sort(List)`, uses the natural sort order to sort elements in a collection. This means that the elements must implement the Comparable interface. Refer to TREE MAP for an example of implementing Comparable.

The merge sort is in place, which means that you will lose any ordering that the collection currently has. You may wish to create a copy of the collection before sorting it.

The example in **Listing 4.59** creates an ArrayList and then copies it (line [40]). It sorts a copy of the list (line [41]), and displays the results of iterating against both the TEMPORARILY SORTED COLLECTION and the original list.

Listing 4.59   *TEMPORARILY SORTED COLLECTION* **Example**

```
List list = new ArrayList();
list.add(new Department("300", "Accounting"));
list.add(new Department("500", "Billing"));
list.add(new Department("100", "Mailroom"));
list.add(new Department("200", "Human Resources"));
list.add(new Department("400", "Info Technology"));
list.add(new Department("600", "Cryogenics"));
```

(40)
```
List temporarilySortedList = new ArrayList(list);
```

(41)
```
Collections.sort(temporarilySortedList);
```

```
System.out.println("temporarily sorted list:");
Iterator iterator = temporarilySortedList.iterator();
while (iterator.hasNext())
    System.out.println(iterator.next());

System.out.println("\noriginal:");
iterator = list.iterator();
while (iterator.hasNext())
    System.out.println(iterator.next());
```

The output produced by running the code in **Listing 4.59** is:

```
temporarily sorted list:
100: Mailroom
200: Human Resources
300: Accounting
400: Info Technology
500: Billing
600: Cryogenics

original:
300: Accounting
500: Billing
100: Mailroom
200: Human Resources
400: Info Technology
600: Cryogenics
```

QUEUE

Answers the Question	How do you maintain a list of elements which the first element added to the list is the first element processed?
Solution	Use a LinkedList to emulate the standard operations. Add elements to the end of the LinkedList; remove elements from the beginning of the LinkedList.
Category	Collections
Related Patterns	Stack

QUEUES are the opposite of STACKS. They provide first-in, first-out (FIFO) processing.

Unfortunately, the JDK does not contain a QUEUE implementation. A QUEUE is very easily emulated using a LINKED LIST. Unless you are building a QUEUE that will be used outside your package, you can get away with not even creating a separate Queue class. The LinkedList class is sufficient for internal needs. You could also use an ArrayList, but adding elements to the front of the list is considerably expensive.

Using a LinkedList object as the basis for a QUEUE, you tack an element to the end with `addLast(Object)`. To retrieve an element from the beginning of a Queue, use `removeFirst()`. All of the other operations you will need (`isEmpty()` and `size()`, for example) are provided directly by the Collection interface.

One use of a QUEUE is to manage events that are coming in too fast to process. A queue might capture an event that has just been received. This event would be added to the back of the queue. Meanwhile, a separate thread would remove events from the front of the queue (as long as they existed) and process them at its leisure.

Listing 4.60 provides a Processor class that can run as a daemon. It takes a LinkedList object to represent the QUEUE as a constructor parameter. In a separate thread, it constantly pulls any existing Event items off the QUEUE, using the LinkedList's `removeFirst()` method. Each event is sent to the `process()` method, where a delay exists to emulate a three-second processing time for the event.

Listing 4.60 *Processor.java*

```
import java.util.LinkedList;
public class Processor
    implements Runnable
{
```

(continued)

Listing 4.60 (cont.) *Processor.java*

```java
LinkedList queue;
Thread processorThread;

public Processor(LinkedList _queue)
{
    queue = _queue;
    processorThread = new Thread(this);
    processorThread.start();
}

public void run()
{
    while (true)
    {
        try
        {
            while (queue.size() > 0)
                process(
                    (Event)queue.removeFirst());
        }
        catch (Exception e)
        {
            System.out.println(e.getMessage());
            System.exit(-1);
        }
    }
}

protected void process(Event event)
    throws Exception
{
    System.out.print("processing " +
                        event + "... ");
    try
    {
        Thread.sleep(3000);
    }
    catch (InterruptedException e) {}
    System.out.print(event + " done. ");
}
}
```

The second class file, EventGenerator.java, in **Listing 4.61** provides another thread to simulate the generator of events. The main() method creates an instance of EventGenerator (line [42]), then passes its associated QUEUE to a new Processor instance (line [43]), where the QUEUE will be monitored. EventGenerator's thread spews five events at a time every 10 seconds. Each event is added to the QUEUE via LinkedList's addLast() method (line [45]).

Listing 4.61   *EventGenerator.java*

```java
import java.util.LinkedList;

public class EventGenerator
   implements Runnable
{
   LinkedList queue = new LinkedList();
   public static void main(String[] args)
   {
      EventGenerator generator =
         new EventGenerator();
      new Processor(generator.getQueue());
   }

   public EventGenerator()
   {
      new Thread(this).start();
   }

   public LinkedList getQueue()
   {
      return queue;
   }

   public void run()
   {
      for (int i = 0; i < 10; i++)
      {
         try
         {
            for (int j = 0; j < 5; j++)
            {
               Event event =
                  new Event(i + "." + j);
               System.out.println(
                  "queueing " + event + "...");
               synchronized(queue)
               {
                  getQueue().addLast(event);
               }
            }
         }
         catch (Exception e)
         {
            System.out.println(
               "Add to queue failed " +
               e.getMessage());
            System.exit(-1);
         }

         try
         {
            Thread.sleep(10000);
         }
         catch (InterruptedException e) {}
      }
   }
}
```

(42)

(43)

(44)

(45)

Note at line [44] in **Listing 4.61** that access to the queue is done in a synchronized block. Why not use a synchronization wrapper around the LinkedList object? The answer is because the synchronization wrappers only support operations declared in the collection interfaces. Thus if you need any operations added in a concrete subclass, they are not supported. This includes the method addLast() in our use of LinkedList. We can easily use the add() method, but other operations such as removeFirst() would not be available.

One possible solution would be to access the LinkedList as a generic synchronized list in EventGenerator, while using it as a LinkedList in a QUEUE. I don't recommend this solution because it can introduce considerable confusion.

A portion of a sample Event class is provided in **Listing 4.62**, in case you wanted to try the above code.

Listing 4.62   Event.java

```java
public class Event
{
    String id;
    public Event(String _id)
    {
        id = _id;
    }
    public String getId()
    {
        return id;
    }
    public boolean equals(Object object)
    {
        if (!(object instanceof Event)) return false;
        Event event = (Event)object;
        return getId().equals(event.getId());
    }
    public int hashCode()
    {
        return id.hashCode();
    }
    public String toString()
    {
        return id;
    }
}
```

LOOKUP CACHE

Answers the Question	How can you optimize expensive serial searches against a list?
Solution	Create a HASH MAP that will store elements as they are found in the list. For each lookup, search first in this HASH MAP.
Category	Collections
Related Patterns	List Hash Map

LISTS are great tools, but they come with a cost. As with every tool, there are tradeoffs that you must make. No one tool solves all problems. LISTS are able to maintain an order by trading away performance. HASH MAPS gain better performance at the cost of being unable to maintain an order. TREE MAPS end up somewhere in the middle. Part of your job as the experienced developer is to determine the most appropriate collection class to use.

Sometimes you choose one extreme but find yourself occasionally wishing you had the opposite characteristic. For instance, you may have stored your customer objects in a large LIST but need the ability to rapidly look up a set of customers. LOOKUP CACHE is a pattern that gives you the best of both worlds.

A cache operates on the basis that recently accessed information has a higher likelihood of being accessed again. In a list of customer objects, there are usually customers that are accessed more frequently because their purchase volume is higher.

Suppose your customer lookup is based on the customer name. Your unoptimized method of finding the matching customer within the large list might be as shown in **Listing 4.63**.

Listing 4.63 *Customer Lookup*

```
public Customer findByName(String name)
{
    Iterator iterator = getCustomers().iterator();
    while (iterator.hasNext())
    {
        Customer customer =
            (Customer)iterator.next();
        if (customer.getName().equals(name))
            return customer;
    }
    return null;
}
```

For LOOKUP CACHE, the expensive serial scan of the customer list becomes a secondary operation. Instead, you first perform a lookup into a HASH MAP that represents the cache, to see if the customer has previously been accessed. If the customer is not there, the serial lookup against the list is performed. The customer, if found, is then placed in the HASH MAP. **Listing 4.64** provides an implementation example for LOOKUP CACHE.

Listing 4.64 *LOOKUP CACHE*

```
public Customer findByName(String name)
{
    Customer customer =
        (Customer)customerCache.get(name);
    if (customer == null)
    {
        customer = lookupByName(name);
        if (customer != null)
            customerCache.put(name, customer);
    }
    return customer;
}

private Customer lookupByName(String name)
{
    Iterator iterator = getCustomers().iterator();
    while (iterator.hasNext())
    {
        Customer customer =
            (Customer)iterator.next();
        if (customer.getName().equals(name))
            return customer;
    }
    return null;
}
```

The `customerCache` instance variable shown in **Listing 4.64** stores a HashMap object. Note that the original public serial lookup, `findByName(String)` in **Listing 4.63**, becomes a private method that is renamed to `lookupByName(String)`. It is invoked by the public method `findByName(String)` in **Listing 4.64** only if the customer was not found in the cache.

The old school implementation for LOOKUP CACHE is to rotate the most recently used elements to the front of the list. Performance-wise, this can be a costly process using Java's implementation of LIST, but is less expensive in terms of memory. A LINKED LIST would be ideal for the base collection in this sort of in-place LOOKUP CACHE.

Chapter 5   CLASSES

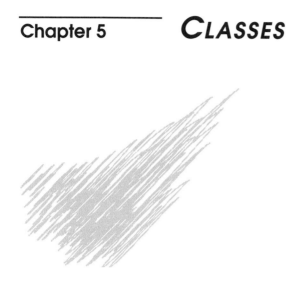

As with state, decisions about class are more related to design than to implementation. What this means is that the patterns in this chapter will have a bit of overlap with design. It also means that this chapter will be extremely short.

All four patterns contained here are about naming: SIMPLE SUPERCLASS NAME, QUALIFIED SUBCLASS NAME, TYPING INTERFACE NAME, and SCOPING PACKAGE NAME. While your class names should already have been chosen in the design phase, change them based on these patterns if necessary. The decision as to what to name a class ripples endlessly throughout coding. Class names are not changed easily and rarely go away.

The patterns in this chapter define a standard for naming your classes, interfaces, and packages.

SIMPLE SUPERCLASS NAME

Answers the Question	What name do you give a class that will be inherited by a subclass?
Solution	Use a concise name that imparts the role the superclass will play as the root of an inheritance hierarchy.
Category	Classes
Related Patterns	Qualified Subclass Name

The biggest problem with inheritance is that your superclasses instantly become legacies. Once you have other developers creating classes that inherit from your superclass, that's it. You better have made sure that your superclass is all that it's cracked up to be. Effecting a change can be impossible with dozens of classes depending on the original definition of not only your superclass's public behavior but also its protected methods.

The very first thing that becomes ingrained is the name of the superclass. You are stuck with it as soon as that first subclass codes the extends keyword. The name of the class will be used in countless programs, in extends phrases and possibly in method signatures.

As with INTENTION-REVEALING METHOD NAME, your superclass name should describe the role of the superclass. It represents objects, so it should have a noun for a name. The name should be concise. Use the shortest word possible that accurately describes what kind of objects your class produces. For instance, if you are building a superclass that will wrap an HttpSession object in order to cleanly manage a web connection, you don't need to call it something wordy like UserHttpSessionManager or HttpSessionCoordinator. For this example, Session would suffice.

Since you know that your class will be inherited, give it a name that sounds good in an expression of the "is a" relationship. For example, if you have created a superclass to represent a web page, the simplest name to give it is Page. Then you can say a specific page subclass, LoginPage for example, *is a* Page. If you named the superclass PageManager instead, it sounds wrong to say that a LoginPage is a PageManager. To make the phrasing sound accurate, LoginPage would have to be called LoginPageManager. The end result is that everyone else will need to name their classes with the unnecessary suffix.

Avoid tacking on prefixes or suffixes. Any sort of prefix is better reflected in the package name (see SCOPING PACKAGE NAME). By adding a prefix, you are limiting the concept of object reusability. For example, if you append a project name to the class name, it implies that the class is only useful in the context of that project.

Most suffixes add unnecessary words without adding value to the superclass name. "Manager" and words like it can usually dropped with a bit of
creativity. The suffix "Object" is outright confusing, especially when you
start talking about classes and instances: "I created an object from the
PageObject class."

Finally, avoid abbreviations. The rule of thumb is that abbreviations
should only be used if they are used in everyday speech. This means that
EntryFld is an unacceptable abbreviation for EntryField, but IdBadge is
preferable to IdentifierBadge. It is not worth a minimally smaller number of
keystrokes to muddle the meaning of your class.

I will reiterate that naming things is one of the most important aspects of
development. Names should always impart meaning of some sort. Just as
with writing, your goal should be conciseness and clarity. Take the time to
choose the perfect identifier or class name. Eliminate unnecessary or
"noise" words. Avoid words that have ambiguous meanings. Above all,
consider your audience. You are writing code that will almost certainly be
used and maintained by someone else.

QUALIFIED SUBCLASS NAME

Answers the Question	What name do you give to a subclass?
Solution	Use the superclass to provide a more specific name that implies the relationship to the superclass.
Category	Class
Related Patterns	Simple Superclass Name

If you have an ideal simple name for a subclass, go ahead and use it. The QUALIFIED SUBCLASS NAME pattern is designed to help you when there is no commonly recognized name to describe your subclass.

Since inheritance represents an "is a" or an "is kind of" relationship, the subclass name can help enforce this relationship. The solution is to prepend an adjective to the superclass name that describes the specialization of the superclass. For example, a web page that presents a login screen and inherits from the Page class is a LoginPage. A user preferences screen is a PreferencesPage, and so on.

The benefit of naming your classes this way is that the inheritance relationship is clearly imparted to a code maintainer. This allows the developer to understand what sort of behaviors to expect from the subclass.

QUALIFIED SUBCLASS NAME works well if your class is a "leaf" class, one that will probably not be inherited from (or one that is explicitly declared as final). If your class is somewhere in the middle of a hierarchy, use SIMPLE SUPERCLASS NAME instead.

As with all naming, avoid those abbreviations!

TYPING INTERFACE NAME

Answers the Question	What name do you give an interface?
Solution	Use the SIMPLE SUPERCLASS NAME pattern to derive a name for your interface.
Category	Class
Related Patterns	Simple Superclass Name

You can take one of two tactics when naming interfaces. One, you can make it explicitly clear that an interface is an interface. Two, you can treat an interface like any other class.

If you want to make it clear that an interface is an interface, there is already a convention adopted in the Java world. Use SIMPLE SUPERCLASS NAME to provide a concise name for your interface, and then append the letters IF (InterFace) to the end of the name. Distinguishing between a class declaration and an interface is thus very easy for the reader.

The other solution is to treat interfaces much like any other class when naming them. Thus, you just use the SIMPLE SUPERCLASS NAME pattern to come up with a name for an interface. I'll go out on a limb here and state this as my preference, mostly because it is yet another example of encapsulation — hiding the implementation details.

An interface is a contract to enforce methods to be implemented by a class. What this does is to add an additional type to a class. A class that implements Comparable method *is a* Comparable object. Anywhere a Comparable object is expected, that class can be passed. So for all intents and purposes, Comparable defines a new class. A method that takes a Comparable object as a parameter does not need to know that the parameter represents an interface.

Take your example from the JDK itself, which does not differentiate interface names from class names. TYPING INTERFACE NAME means you should name your interfaces solely based on their type.

SCOPING PACKAGE NAME

Answers the Question	What name do you give to a package?
Solution	Create a package hierarchy that goes from general to specific, starting with an organizational name and moving to the name of a component package to which similar classes will belong.
Category	Class
Related Patterns	None

Packages in Java, while initially confusing to the seasoned C or C++ developer, are a great organizational tool. Packages are useful for grouping related classes. A class on its own is not often a very reusable thing. Frequently classes have to coexist with other classes in order to provide a complete reusable component. The GregorianCalendar class is of little use without the Calendar or Date classes.

Packages also provide a good solution to avoiding namespace collisions. There are thousands of classes named Customer out there in the Java development world, and if you work for a large firm there are probably dozens of departments that have built a Customer class. Working with the other departments' objects would be impossible if it weren't for packages. Packages allow for classes with common names to coexist in the same application.

As with inheritance hierarchies, don't get too out of hand with the levels of package naming. Switching through a lot of directories to get to corresponding code locations can become tedious after a while. A package name with five or six levels is probably an optimal length. Use more levels if you need them, but the rule of thumb is that each level should be meaningful and include at least some files.

The scope of package naming is from general to specific. The trend is to start with your Web site's domain name in reverse. If you are `http://www.gmssolutions.com`, your package name should start with `com.gmssolutions`. A subsequent name can identify the workgroup or product. Any further names should provide the reusable component group to which the class belongs.

For example, if you are building an Employee object for a personal information manager (PIM) product for Bozo Industries, an appropriate fully scoped class name might be `com.bozo.pim.personnel.Employee`.

Package names should be comprised of lowercase characters. This will clarify whether or not something is the name of a package, such as:

```
java.beans.beancontext
```

versus being a reference to a class within a package:

```
java.beans.BeanDescriptor
```

Abbreviations are still to be avoided, as with SIMPLE SUPERCLASS NAME. But because there can be several levels of package names, abbreviations can make a package name more workable. The package name is used only infrequently in code and can afford to be a bit terse.

Chapter 6 *FORMATTING*

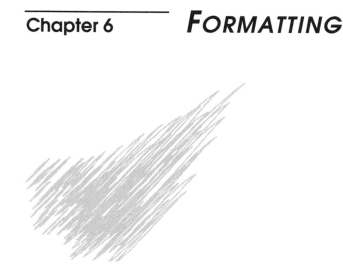

I don't dare come down with a final word on formatting. Most developers are pretty intent on using their own personal formatting style. Heated debates can ensue when you try to tell someone that your way of formatting code is better.

The problem to be solved with formatting patterns is not so much a question of determining which one is "right." You will never reach agreement on that score. Instead, the solution needed is to come up with a set of patterns that can be agreed upon by your workgroup. Consistency is the key word here.

No matter what standards you decide upon, there will always be some people who disagree with the formatting decisions made. I personally have a hard time reading code written with some of the more common "standards." If it comes down to having to comprehend a difficult section of code, I will frequently reformat the code as I merrily refactor my way into a better understanding of it.

The problem with letting people do this, however, is that it can cause headaches for everyone else in the workgroup. Perhaps my style is unique; should everyone else suffer because of my quirky need to read code? Who decides what patterns are acceptable? Your workgroup will have to determine the answers to these questions.

I recommend that you do not proceed a minute further until you have figured this out. Use the patterns in this chapter as a starting point. I have chosen not to reinvent the wheel and provide every possible formatting pattern. You will want to refer to one of the many style guidelines available on the web for the rest of your common formatting standards. Go ahead, I'll wait.

An overlooked point about varying formatting styles is the way it negatively affects revision comparison operations. Suppose you check out a class file from a source repository, reformat the code considerably, and check it back in. A diff comparison between my code and the previous revision will likely show lots of changes based on formatting alone, making it difficult to determine just what logic has changed.

A possible solution might be to invest in a pretty-print program. These tools are fairly commonplace in the C world, but I have not come across many for Java. Each developer could run the pretty-print, using personal preferences, against code being checked out from the repository. Putting code back in would require a pretty-print pass against the code, using a standard set of preferences.

If you have already followed the rest of the patterns within *Essential Java Style*, many of the formatting questions become less important. The question of how to treat multiple nested if statements is moot if you use COMPOSED METHOD to eliminate the nesting. Vertical white space (i.e., blank lines) becomes less necessary if your methods are short and perform a single level of abstraction. Patterns for comments are less important if your code does not require as many comments.

There are a limited number of patterns in this chapter. Many of the patterns that have long been commonplace in C coding are not discussed here. Most of the patterns here have a unique Java perspective. A few of the patterns are C leftovers that are still hotly debated. But patterns on cascading if/else indentation are omitted, for example, and so are patterns on when to use parentheses in a complex expression. In general, if a pattern is not here to help you make a decision, it's probably because a good standard already exists and is commonly accepted.

In fact, the majority of seasoned (old) programmers doing Java are C or C++ coders. The easiest and least controversial decision in your workgroup may be to stick with established convention for doing things. This is especially true when there is no definite reason for choosing one solution over the other. Just be consistent.

Use the patterns in this chapter to provide a basis for some of your workgroup's decisions on formatting. The patterns should shed a bit of light on why one alternative might be preferable to another.

METHOD SIGNATURE

Answers the Question	How do you format a method signature?
Solution	Put the complete signature, minus the throws clause (if any), on a single line.
Category	Formatting
Related Patterns	None

Method signatures have gotten longer, in progression from C to C++[1] to Java. A typical `main()` method in Java might be written out as:

```
public static void main(String[] args) throws IOException
```

If you have methods with more than a parameter or two, things can quickly become unwieldy. You may find that a signature has to span more than one line to be complete.

When scanning code in a single class file, you are typically looking for where each method begins. In order to be visually identified quickly, a METHOD SIGNATURE, has to stand out. The most important part of recognizing a method is its access specifier (`public`, `private`, or `protected`[2]). After a line has been identified as being a METHOD SIGNATURE, the name of the method is what you look for next. And for final identification as to whether a METHOD SIGNATURE is a match for what you are looking for, the parameter list uniquely identifies the method.

It would seem then that it is fairly important to keep these three items — access specifier, method name, and parameters — on a single line if possible. Not only are visual searches enhanced, but find operations are much easier if the information appears on a single line. Throws clauses can be placed on a separate line, since they do not help uniquely identify the method. The other parts of the signature, the static keyword if it exists and the return type, are pretty much stuck between the access specifier and the method name.

The other question is that of order. The return type must appear before the method name. But the access specifier and static keyword, if any, can be switched. I prefer the visual consistency of always having the access specifier appear first.

---

1 If you can call moving from C to C++ a "progression."

2 The omission of `package` as a keyword is yet another questionable Java design decision. Sometimes the explicit declaration of a default value can go a long way in declaring intent. With access specifiers, you otherwise need a clear understanding that package level protection is the default. For visual recognition purposes, it would have helped a lot to allow the word "package" to be explicitly used.

Using these rules, the declaration of the main() method is not very different from the first cut above:

```
public static void main(String[] args)
    throws IOException
```

If I am using a class browser such as the one in VisualAge for Java, it becomes equally important to keep the signature on a single line, but for a different reason. The bottom pane that contains the method code is limited in height. If the signature is allowed to break a line for each parameter, the code invariably ends up scrolling off the bottom. Any time that you can avoid making someone scroll, it's a good thing.

Reality always intervenes, however. Often, your parameter list will not fit on a single line. Either you can choose to allow the line to wrap, or you can place each parameter on a separate line. I prefer the wrap option; this way I am always assured that the METHOD SIGNATURE (minus any throws clauses) can always be found on a single line.

Of course, I can come up with an equally strong argument in the other direction. Part of the problem with method signatures being as long as they are is that METHOD SIGNATURES with more than one or two parameters will rarely fit on a single line. The use of inner classes can make things worse by requiring a new level of indentation. Using descriptive ROLE-SUGGESTING PARAMETER NAMES also tends to lengthen the signature. The result is that most METHOD SIGNATURES end up wrapping, which can ultimately make things more difficult to read. If it comes down to making terse parameter names versus putting each parameter on a separate line, it is more important that your parameter names are meaningful.

ROLE-SUGGESTING PARAMETER NAME

Answers the Question	What do you name each parameter in a method?
Solution	Name each parameter after the role it plays in the method. Use an underscore to distinguish SETTING METHOD parameters from the instance variable they are setting.
Category	Formatting
Related Patterns	Role-Suggesting Instance Variable Name

In Smalltalk, a parameter or variable can hold any class of object. Imparting the expected type of a parameter can be very important in clarifying a method. In Java, parameters and variables must be defined with a specific type. It is clear just what class or native type will be stored in a parameter.

Since the type of a parameter is clearly available, it is more useful to define the role a parameter will play in a method. The rules for ROLE-SUGGESTING PARAMETER NAME then become the same as with ROLE-SUGGESTING INSTANCE VARIABLE NAME.

For the rectangle example in the MESSAGE SEND pattern, a constructor signature that demonstrates ROLE-SUGGESTING PARAMETER NAME appears in **Listing 6.1**.

Listing 6.1 *ROLE-SUGGESTING PARAMETER NAME*

```
Rectangle(int left, int right, int top, int bottom)
{
    // ...
}
```

You want your parameter name to remain implementation-neutral. I learned this lesson some years ago while doing OS/2 SDK development. In doing C development, one of the favored trends was to name variables using Hungarian notation. The concept of Hungarian notation is to prefix each variable with an abbreviation that suggests the variable type. Using Hungarian notation, names for zero-terminated strings start with `sz` (`szName`), shorts start with `s` (`sCount`), unsigned shorts start with `us` (`usHeight`), and so on.

Well, under OS/2 1.x, the message parameter sent to every window procedure was an unsigned short quantity, so we called these things `usMsg`. When OS/2 2.0 came out, IBM changed this parameter to a 32-bit-long value. It was easy enough to go through all the code and change the parameter's types to ULONG, but the new parameter name usMsg was misleading. Unfortunately, use of usMsg was pretty pervasive, and to make it worse, "Msg" was one of those very overloaded variable name prefixes. Thus we were unable to just do an automated global search and replace.

Lesson learned: Hungarian notation violates encapsulation. Don't use it.

Setting Methods

So, what should you name the parameter to a SETTING METHOD? I had been using the following technique for my setters:

```
public void setVarName(Object varName)
{
    this.varName = varName;
}
```

This basically involved giving the parameter the same name as the instance variable and using this to distinguish beneath the two. This technique appears to be the most commonly accepted. But after a bad experience (which is usually what triggers this kind of radical change), I now use a different convention, which is to prepend an underscore to the parameter name:

```
public void setVarName(Object _varName)
{
    varName = _varName;
}
```

I really don't care for underscores, but since setters are not modified very often, I am willing to put up with them. Here's the code that caused me to change my mind.

```
public void setValue(Object Value)
{
    this.value = value;
}
```

It should be obvious in this limited context that I accidentally capitalized the parameter Value. In the midst of dozens of other accessor methods, though, a typographical error like this is fairly easy to overlook. Unfortunately, I missed it and so did the compiler. The nature of this idiom is such that I got no compilation errors or warnings. What I did was perfectly acceptable to javac: that is, value is an unused parameter, and the statement this.value = value ends up being equivalent to value = value.

The insidious result was that `value` remained pointing at whatever it was already pointing at. My subsequent executions produced some very unexpected results. Debugging this problem was difficult, because I made the common assumption that my setter methods were correct.

Using an underscore to prefix your parameters will at least ensure that your constructor or setter method causes the compilation to fail if the formal parameter was mistyped. Use of an underscore is a no-no in the eyes of some developers, especially for those for whom the convention implies something else in C/C++. If `_varName` is not your bag, adopt a different pattern and stick with it. For example, append "Parm" to the name:

```
public void setName(String nameParm)
{
    name = nameParm;
}
```

Again, there are no hard-and-fast rules here. Feel free to use `this.value = value` if you must, but my preference is to catch as much at compile time as possible. A good lint program should be able to ferret out things of this sort. Regardless of your choice, adopt it as the standard for your development workgroup.

MESSAGE SEND

Answers the Question	How do you format an invocation of a method or constructor?
Solution	If the parameters are unclear, put each parameter on a separate line and annotate it with a line comment. Otherwise use EXPLAINING TEMPORARY VARIABLES to clarify the role of a parameter in a message send.
Category	Formatting
Related Patterns	Explaining Temporary Variable

One of my favorite constructs in Objective C and Smalltalk is the ability to name the parameters to a message send. In Smalltalk, you create a rectangle object using the following message send:

```
Rectangle left: 1 right: 10 top: 5 bottom: 25
```

This returns a new Rectangle object with the upper left corner at $(1, 5)$ and the lower right corner at $(10, 25)$. A corresponding message send in Objective C might be:

```
[[Rectangle alloc]
   initLeft: 1 right: 10 top: 5 bottom: 25]
```

In both languages, it is clear just what the value is for each parameter. In contrast, the corresponding message send in Java is shown in **Listing 6.2**.

Listing 6.2   Unadorned MESSAGE SEND

```
new Rectangle(1, 10, 5, 25);
```

Unless you already know the order of the arguments in Rectangle's constructor, you will have to look up the method signature using javadoc to determine what each parameter is expected to represent.

When initially coding MESSAGE SENDS, you might choose to comment what each parameter is in the message send. Another option is to use EXPLAINING TEMPORARY VARIABLES to describe each parameter. Finally, you can choose to ignore the problem and ultimately make maintenance more costly.

If you opt to ignore the problem, just put all the parameters on a single line, as in **Listing 6.2**. There is no reason to break the MESSAGE SEND up into multiple lines.

If you choose to annotate the MESSAGE SEND with comments, each parameter should appear on a separate line, along with a line comment that describes it. To be consistent with my ravings about comments in the rest of this book, I am not thrilled with this solution. However, it can be preferable to introducing a lot of temporary variables that will only be used for a single MESSAGE SEND. An example is shown in **Listing 6.3**.

Listing 6.3 *MESSAGE SEND with Comments*

```
new Rectangle(1,    // left
              10,   // right
              5,    // top
              25);  // bottom
```

Lining up all the parameters can get old after a while. The other adverse effect of the solution in **Listing 6.3** is that it can quickly eat up many lines of vertical white space, something that is not in as much visual abundance as horizontal space.

If you elect to use EXPLAINING TEMPORARY VARIABLES, the MESSAGE SEND will again be all on a single line. This is demonstrated in **Listing 6.4**.

Listing 6.4 *MESSAGE SEND with EXPLAINING TEMPORARY VARIABLES*

```
int left = 1;
int right = 10;
int top = 5;
int bottom = 25;
new Rectangle(left, right, top, bottom);
```

It is also possible that instance or temporary variables themselves do not clarify a MESSAGE SEND. Suppose you have a method to copy the contents of one object into another. Its form is `copy(Object, Object)`. Which is the source and which is the target? Should you really be creating temporaries to alias a reference? In this case, my preference is definitely to annotate the message send with comments, as in **Listing 6.3**.

As you can see, the alternatives in this formatting pattern show the difficulty of deciding on a single solution that will make all developers happy. A consensus decision should be made and developers should be required to adhere to it, with exceptions for extenuating circumstances. Like most rules, there are always valid reasons to break them.

A Note on Parentheses

Another question frequently arises with MESSAGE SENDS and parentheses. How should the method name, parentheses, and parameters be separated? There are three basic options, all shown in **Listing 6.5**.

Listing 6.5 *Message Send Spacing*

```
(1)    new Rectangle (left, right, top, bottom);
(2)    new Rectangle(left, right, top, bottom);
(3)    new Rectangle( left, right, top, bottom );
```

I don't particularly care for the first option (line [1]), for several reasons. First, in mathematics it is common practice to declare a function by immediately appending a (to the function name, with no intervening space. Second, searches for all occurrences of construction of a Rectangle object are much easier if you know that a left parenthesis will always be tacked onto the end of the class name.

I code using the second option (line [2]), probably for its terseness. But the third option (line [3]) has a slight advantage if you want to search for all occurrences of the identifier left. If you can assume there will always be a leading space, you can include that in your search to avoid getting matches against the identifier cleft, for example.

Parentheses really provide two roles in C/C++/Java programming: to set off the parameters in a function call, and to logically group statements or expressions, as shown in **Listing 6.6**. These are standard syntactical constructs, not functions. The space between the keyword (if, for, etc.) and the statement/expression group serves to point the construct out as such — no chance to confuse it with a message send.

Listing 6.6 *Separated Opening Parenthesis*

```
if (...)
for (...)
while (...)
```

LEFT-ALIGNING BLOCK

Answers the Question	How do you format the braces in a block statement?
Solution	Left-align both braces so that they are flush with the first character of the block enclosing statement.
Category	Formatting
Related Patterns	None

The alignment of braces in a block statement is another hot button for many people. There are two widely used forms, and a handful of others that are less frequently used. I will only cover the two most popular. If you happen to use one of the other forms . . . sorry.

The block form that I have encountered the most is shown in **Listing 6.7**. Both the method signature and `for` statement in the example demonstrate this block form. The opening brace is placed at the end of the enclosing statement, and the closing brace appears flush with the left side of the enclosing statement. I'll refer to this as a *wrapping block*.

Listing 6.7 *Wrapping Block*

```
public static void main(String[] args) {
    System.out.print("parms: ");
    for (int i = 0; i < args.length; i++) {
        if (i > 0)
            System.out.print(" ");
        System.out.print(args[i]);
    }
    System.out.println();
}
```

The second most common block form is shown in **Listing 6.8** on the next page. The only difference from the form in **Listing 6.7** is that the opening brace appears on a separate line, flush-left with the enclosing statement. This is a LEFT-ALIGNING BLOCK, for lack of a better name. And since this also happens to be the name of the pattern, you can guess my preference.

Listing 6.8 Lᴇꜰᴛ-Aʟɪɢɴɪɴɢ Bʟᴏᴄᴋ

```
public static void main(String[] args)
{
    System.out.print("parms: ");
    for (int i = 0; i < args.length; i++)
    {
        if (i > 0)
            System.out.print(" ");
        System.out.print(args[i]);
    }
    System.out.println();
}
```

So why might a Lᴇꜰᴛ-Aʟɪɢɴɪɴɢ Bʟᴏᴄᴋ be better than a wrapping block? Part of the answer is white space. **Listing 6.7** saves a couple of lines at the cost of readability. The added white space provided by putting opening braces on their own lines gives the method some breathing room, whereas using wrapping blocks can make a method look cramped. While vertical white space is at a slight premium, if you have used Cᴏᴍᴘᴏꜱᴇᴅ Mᴇᴛʜᴏᴅ this is not as much of a concern.

The other part of the answer is that left-aligning both the opening and closing brace makes it much easier to visually recognize the block construct. With a wrapping block, your eyes cannot match a closing brace as quickly with the somewhat random character that begins the enclosing statement. Locating a pair of matching braces should be easier.

Beauty is in the eyes of the beholder, of course.

GUARD CLAUSE

Answers the Question	How do you format control flow when an alternate condition is encountered?
Solution	Have exceptional conditions return directly out of the method as soon as they occur.
Category	Formatting
Related Patterns	None

The slogging that goto has received ever since Dijkstra's paper, "Goto Statement Considered Harmful," is probably well-deserved. Even if you have a legitimate use for a goto, it's not worth the grief you will receive when someone else finds it. Somewhere along the line, I also remember a platitude about not returning out of a routine in its middle. Of course, this was back in the days when functions or subroutines were dozens of lines long, and the cardinal rule was to keep all functions under a single printed page.

With the use of COMPOSED METHOD, your Java methods will be short, hopefully less than a dozen lines. The procedural nature of code is lessened while the object-oriented aspect of message sending is increased. If you do a good job of applying patterns like CHOOSING MESSAGE or DISPATCHED INTERPRETATION to your code, you will not need nearly as many branching statements.

Within the context of a brief method, then, a return statement is not nearly as obscured as one within a large nesting of other statements. GUARD CLAUSE, one of my favorite formatting patterns, promotes early exits from methods. As opposed to making a method more difficult to follow, it goes a long way towards improving the readability and understanding of a method.

The premise of GUARD CLAUSE is that a method has a standard, happy-path flow, just like a use case. Certain conditions are regarded as exceptional. Perhaps a parameter passed to the method is null, or maybe the employee classification is not the one you were expecting. Without GUARD CLAUSE, the typical way to code this is demonstrated in **Listing 6.9**. The method nxxFrom(String) extracts the nxx[3] from a phone number string, accounting for hyphens in the phone number if they exist.

Listing 6.9 Top-Down Approach

```
public String nxxFrom(String phoneNumber)
{
    String result = null;
    if (phoneNumber.length() >= 10)
    {
```

(continued)

---

3 An *nxx* is the second set of three digits in a U.S. phone number. For example, the nxx in 719-555-9999 is 555.

Listing 6.9 (cont.)   *Top-Down Approach*

```
        int start;
        int end;
        if (phoneNumber.indexOf('-') > -1)
        {
            start = 4;
            end = 7;
        }
        else
        {
            start = 3;
            end = 6;
        }
        result = phoneNumber.substring(start, end);
    }
    return result;
}
```

GUARD CLAUSE treats phone number strings of fewer than 10 characters as an unhappy path; it *guards* the rest of the method from this exceptional condition. Refer to **Listing 6.10**.

Listing 6.10   GUARD CLAUSE

```
public String nxxFrom(String phoneNumber)
{
    if (phoneNumber.length() < 10)
        return null;
    int start;
    int end;
    if (phoneNumber.indexOf('-') > -1)
    {
        start = 4;
        end = 7;
    }
    else
    {
        start = 3;
        end = 6;
    }
    return phoneNumber.substring(start, end);
}
```

(4)

The GUARD CLAUSE at line [4] causes method execution to make an early exit if the phone number string is not long enough. There are a few advantages to this. First, the braces for the large if statement in **Listing 6.9** are no longer required. This also means that additional indentation is not needed for the bulk of the code. The temporary variable result used in **Listing 6.9** is not needed. Most importantly, however, the intent of this method becomes clear: the GUARD CLAUSE presents a condition under which this method is no longer allowed to execute.

CONDITIONAL EXPRESSION

Answers the Question	How do you code conditionals which the return value of the result is required in an assignment, return value, or longer expression?
Solution	Use the ternary operator to eliminate unnecessary if/else statements.
Category	Formatting
Related Patterns	None

The ternary operator in C and Java is often ignored or looked upon with scorn. Syntactically it is one of the more cryptic constructs in Java. It is a perfectly legitimate operator, however, and used appropriately it can help clarify your code. A CONDITIONAL EXPRESSION uses branching logic to return the result of one of two possible expressions. Java's ternary operator provides a succinct idiom for CONDITIONAL EXPRESSION.

The following example demonstrates how to use a ternary operator to return an absolute value:

```
int absoluteOfNumber =
   number < 0 ? -number : number;
```

This is a fairly straightforward use of the construct, although the code:

```
int absoluteOfNumber = Math.abs(number)
```

would be preferred in this example. In fact, in most cases, you should use COMPOSED METHOD and make the expression into its own method.

The ternary operator can easily be abused, as shown in the code in **Listing 6.11**.

Listing 6.11 *Abusing the Ternary Operator*

```
int pointTotal =
   isTouchdown ?
      (conversionSuccessful ?
         (twoPointConversion ? 8 : 7) : 6) :
      (safety ? 2 : (fieldGoal ? 3 : 0));
```

Use it judiciously!

There are two places where the ternary operator is ideal. First is in simple assignments and return values:

```
String genderString = null;
if (gender == Gender.FEMALE)
   genderString = "women";
else
   genderString = "men";
```

Applying CONDITIONAL EXPRESSION, this becomes:

```
String genderString =
   (gender == Gender.FEMALE ? "women" : "men");
```

CONDITIONAL EXPRESSION is also very useful in the context of string concatenation operations:

```
System.out.println("There are " +
                   count +
                   (gender == Gender.FEMALE ?
                     " women" : " men") +
                   " in the group");
```

Two of the alternatives are either wasteful:

```
if (gender == Gender.FEMALE)
   System.out.println("There are " + count +
                      " women in the group.");
else
   System.out.println("There are " + count +
                      " men in the group.");
```

or produce cluttered code:

```
System.out.print("There are ");
if (gender == Gender.FEMALE)
   System.out.print("women");
else
   System.out.print("men");
System.out.println(" in the group.");
```

The second situation in which a ternary operator is useful is within the context of a longer expression, where a separate function might be considered overkill:

```
int totalPrice = basePrice +
                 deliveryCharge +
                 dealerPrep +
                 obsceneProfit +
                 (isTaxExempt ? 0 : salesTax) +
                 costOfTags;
```

SIMPLE ENUMERATION VARIABLE NAME

Answers the Question	What do you call the temporary variable that holds each element extracted via an ENUMERATION?
Solution	Name it each.
Category	Formatting
Related Patterns	Enumeration

With all these patterns that I am espousing, I manage to break most of them on some occasion or other. Certain deviations from standard practice can become patterns in themselves. For example, I have repeated a few times now that you should not use abbreviations or terse, meaningless variable names. Yet almost every time I have to write a for loop to directly iterate through a collection, I use the identifier i as the collection index, as in **Listing 6.12**. I have been sneaky about it in this book, expanding it to index whenever I noticed my supposed gaffe.

Listing 6.12 The Author's Guilty Pleasure

```
for (int i = 0; i < args.length; i++)
    System.out.println(args[i]);
```

I used to code so many for loops, whipping one of these out was second nature. Use of the index i is so pervasive and so commonplace that I still feel little remorse for using it. The commonness of the idiom reinforces the intent. In fact, if you have seen a hundred for loops in code with the use of i and suddenly you come across one that uses index, it makes you stop and wonder if there is a special reason for this. Idioms work only if they are expressed in a consistent manner.

SIMPLE ENUMERATION VARIABLE NAME is a pattern that actually eliminates contextual meaning from a variable name in favor of a standard that makes the pattern all the more recognizable.

The question that SIMPLE ENUMERATION VARIABLE NAME answers is what to name the object extracted with each next() message send to an iterator object. Your garden-variety ENUMERATION, the procedural form of a Do loop, is shown in **Listing 6.13**.

Listing 6.13 Do We Even Need a Variable?

```
Iterator iterator = list.iterator();
while (iterator.hasNext())
{
    Customer each =
        (Customer)iterator.next());
    do(each);
}
```

(5)

In **Listing 6.13**, I named the instance variable to hold the object extract-ed each (line [5]). This convention derives from the Smalltalk world, but it works equally well in Java. It is an arbitrary decision; I might have chosen the variable name object, current, or something else. I could also have chosen customer to make the instance variable name more meaningful. In the spirit of the idiom, however, using each for every enumeration you write ultimately simplifies your coding. Not to mention that every time I write something like the code in **Listing 6.14** — typing the word "customer" three times in a row — I get a bit annoyed.

Listing 6.14 *Repetitive Repetitive Repetitive*

```
Customer customer = (Customer)iterator.next();
```

There is also a social engineering aspect of getting you to use each for your variable name. You will be processing the Customer object retrieved by sending it messages. Sending messages to an instance variable called each is unclear. So you are encouraged to use COMPOSED METHOD (again) and break the processing of each Customer object into its own method. In this example the method is do().

But now, taking a second look at **Listing 6.13**, the need for a temporary variable is questionable. Creating a temporary variable simply to pass it to a method is unnecessary in this case, especially since the temporary variable name has no contextual meaning. The revised ENUMERATION is shown in **Listing 6.15**.

Listing 6.15 *A Cleaner ENUMERATION*

```
Iterator iterator = list.iterator();
while (iterator.hasNext())
    do((Customer)iterator.next());
```

No temporary variable is needed. The braces go away (a personal choice of mine; I know some of you prefer the braces regardless of whether or not they are necessary), leaving things a bit cleaner.

But if you have chosen to use the object-oriented ENUMERATIONS, such as DO and DETECT, described in Chapter 4, the SIMPLE ENUMERATION VARIABLE NAME pattern finally applies. **Listing 6.16** shows a DO loop. Note that the Object parameter to the exec() method is named each.

Listing 6.16 *SIMPLE ENUMERATION VARIABLE NAME in DO*

```
list.forEachDo(
    new Block() {
        int i = 0;
        public void exec(Object each) {
            show(each, i++);
    }});
```

Chapter 7   DEVELOPMENT EXAMPLE

The implementation patterns in *Essential Java Style* are the "make it right" part of the mantra described in COMPOSED METHOD. For me, this is the most enjoyable part of coding. Getting something to work is certainly fun, but it is a more rewarding challenge to make code clean and cost-effective. The work you accomplish will probably be around for some time and may be viewed by dozens of people over its lifetime. Some code never disappears.

Unlike good artwork, which is designed to provoke you and make you think, good code is the exact opposite. Code should be as simple as possible. The simpler the code, the easier it is to comprehend and maintain. Occasionally you will come across a difficult problem that has a complex solution. Your goal is to make the solution as comprehensible as possible to the next person. If your code is not simple enough, the next person will ultimately have to re-solve the original problem in order to understand your code.

This chapter contains a small portion of an example of how the patterns can be applied in an actual development project. The example is a utility program to expedite the creation of Java source code for domain classes. I use this command-line utility to give me a quick start on coding when I start a project.

The Class Definer Utility

The goal of the class definer utility is to produce a skeleton Java source file that contains private instance variable declarations, GETTING METHODS, and SETTING METHODS for a domain class. It creates stub javadoc comments as well. The class definer as I present it here is a very bare-bones utility that could use a lot more bells and whistles. Feel free to use it as a starting point for your own needs.

The class definer takes as input a text file with two keywords on each line. This file is referred to as the class definition file.

Within the class definition file, one line should be in the form:

```
class ClassName
```

where *ClassName* represents the class name for the Java source file to be produced. Another line should be in the form:

```
package packageName
```

There should be one line per instance variable to be declared, in the form:

```
Class instanceVariableName
```

An example of how to create a Customer class in the package `smelt.core.domain`, with three instance variables, is shown in **Listing 7.1**. For the example, this file is named Customer (with no extension).

Listing 7.1 *Customer Class Definition File*

```
package smelt.core.domain
class Customer
String ssn
ArrayList addresses
Date effectiveDate
```

The output produced by running the class definer against the Customer file in **Listing 7.xa** is the source file Customer.java, shown in **Listing 7.2**. Note that the javadoc comments are stubs, and will need to be filled in.

Listing 7.2 *Customer.java*

```
package smelt.core.domain;

import java.util.ArrayList;
import java.util.Date;
```

```
/**
 *
 * Customer is the domain class that represents .
 *
 * @author Jeff Langr
 * @version
 * @date
 */
public class Customer
{

    /**
     * Creates a new object in which to store Customer data.
     *
     */
    public Customer()
    {
    }


    /**
     * Sets .
     *
     * @param    ssn    .
     */
    private void setSsn(String _ssn)
    {
        ssn = _ssn;
    }


    /**
     * Returns .
     *
     * @return    String representing .
     */
    private String getSsn()
    {
        return ssn;
    }


    /**
     * Sets .
     *
     * @param    addresses    .
     */
    private void setAddresses(ArrayList _addresses)
    {
        addresses = _addresses;
    }
```

(continued)

Listing 7.2 (cont.) *Customer.java*

```
/**
 * Returns .
 *
 * @return   ArrayList representing .
 */
private ArrayList getAddresses()
{
    return addresses;
}


/**
 * Sets .
 *
 * @param    effectiveDate   .
 */
private void setEffectiveDate(Date _effectiveDate)
{
    effectiveDate = _effectiveDate;
}


/**
 * Returns .
 *
 * @return   Date representing .
 */
private Date getEffectiveDate()
{
    return effectiveDate;
}

private String ssn;
private ArrayList addresses;
private Date effectiveDate;
}
```

My initial hack at the code is shown in **Listing 7.3**. It works, but it certainly is difficult to maintain. Being able to derive a useful subclass off this first cut would be impossible.

Listing 7.3 *Pass 1: ClassDef.java*

```
import java.io.*;
import java.util.*;
import java.sql.*;
import java.text.*;
public class ClassDef
{
    private BufferedWriter writer;
```

```java
private class Attribute
{
   String name;
   String className;
}

ClassDef(String filename)
   throws IOException
{
   BufferedReader reader =
      new BufferedReader(
         new FileReader(filename));
   String line;
   String className = "";
   String packageName = "";
   Set imports = new HashSet();
   List attributes = new ArrayList();
   String[] tryPackages =
   {"java.util", "java.io",
    "java.sql", "java.text"};
   while ((line = reader.readLine()) != null)
   {
      StringTokenizer tk =
         new StringTokenizer(line, " ");
      int numTokens = tk.countTokens();
      if (numTokens >= 2)
      {
         String token1 = tk.nextToken();
         String token2 = tk.nextToken();
         if (token1.equals("class"))
            className = token2;
         else if (token1.equals("package"))
            packageName = token2;
         else
      // assume this is an attribute definition
         {
            Attribute attribute =
               new Attribute();
            attribute.className = token1;
            attribute.name = token2;
            attributes.add(attribute);
            if (token1.indexOf('.') != -1)
               imports.add(token1);
            else
            {
               Class javaClass = null;
               for (int i = 0;
                    i < tryPackages.length;
                    i++)
               {
                  try
                  {
```

(continued)

Listing 7.3 (cont.)   *Pass 1: ClassDef.java*

```
                    javaClass =
Class.forName(tryPackages[i] + "." + token1);
                        break;
                    }
                    catch (
                        ClassNotFoundException e)
                    { }
                }
                if (javaClass != null)
                    imports.add(
javaClass.getPackage().getName() + "." + token1);
                }
            }
        }
    }
    reader.close();

    writer =
        new BufferedWriter(
            new FileWriter(filename + ".java"));
    if (!packageName.equals(""))
        outln("package " + packageName + ";\n");

    Iterator iterator = imports.iterator();
    while (iterator.hasNext())
    {
        String importName =
            (String)iterator.next();
        outln("import " + importName + ";");
    }

    outln("");
    outln("/**");
    outln(" *");
    outln(" * " + className +
" is the domain class that represents .");
    outln(" *");
    outln(" * @author Jeff Langr");
    outln(" * @version");
    outln(" * @date");
    outln(" */");
    outln("public class " + className);
    outln("{");

    outln("");
    outln("\t/**");
    outln(
"\t * Creates a new object in which to store " +
className + " data.");
    outln("\t *");
    outln("\t */");
    outln("\tpublic " + className + "()");
    outln("\t{");
    outln("\t}");
```

```
Iterator iterator2 = attributes.iterator();
while (iterator2.hasNext())
{
    outln(""); outln("");
    Attribute attrib =
        (Attribute)iterator2.next();
    outln("\t/**");
    outln("\t* Sets .");
    outln("\t*");
    outln("\t* @param    " +
        attrib.name + "    .");
    outln("\t*/");
    outln("\tprivate void set" +
        upFirst(attrib.name) +
        "(" + attrib.className +
        " _" + attrib.name + ")");
    outln("\t{");
    outln("\t\t" + attrib.name +
        " = _" + attrib.name + ";");
    outln("\t}");

    outln(""); outln("");
    outln("\t/**");
    outln("\t* Returns .");
    outln("\t*");
    outln("\t* @return    " +
        attrib.className +
        " representing .");
    outln("\t*/");
    outln("\tprivate " +
        attrib.className +
        " get" +
        upFirst(attrib.name) + "()");
    outln("\t{");
    outln("\t\treturn " + attrib.name + ";");
    outln("\t}");
}

outln("");
iterator2 = attributes.iterator();
while (iterator2.hasNext())
{
    Attribute attrib =
        (Attribute)iterator2.next();
    outln("   private " +
        attrib.className + " " +
        attrib.name + ";");
}

outln("}");
writer.close();
}
```

(continued)

Listing 7.3 (cont.) *Pass 1: ClassDef.java*

```
        private String upFirst(String string)
        {
            StringBuffer s = new StringBuffer();
            char c = string.charAt(0);
            s.append(Character.toUpperCase(c));
            s.append(string.substring(1));
            return s.toString();
        }


        private void outln(String s)
            throws IOException
        {
            writer.write(s, 0, s.length());
            writer.newLine();
        }


        static public void main(String[] args)
        {
            if (args.length < 1)
            {
                System.out.println(
"USAGE:\n\tjava ClassDef classDefFile");
                System.exit(-1);
            }
            try
            {
                new ClassDef(args[0]);
            }
            catch (IOException e)
            {
                System.out.println(
"Unable to open " + args[0]);
            }
        }
}
```

(1)

You should notice immediately that the formatting in **Listing 7.3** leaves something to be desired. I have forced line breaks throughout the code in order to make things fit, partly due to the tight margins in this book. Note that after I have applied all the patterns, the source will require fewer unnecessary line breaks.

The very first problem with the class is the class name itself. Noting that SIMPLE SUPERCLASS NAME recommends avoiding abbreviations, I renamed the class from ClassDef to ClassDefiner (line [2] in **Listing 7.4**).

In a similar vein, I used ROLE-SUGGESTING TEMPORARY VARIABLE NAME to provide better identifiers. Specifically, I changed attrib to attribute (line [6]) and s to buffer (line [13]). I also eliminated the temporary variable c at line [1] in **Listing 7.3**, because it did not provide a lot of value as an EXPLAINING TEMPORARY VARIABLE.

Organizationally, I applied SMALL CAPS COMPOSED METHOD to break the constructor up into two protected methods: `loadClassDefinition()` (line [3]) and `writeJavaSource()` (line [10]). This provides a high-level decomposition into the two steps that the utility takes to accomplish its goal. Each method takes the input filename as its parameter.

This also drove the changing of the BufferedWriter instance variable `writer` into a temporary variable (line [11]), because it is only needed in `writeJavaSource()`. That in turn meant that all calls to the `outln()` method (line [14]) needed to be passed a BufferedWriter (line [12], for example).

Next, I identified the important outputs that were being populated in `loadClassDefinition()`: `className` (line [4]), `packageName` (line [5]), `imports` (lines [8, 9]), and `attributes` (line [7]). These are all things that result from loading and parsing through the class definition file. They are required for `writeJavaSource()` to be able to output a source file. As a temporary measure, I decided to make these into instance variables (line [15]), as they represent the essence of the data that the class definer stores.

Finally, I changed the inner class Attribute so that it provided a constructor to set its instance variables (line [16]).

Listing 7.4   *Pass 2: ClassDefiner.java*

```
          import java.io.*;
          import java.util.*;
          import java.sql.*;
          import java.text.*;
(2)       public class ClassDefiner
          {
              ClassDefiner(String filename)
                 throws IOException
              {
                 loadClassDefinition(filename);
                 writeJavaSource(filename);
              }

(3)           protected void loadClassDefinition(String filename)
                 throws IOException
              {
                 BufferedReader reader =
                    new BufferedReader(
                       new FileReader(filename));
                 String line;
                 String[] tryPackages =
                    {"java.util", "java.io",
                     "java.sql", "java.text"};
                 while ((line = reader.readLine()) != null)
                 {
```

(continued)

Listing 7.4 (cont.) *Pass 2: ClassDefiner.java*

```
                StringTokenizer tk =
                    new StringTokenizer(line, " ");
                int numTokens = tk.countTokens();
                if (numTokens >= 2)
                {
                    String token1 = tk.nextToken();
                    String token2 = tk.nextToken();
                    if (token1.equals("class"))
(4)                     className = token2;
                    else if (token1.equals("package"))
(5)                     packageName = token2;
                    else
                // assume this is an attribute definition
                    {
(6)                     Attribute attribute =
                            new Attribute(token2, token1);
(7)                     attributes.add(attribute);
                        if (token1.indexOf('.') != -1)
(8)                         imports.add(token1);
                        else
                        {
                            Class javaClass = null;
                            for (int i = 0;
                                 i < tryPackages.length;
                                 i++)
                            {
                                try
                                {
                                    javaClass =
        Class.forName(tryPackages[i] + "." + token1);
                                    break;
                                }
                                catch (
                                    ClassNotFoundException e)
                                { }
                            }
                            if (javaClass != null)
(9)                             imports.add(
        javaClass.getPackage().getName() + "." + token1);
                        }
                    }
                }
            }
            reader.close();
        }


(10)    protected void writeJavaSource(String filename)
            throws IOException
        {
(11)        BufferedWriter writer =
                new BufferedWriter(
                    new FileWriter(filename + ".java"));
```

```
        if (!packageName.equals(""))
            outln(writer, "package " +
                packageName + ";\n");

        Iterator iterator = imports.iterator();
        while (iterator.hasNext())
        {
            String importName =
                (String)iterator.next();
            outln(writer, "import " +
                importName + ";");
        }
```

(12)
```
        outln(writer, "");
        outln(writer, "/**");
        outln(writer, " *");
        outln(writer, " * " + className +
    " is the domain class that represents .");
        outln(writer, " *");
        outln(writer, " * @author Jeff Langr");
        outln(writer, " * @version");
        outln(writer, " * @date");
        outln(writer, " */");
        outln(writer, "public class " + className);
        outln(writer, "{");

        outln(writer, "");
        outln(writer, "\t/**");
        outln(writer,
    "\t * Creates a new object in which to store " +
    className + " data.");
        outln(writer, "\t *");
        outln(writer, "\t */");
        outln(writer, "\tpublic " +
                className + "()");
        outln(writer, "\t{");
        outln(writer, "\t}");

        Iterator iterator2 = attributes.iterator();
        while (iterator2.hasNext())
        {
            outln(writer, "");
            outln(writer, "");
            Attribute attribute =
                (Attribute)iterator2.next();
            outln(writer, "\t/**");
            outln(writer, "\t* Sets .");
            outln(writer, "\t*");
            outln(writer, "\t* @param    " +
                attribute.name + "    .");
            outln(writer, "\t*/");
            outln(writer, "\tprivate void set" +
```

(continued)

Listing 7.4 (cont.)   *Pass 2: ClassDefiner.java*

```
                    upFirst(attribute.name) + "(" +
                    attribute.className + " _" +
                    attribute.name + ")");
            outln(writer, "\t{");
            outln(writer, "\t\t" + attribute.name +
                " = _" + attribute.name + ";");
            outln(writer, "\t}");

            outln(writer, ""); outln(writer, "");
            outln(writer, "\t/**");
            outln(writer, "\t* Returns .");
            outln(writer, "\t*");
            outln(writer, "\t* @return    " +
                attribute.className +
                " representing .");
            outln(writer, "\t*/");
            outln(writer, "\tprivate " +
                attribute.className + " get" +
                upFirst(attribute.name) + "()");
            outln(writer, "\t{");
            outln(writer, "\t\treturn " +
                attribute.name + ";");
            outln(writer, "\t}");
        }

        outln(writer, "");
        iterator2 = attributes.iterator();
        while (iterator2.hasNext())
        {
            Attribute attribute =
                (Attribute)iterator2.next();
            outln(writer, "    private " +
                attribute.className + " " +
                attribute.name + ";");
        }

        outln(writer, "}");

        writer.close();
    }


    private String upFirst(String string)
    {
        StringBuffer buffer = new StringBuffer();
        buffer.append(
            Character.toUpperCase(string.charAt(0)));
        buffer.append(string.substring(1));
        return buffer.toString();
    }
```

(13)

```
(14)        private void outln(BufferedWriter writer, String string)
               throws IOException
            {
               writer.write(string, 0, string.length());
               writer.newLine();
            }


            static public void main(String[] args)
            {
               if (args.length < 1)
               {
                  System.out.println(
         "USAGE:\n\tjava ClassDefiner classDefFile");
                  System.exit(-1);
               }
               try
               {
                  new ClassDefiner(args[0]);
               }
               catch (IOException e)
               {
                  System.out.println(
         "Unable to open " + args[0]);
               }
            }

(15)        private String className = "";
            private String packageName = "";
            private Set imports = new HashSet();
            private List attributes = new ArrayList();

            private class Attribute
            {
               String name;
               String className;
(16)           private Attribute(String _name, String _className)
               {
                  name = _name;
                  className = _className;
               }
            }
         }
```

Once I had refactored to the source in **Listing 7.4,** I made sure that my
output was still correct. I used a different program to test that the source
file created with the new version of the code was the same as the one created by the original version. Having automated tests is almost essential to
proper refactoring, because it is very easy to introduce new problems by
moving things around.

So far, I had incorporated a good number of changes, but the code was still nowhere near what it needed to be. **Listing 7.5**, my final stab at this for the time being, shows a radically refactored solution.

First, the high-level representation of the processing accomplished in the ClassDefiner has been removed from the constructor. The constructor in general should be a place for putting together your objects, not for accomplishing work. Thus, a new method called `createJavaSource()` (line [17]) was created to execute both COMPOSED METHODS `writeJavaSource()` (line [21]) and `loadClassDefinition()` [17], through a series of DECOMPOSING MESSAGES.

The `tryPackages` temporary variable has become an instance variable, `packagesToTry` (line [24]), that stores the list of package names. This list is initially populated via LAZY INITIALIZATION (line [20]).

The tab characters ("\t") embedded in the output strings have been removed from the strings, as it makes them difficult to read. The `write()` method has been modified to take a number of tabs as a parameter (line [23]). To simplify coding when no tabs are required, a method to supply DEFAULT PARAMETER VALUES is supplied (line [22]).

A GUARD CLAUSE has been used to allow an early exit from the `parse()` method if there are fewer than two tokens (line [19]).

Listing 7.5 *Pass 3: ClassDefiner.java*

```
public class ClassDefiner
{
    ClassDefiner(String _filename)
    {
        filename = _filename;
    }


    static public void main(String[] args)
    {
        if (args.length < 1)
        {
            System.out.println(
"USAGE:\n\tjava ClassDefiner classDefFile");
            System.exit(-1);
        }
        try
        {
            String filename = args[0];
            ClassDefiner definer =
                new ClassDefiner(filename);
            definer.createJavaSource();
        }
        catch (IOException e)
        {
            System.out.println(
"Unable to open " + args[0]);
```

```
        }
    }


(17)    public void createJavaSource()
            throws IOException
        {
            loadClassDefinition(filename);
            writeJavaSource(filename);
        }


(18)    protected void loadClassDefinition(String filename)
            throws IOException
        {
            BufferedReader reader =
                new BufferedReader(
                    new FileReader(filename));
            String line;
            while ((line = reader.readLine()) != null)
                parse(line);
            reader.close();
        }


        protected void parse(String line)
        {
            StringTokenizer tokenizer =
                new StringTokenizer(line, " ");
(19)        if (tokenizer.countTokens() < 2)
                return;

            String token1 = tokenizer.nextToken();
            String token2 = tokenizer.nextToken();
            if (token1.equals("class"))
                className = token2;
            else if (token1.equals("package"))
                packageName = token2;
            else
                addAttribute(token1, token2);
        }


        protected void addAttribute(String className, String name)
        {
            Attribute attribute =
                new Attribute(name, className);
            attributes.add(attribute);
            if (className.indexOf('.') != -1)
                imports.add(className);
            else
            {
```

(continued)

Listing 7.5 (cont.)   *Pass 3: ClassDefiner.java*

```
            Class javaClass = getClass(className);
            if (javaClass != null)
                imports.add(
javaClass.getPackage().getName() + "." +
className);
        }
    }


    protected Class getClass(String className)
    {
        Class javaClass = null;
        Iterator iterator =
            getPackagesToTry().iterator();
        while (iterator.hasNext())
        {
            String packageName =
                (String)iterator.next();
            try
            {
                javaClass =
Class.forName(packageName + "." + className);
                return javaClass;
            }
            catch (ClassNotFoundException e)  { }
        }
        return null;
    }


    protected List getPackagesToTry()
    {
(20)    if (packagesToTry == null)
        {
            packagesToTry = new ArrayList(10);
            packagesToTry.add("java.util");
            packagesToTry.add("java.io");
            packagesToTry.add("java.sql");
            packagesToTry.add("java.text");
        }
        return
Collections.unmodifiableList(packagesToTry);
    }


(21)    protected void writeJavaSource(String filename)
            throws IOException
    {
        BufferedWriter writer =
            new BufferedWriter(
                new FileWriter(filename + ".java"));
```

```java
        writePackageInfo(writer, packageName);
        writeImportStatements(writer, imports);
        writeClassHeader(writer, className);
        writeConstructor(writer, className);
        writeAccessorMethods(writer, attributes);
        writeInstanceVariables(writer, attributes);
        writeClassClosing(writer);
        writer.close();
    }

    protected void writePackageInfo(BufferedWriter writer,
String packageName)
        throws IOException
    {
        if (!packageName.equals(""))
            write(writer, "package " +
                packageName + ";\n");
    }

    protected void writeImportStatements(
BufferedWriter writer, Set imports)
        throws IOException
    {
        Iterator iterator = imports.iterator();
        while (iterator.hasNext())
        {
            String importName =
                (String)iterator.next();
            write(writer, "import " +
                importName + ";");
        }
    }


    protected void writeClassHeader(BufferedWriter writer,
String className)
        throws IOException
    {
        write(writer, "");
        write(writer, "/**");
        write(writer, " *");
        write(writer, " * " + className +
" is the domain class that represents .");
        write(writer, " *");
        write(writer, " * @author Jeff Langr");
        write(writer, " * @version");
        write(writer, " * @date");
        write(writer, " */");
        write(writer, "public class " + className);
        write(writer, "{");
    }
```

(continued)

Listing 7.5 (cont.) *Pass 3: ClassDefiner.java*

```java
    protected void writeInstanceVariables(BufferedWriter writer,
List attributes)
        throws IOException
    {
        write(writer, "");
        Iterator iterator = attributes.iterator();
        while (iterator.hasNext())
        {
            Attribute attribute =
                (Attribute)iterator.next();
            write(writer,
                "    private " +
                attribute.className +
                " " + attribute.name + ";");
        }
    }


    protected void writeConstructor(BufferedWriter writer,
String className)
        throws IOException
    {
        write(writer, "");
        write(writer, "/**", 1);
        write(writer,
" * Creates a new object in which to store " +
className + " data.",
            1);
        write(writer, " *", 1);
        write(writer, " */", 1);
        write(writer, "public " + className +
            "()", 1);
        write(writer, "{", 1);
        write(writer, "}", 1);
    }


    protected void writeAccessorMethods(BufferedWriter writer,
List attributes)
        throws IOException
    {
        Iterator iterator = attributes.iterator();
        while (iterator.hasNext())
        {
            Attribute attribute =
                (Attribute)iterator.next();
            writeSetter(writer, attribute);
            writeGetter(writer, attribute);
        }
    }
```

```
    protected void writeSetter(BufferedWriter writer, Attribute
attribute)
        throws IOException
    {
        write(writer, "");
        write(writer, "");
        write(writer, "/**", 1);
        write(writer, "* Sets .", 1);
        write(writer, "*", 1);
        write(writer,
            "* @param   " + attribute.name +
            "    .",
            1);
        write(writer, "*/", 1);
        write(writer,
            "private void set" +
            upFirst(attribute.name) +
            "(" + attribute.className + " _" +
            attribute.name + ")",
            1);
        write(writer, "{", 1);
        write(writer,
            attribute.name + " = _" +
            attribute.name + ";",
            2);
        write(writer, "}", 1);
    }


    protected void writeGetter(BufferedWriter writer, Attribute
attribute)
        throws IOException
    {
        write(writer, "");
        write(writer, "");
        write(writer, "/**", 1);
        write(writer, "* Returns .", 1);
        write(writer, "*", 1);
        write(writer,
            "* @return   " + attribute.className +
            " representing .",
            1);
        write(writer, "*/", 1);
        write(writer,
            "private " + attribute.className +
            " get" + upFirst(attribute.name) +
            "()",
            1);
        write(writer, "{", 1);
        write(writer, "return " + attribute.name +
            ";", 2);
        write(writer, "}", 1);
    }
```

(continued)

Listing 7.5 (cont.)   *Pass 3: ClassDefiner.java*

```
        private String upFirst(String string)
        {
            StringBuffer buffer = new StringBuffer();
            buffer.append(
                Character.toUpperCase(string.charAt(0)));
            buffer.append(string.substring(1));
            return buffer.toString();
        }


        protected void writeClassClosing(BufferedWriter writer)
            throws IOException
        {
            write(writer, "}");
        }
```

(22)
```
        private void write(BufferedWriter writer, String string)
            throws IOException
        {
            write(writer, string, 0);
        }
```
(23)
```
        private void write(BufferedWriter writer, String string,
                int tabs)
            throws IOException
        {
            for (int i = 0; i < tabs; i++)
                writer.write("\t", 0, 1);
            writer.write(string, 0, string.length());
            writer.newLine();
        }

        private String filename;
        private String className = "";
        private String packageName = "";
        private Set imports = new HashSet();
        private List attributes = new ArrayList();
```
(24)
```
        private List packagesToTry = null;

        private static class Attribute
        {
            String name;
            String className;
            private Attribute(String _name, String _className)
            {
                name = _name;
                className = _className;
            }
        }
    }
```

Listing 7.5 would probably not be my final word in refactoring. There are still lots of things that could be done to improve this class. I could add more constructor parameters to improve flexibility. PARAMETER OBJECT could be incorporated instead of making `className`, `packageName`, `imports`, and `attributes` into instance variables. Many of the string constants in the various `writeXxx()` methods could be cleaned up and made into CONSTANTS or CONSTANT METHODS.

The important thing at this point is that I now have a class that can be casily maintained and subclassed without too many headaches. Now, go and have fun ripping up your own code.

Appendix A   PERFORMANCE

Performance is almost always a subjective criterion. My goal as a developer is to follow the mantra, "make it run, make it right, make it fast." Making it run is the first, most obvious goal. I typically jam lots of code into a single method, get it to work, and only then do I go back and use COMPOSED METHOD to refactor my code (i.e. "make it right"). Making it fast only comes into consideration once the code is right. Usually it is difficult to tell that a certain piece of code will need performance improvements. Unless a user (an end user, a tester, another developer, or perhaps me) complains, I do not complicate my code with performance enhancements.

I tested several of the constructs promoted by *Essential Java Style* patterns for performance considerations. One example was from METHOD COMMENT, where the line of code:

```
if (ftpResponse.charAt(0) == '2')
```

was factored into its own method:

```
public boolean wasSuccessful(String ftpResponse)
{
    return ftpResponse.charAt(0) == '2';
}
```

I could hear the complaining when you came across this code: "What about performance?" Well, adding a method call does increase execution time. And Java certainly does concern me regarding performance. But I am not so concerned that I will sacrifice the more valuable aspect of maintainability by eliminating every precious microsecond of execution time. Java's currently lame performance is not an excuse to obfuscate code. Remember that in most cases you are crafting code that someone else will have to maintain.

The refactoring of the conditional into a separate method results in a performance sink of about 35%, with optimizations turned off. That sounds like a lot, but we are talking microseconds here. In fact, running 1,000,000 iterations on my machine against the above example results in a difference of about 30 milliseconds. Your use of method refactoring would have to be extremely pervasive and your iterations very high before the performance loss would even raise an eyebrow.

With optimization turned on (`javac -O`) and the `final` keyword on the method signature, the performance should be equivalent. Be forewarned, however, that `final`, just like `inline` in C++ is only a request to the compiler. If your compiler is javac, for example, it will not inline if you use local variables in your method.

Get to know your compiler. Take a look at the byte codes it generates by using the javap program:

```
javap -c ClassName > ClassName.bytes
```

This command generates a file named `ClassName.bytes`. You should be able to quickly determine if your method has been inlined by looking at the annotated byte codes in this file. For details on how to read the byte codes, refer to the Java Virtual Machine Specification provided by Sun.

There are places in this book where I ignore my own mandate of not coding for performance unless necessary. Coding for performance usually causes your code to suffer in terms of understandability. In many cases, however, coding for performance does nothing detrimental the readability of your code. For instance, the use of a CACHING TEMPORARY VARIABLE can actually make your code clearer in addition to improving performance.

If there is a commonly accepted performance solution that does not adversely affect your code's intent, by all means use it. Do not make your code more confusing with performance enhancements in order to shave off a few insignificant microseconds.

Java Optimizations

The following are a small number of optimization techniques geared specifically toward Java coding. I do not cover standard optimizations that can be done in most languages, such as eliminating common sub-expressions, unrolling loops, or extracting invariant calculations from loops. There are whole books on the subject of performance.

Before you spend lots of time optimizing the wrong section of code, make sure you run a performance profiler against your code. Be sure to write down the performance results before applying optimizations. Compare these initial performance results to the results obtained after optimizations were applied. If an optimization provided no significant time saving, remove it.

The JDK provides a rudimentary profiling option on java.exe, `-prof`[1], which produces a raw dump of how many times each method was invoked during an execution. You may want to write a utility program to make better use of the data provided. There are also a good number of tools available that do a much better job of performance profiling.

Finally, before you start applying tricks that muddle your code, look at the algorithm you are using. For small amounts of data, some algorithms may be fine but may introduce severe performance problems as the size of the data grows. The data structure used can also make a significant difference.

Don't forget to use the -O option to turn on optimizations when you compile with javac.

Minimize Casting

Casting is not a free operation. The three casts in the following code:

```
int length = ((String)object).length();
char ch1 = ((String)object).charAt(0);
char ch2 = ((String)object).charAt(length - 1);
```

can be minimized to a single cast through the use of a temporary variable:

```
String string = (String)object;
int length = string.length();
char ch1 = string.charAt(0);
char ch2 = string.charAt(length - 1);
```

Minimize Synchronization

Synchronization blocks are considerably expensive. Use synchronization only when necessary. In JDK 1.1, realize that the collections are synchronized by default whereas in JDK 1.2, you must explicitly wrap a collection in a synchronization wrapper. Using synchronizing methods is somewhat less expensive than synchronizing individual blocks of code.

---

1 Apparently this option is not available on the Macintosh™. Sorry.

Minimize Use of `instanceof`

Excessive use of `instanceof` will slow your program, as will most reflection operations. CHOOSING MESSAGE demonstrates how to reorganize things so that the use of `instanceof` can be minimized.

Minimize Instantiation

Object instantiation is one of the costlier operations in Java. The fewer objects you have to create, the faster your program will be. Also, each object instantiation ultimately results in increased garbage collection time. Note that the more superclasses there are of the class being instantiated, the costlier the instantiation time.

Most objects cannot be effectively reused; there is too much risk in ensuring that the contents have been correctly cleared and replaced. Many collection classes, including ArrayList and HashMap, do support the `clear()` operation to remove all elements.

Iterate Through Loops in Reverse

The standard idiom for iterating through a loop is to start counting upward from 0:

```
for (int i = 0; i < list.length(); i++)
    list.get(i).process();
```

For each iteration, the length of the referenced list must be determined and compared to the index `i`. This involves a message send, not terribly expensive but not free either.

If you do not need to access the elements of a collection in forward order, it is just as easy to access them in reverse order:

```
for (i = list.length(); i >= 0; i--))
    list.get(i).process();
```

Comparing `i` to 0 for each iteration is less expensive than comparing it to the list's length. With large numbers of iterations, it can be at least three times slower to do forward loop iteration.

Another technique is to store the length of the list in a CACHING TEMPORARY VARIABLE:

```
int length = list.length();
for (int i = 0; i < length; i++)
    list.get(i).process();
```

Manually Inline Methods

If you need performance, you may not want to depend on the compiler or VM to inline a method. Inlining may disappear if you switch environments. Someone could introduce a change that inadvertently causes the inlining to go away.

If you want to ensure improved performance with a method that is invoked a significant number of times, pull the code out of the method and inline it directly from where it was invoked. Using COMPOSED METHOD will introduce more method calls, but until you do so, it will be difficult to determine just which portion of code is the source of the performance problem.

Once you have identified a method as a performance hog, determine the source of the problem. It will be either code in the method itself or the fact that the method is getting invoked a significant amount of times. If the code in the method is proven to execute quickly, eliminate all message sends that invoke the method. To do this, replace the message send directly with the called method's code.

If the method that you manually inline is not private, you will need to retain the original method, in case a subclass or other object invokes it. Proving that no other object needs the method can be difficult, especially when reflection capabilities have been used.

Use the `static` and `final` Modifiers

Use of `static` and `final` will improve the performance of your method if it can be inlined. Inlining will not occur unless one of these is used.

Use a `StringBuffer` Instead of +

This is a performance enhancement that is often used when not necessary. To concatenate strings, the simplest technique is to use the concatenation (+) operator to add them together:

```
String selectClause =
    "select name from " + tableName +
    " where ssn = '" + ssn + "'";
```

Some developers insist that this is bad for performance and that you should use a `StringBuffer` to perform this operation:

```
return
    new StringBuffer("select name from ")
        .append(tableName)
        .append(" where ssn = '")
        .append(ssn)
        .append("'")
        .toString();
```

Nonsense. The byte codes produced by using the concatenation operator in the first example are exactly the same as those produced by the second example. The javac compiler creates a `StringBuffer` object in the first example behind the scenes.

So which one should you use? The answer should be obvious: if there is no difference in performance, use the concatenation operator. Your code will be much clearer.

This does not mean that the concatenation operator should always be used. The `StringBuffer` is ideal when either the string cannot be put together in one initialization statement, or when you want to repetitively tack on strings to a single existing string. For example, suppose you want to create a very large string that represents a list of words. A method using the concatenation operator might read:

```
public final String cat(List words)
{
   String allWords = "";
   Iterator iterator = words.iterator();
   while (iterator.hasNext())
      allWords += (String)iterator.next() + " ";
   return allWords;
}
```

The corresponding method using a `StringBuffer`:

```
public final String catB(List words)
{
   StringBuffer buffer = new StringBuffer();
   Iterator iterator = words.iterator();
   while (iterator.hasNext())
      buffer.append((String)iterator.next() + " ");
   return buffer.toString();
}
```

For shorter lists of words, there is little difference in performance. But with longer lists (10,000 words and up), the `StringBuffer` solution performs over 50 times faster than the concatenation operator. The reason is that when you use the concatenation operator, a new string is created each time as a result of appending the next word to the existing string.

Do Not Throw Exceptions for Normal Processing

Throwing an exception is costly and should be reserved for exceptional situations. Something that you expect to happen normally during the execution of your code is not exceptional. For example, if you are writing validation rules that either pass or fail, you should not generate an exception on a rule failure. Control anything you can directly with code. Exceptions are designed to handle situations for which you cannot possibly code.

One purported optimization technique actually recommends using exception handling to control iterating through an array. You avoid testing the array bounds manually, and just wait until Java throws an out-of-bounds exception. The premise is that `try` and `catch` blocks do not have any "cost" associated with them until an exception is thrown.

Unfortunately, I haven't been able to derive any performance benefit from doing things this way, optimizations or not. Ten million iterations showed virtually no difference between either technique. The moral of the story is: Don't believe someone else's optimizations unless you try them yourself. Even mine. If there is no performance benefit, there is no point in making your code more confusing, as shown in the example:

```
try  // DON'T DO THIS
{
    int i = 0;
    while (true)
        process(array[i++]);
}
catch (ArrayIndexOutOfBoundsException e)
{
}
```

HotSpot

Perhaps the final word on optimizing Java will come from Sun and other third-party VM vendors. HotSpot is Sun's second-generation virtual machine (VM). Performance approaching that of native-compiled C++ code has been claimed for HotSpot.

One of the key features of HotSpot is known as adaptive optimization. As your program executes, the HotSpot VM identifies critical performance areas in code — "hot spots" — and does some native-level optimization on that code. Contrast this with the JIT (Just In Time) compilers, which compile methods into native code upon their first execution.

The small virtual methods you create using COMPOSED METHOD will no longer be a source of performance problems. HotSpot will dynamically inline code during execution. The code muddling you do in the name of performance, such as the techniques described briefly in this appendix, will no longer be necessary.

Further details on HotSpot are available in a Sun white paper at:
`http://www.javasoft.com/products/hotspot/whitepaper.html`

Big O

In a few patterns in this book, I have mentioned Big-O notation. For example, the performance of bubble sort is described as $O(n^2)$. This is a standard way of describing the complexity of an algorithm. This section describes just what Big-O is and what the different complexity levels mean.

Big-O notation measures the complexity of an algorithm (not the implementation) in respect to the number of elements n on which the algorithm operates. It describes the maximum time or space in which an algorithm will run, for large enough values of n. For smaller values of n, the constants may end up being dominant over a factor of the size of the collection.

The simplest example is iterating over a collection of n elements, which is an O(n) algorithm.

Big-O notation is based on algorithm performance for large values of n. What this means is that arithmetic multipliers are not taken into consideration. An algorithm has the same complexity, regardless of whether its implementation results in 20 instructions or 50 instructions per element processed. Similarly, an algorithm that requires two or three passes against all n elements is still referred to as O(n). Logarithmic multipliers and powers dominate and thus are the sole modifiers in Big-O notation.

Big-O notation also assumes worst-case performance. If you have to serially search through a collection to locate an element, your *best case* is that the element is the first one iterated over. *Worst case* is that you search all n elements and the one you are looking for is the last element in the list. The *average case* is that the element is in the middle. Big-O notation ignores the specific situation — the complexity is O(n) in either case.

The range of complexity starts at O(1). O(1) means that a constant number of instructions is executed regardless of the size of n. The table shows the range of complexity measurements.

Big-O	Description	# Operations when $n = 1024$	Examples
O(1)	constant	1	ideal hash table lookup
O($\log_2 n$)	logarithmic	10	binary search on a sorted array
O(n)	linear	1024	linear search
O(n $\log_2 n$)	linear-logarithmic	10,240	quick sort, merge sort, heap sort
O(n^2)	quadratic	1,048,576	bubble sort, selection sort
O(n^3)	cubic	1,073,741,824	
O(2^n)	exponential	an extremely large number	the traveling salesman problem[2]

2 A salesman takes a round trip to n cities. Find the shortest complete route.

An "operation" is defined as a linear set of instructions. As you can see, there are very significant differences in magnitude between the various levels of complexity.

The formal definition of Big-O is as follows:

```
f(n)=O(g(n))
if-and-only-if there are positive constants k and n₀
such that f(n)<=k*g(n) for all n, n>= n₀.
```

Expressed in something closer to English: When n is large enough, there is a function k*g(n) that is larger than f(n). The function g(n) acts as a bounding function.

Big O, So What?

The best performance modification you can make is to improve an algorithm's Big-O measurement. If you can swap out an $O(n^2)$ bubble sort and replace it with an $O(n \log_2 n)$ quick sort, you can potentially improve the performance of a sort one-hundred-fold. I sorted 100,000 elements. On my machine, it took more than a minute and a half with a bubble sort. Using a merge sort brought the execution time down to less than a second.

Algorithms that share the same Big-O measurement can produce considerably different execution times with smaller data sets. Also, performance of some algorithms can actually vary depending on the data. A quick sort can actually degrade to $O(n^2)$ if the data is already sorted.

If you have a choice of more than one algorithm with the same Big-O, choose the algorithm that is the least convoluted. Maintenance time is more costly than anything else. Quick sort is often chosen over merge sort because it is a bit easier to code and to understand.

Appendix B   PATTERN SUMMARY

This appendix is provided as a quick reference summary of the patterns in this book. The name, problem, and solution for each pattern is listed. Patterns are grouped by chapter. Within each chapter's summary, the patterns are provided in alphabetical order.

Behavior — Method

Pattern Name	Answers the Question	Solution
Comparing Method	How do you order objects with respect to each other?	Implement the Comparable interface within the objects to be ordered and call Collections.sort (List). Use Collections.sort (List, Comparator) if the elements are to be sorted in a non-natural sequence.
Composed Method	How do you divide a class into methods?	Create small methods, each of which accomplishes a single task that is concisely represented by the method name.
Constructor Method	How do you represent instance creation?	Provide a constructor for each valid way to create an instance; do not provide constructors that allow creation of invalid objects.
Constructor Parameter Method	How do you set instance variables from the parameters to a CONSTRUCTOR METHOD?	Use DIRECT VARIABLE ACCESS; create a private set () method if more than one constructor needs to set common parameters.
Converter Constructor Method	How do you represent the conversion of one object to another, possibly with a different protocol?	Provide constructor methods in the target class that take the source object as a parameter.
Converter Method	How do you represent simple conversion of an object to another with the same protocol but a different format?	Prefer the use of CONVERTER CONSTRUCTOR METHOD if possible. If not, create a method asTargetClass () and have it return a new instance of the target class.
Debug Printing Method	How do you provide a printable representation of an object for debugging purposes?	Override toString () and have it return a concise string that uniquely describes the object.

Behavior — Method (cont.)

Pattern Name	Answers the Question	Solution
Default Parameter Values	How do you set parameters to default values?	Overload the method with all combinations of required parameters. Delegate from the more specific methods with fewer parameters to the methods with more parameters, ultimately delegating to the method that does the actual work.
Intention-Revealing Method Name	What should a method be named?	Name a method after what it does, not how it does it.
Method Comment	How do you comment methods?	Provide a developer-oriented comment, apart from the javadoc comment, at the beginning of a method, *only if necessary*. This comment should only communicate important information that is not obvious from the code. Refactor unclear code using other patterns, including COMPOSED METHOD.
Method Object	How do you code a method where many lines of code share many arguments and temporary variables?	Define an inner class named after the method. Declare an instance variable in the class for each temporary variable in the original method; pass the temporary variables into the class via a single constructor. Define a method compute( ) which triggers the process defined in the original method. Apply COMPOSED METHOD within the METHOD OBJECT.

(continued)

Behavior — Method (cont.)

Pattern Name	Answers the Question	Solution
Parameter Object	How do you code a method where many lines of code share many arguments and temporary variables?	Apply COMPOSED METHOD; use an inner class to store the parameters that need to be passed from method to method. Access the parameters within the PARAMETER OBJECT directly from the COMPOSED METHODS.
Query Method	How do you represent testing the property of an object?	Provide a method named like a query: Prefix the property to be tested with] a form or variant of the verb "be": isOpen(), or variant of the verb "be": isOpen(), hasDependents(), wasDeleted(), for example. Return a boolean from the method.
Reversing Method	How do you code a smooth flow of messages?	Add a new method to the class of a parameter. The new method takes the original receiver as a parameter, and sends a "reversing" message back to the original receiver with this as a parameter.
Shortcut Constructor Method	How can you simplify the construction of objects?	Provide a method that creates an instance of a new object, using its parameter as an initialization value.

Behavior — Message

Pattern Name	Answers the Question	Solution
Choosing Message	How do you execute one of several alternatives?	Send a message to an object; let the class of the object determine its behavior (polymorphism).
Collecting Parameter	How do you return a collection that is the collaborative result of several operations?	Use COMPOSED METHOD to break each operation into its own method. Return the sub-collection from each method and concatenate the results. Optionally, pass a collecting parameter to all of the new methods.
Decomposing Message	How do you invoke parts of a computation?	Send several messages (implicitly) to `this`.
Delegation	What is an alternative to inheritance for reusing implementations?	Delegate work requested of an object to another object.
Dispatched Interpretation	How can two objects cooperate when one wishes to conceal its representation?	Encapsulate the representation within the responsible object. Create an interface that client objects must implement. Client objects dispatch back to the responsible object a request for one of its interface methods to be executed.
Double Dispatch	How do you delegate responsibility based on the classes of two receiving objects?	Send a message to the argument; append the name of this class to the message name, and pass `this` as a parameter to the message.
Extending Super	How do you add to the implementation of a superclass method?	Override the superclass method. Call the superclass method from within the overriding method using `super`.
Mediating Protocol	How do you code the interaction between two objects that need to remain independent?	Refine the protocol between the objects so that the words used are consistent.

(continued)

Behavior — Message (cont.)

Pattern Name	Answers the Question	Solution
Message	How do you invoke computation?	Send a message in the form of a function call to an object or class; let the receiver decide which method to invoke.
Modifying Super	How do you change superclass behavior when you do not have the ability to directly modify the superclass?	Override the superclass method. Invoke it using `super`. Execute code that modifies the results.
Pluggable Method Name	How do you invoke different methods based on another factor?	Create an instance variable to store the name of the appropriate method to be invoked; append "Message" to the end of this variable name. With Java reflection capabilities, create the corresponding java.lang.reflect.Method object using the message name, and execute it via `invoke ( )`.
Self-Delegation	How do you delegate behavior to a secondary object when it needs to be able to send messages back to the original receiving object?	Send along `this` as a parameter to the message being sent to the delegate.
Simple Delegation	How do you delegate behavior when the delegate needs no information from the original receiving object?	Send the message from the original receiving object to the delegate without changing it.
Super	How do you invoke superclass behavior?	Explicitly send a message to `super` as the receiving object.

State

Pattern Name	Answers the Question	Solution
Boolean Property Setting Method	How do you set a boolean property?	Create two methods: one to set the property on and another to set the property off. Neither method takes a parameter.
Caching Temporary Variable	How do you improve the performance of a method?	Assign the value of a costly expression to a TEMPORARY VARIABLE that will act as a cache. Use the variable in the remainder of the method.
Collecting Temporary Variable	How do you collect values that will be used later in a method?	Use a TEMPORARY VARIABLE to hold the values that are collected.
Collection Accessor Method	How do you provide access to an instance variable that holds a collection?	JDK 1.1: Allow access to the collection only through delegated messages. JDK 1.2: Use the unmodifiable wrappers provided by the Collections class.
Common State	How do you represent state?	Provide an instance variable within your class definition.
Constant	How do you represent a constant value?	Declare a final class variable and assign it the constant value.
Constant Method	How do you represent the default value of a variable?	Provide an accessor method that returns the value of the constant.
Constant Pool	How do you share a pool of common constants that are needed by multiple classes?	Define an interface. Declare the pool constants within the interface. Implement the interface in classes that need the constants.
Default Value Constant	How do you represent the default value of a variable?	Provide a CONSTANT that specifies the default value; initialize the variable to this CONSTANT.

(continued)

State (cont.)

Pattern Name	Answers the Question	Solution
Default Value Method	How do you represent the default value of a variable?	Provide a method that returns the default value.
Direct Variable Access	How do you get and set an instance variable's value?	Access and set the instance variable directly.
Enumerated Constants	How do you provide a safe, C-like enum capability?	Create a special class to represent the enumeration.
Enumeration Method	How do you provide safe, general access to collection elements?	Provide a method that takes a closure as a parameter. Iterate through the collection and send a message to the closure for each element of the collection.
Explaining Temporary Variable	How do you simplify a complex expression within a method?	Break subexpressions out of the complex expression. Assign the result of each subexpression to a TEMPORARY VARIABLE that has a ROLE-SUGGESTING TEMPORARY VARIABLE NAME.
Explicit Initialization	How do you initialize instance variables to their default value?	Assign an initial value to the instance variable when it is declared in the class.
Getting Method	How do you provide access to an instance variable?	Provide a method that returns the instance variable. Name it using the pattern: getInstanceVariable().
Indirect Variable Access	How do you get and set an instance variable's value?	Use GETTING METHODS and SETTING METHODS to access and update the value of the instance variable.

State *(cont.)*

Pattern Name	Answers the Question	Solution
Lazy Initialization	How do you initialize instance variables to their default value?	Test the value of the instance variable each time it is accessed in its GETTING METHOD. If it is uninitialized, set the variable to its initial value.
Reusing Temporary Variable	How do you use the results of an expression several times in a method when its value may change?	Assign the results of the expression to a TEMPORARY VARIABLE. The variable may be reused throughout the remainder of the method.
Role-Suggesting Instance Variable Name	What do you name an instance variable?	Name the instance variable after the role it plays as an attribute of an object, not after how it is implemented.
Role-Suggesting Temporary Variable Name	What do you name a TEMPORARY VARIABLE?	Name it after the role it performs in the computation.
Setting Method	How do you change the value of an instance variable?	Provide a method to set the value of the variable. Name the method using the pattern `setInstanceVariable(Object)`.
Temporary Variable	How do you store a value for later use in a method?	Declare a locally scoped variable and assign it a value.
Variable State	How do you represent state that can vary between instances of a single class?	Use a HashMap to store the attributes as key-value pairs. Allow access to the attributes via a `getProperty()` method; allow updates to the attributes via a `setProperty()` method.

Collections

Pattern Name	Answers the Question	Solution
Array	How do you store a fixed-size ordered collection of elements?	Use an Array object.
Collect	How do you return a new collection that is a transformation of each object in the original collection?	*Procedural:* Create an empty list. Iterate through the collection using a `while()` loop, extracting each element within. Transform each element and add it to the new collection. *Object-oriented:* Create a `collect()` method in the list class that takes a closure as a parameter. `collect()` iterates over the collection and sends a message back to the closure for each element. The closure in turn transforms the element and returns an object to be added to a new list in `collect()`. `collect()` returns a new list of transformed elements.
Collection	How do you represent aggregations of objects?	Use a collection.
Concatenation	How do you append one collection to another?	Create a list at least large enough to hold both collections. Use `addAll()` to concatenate each collection to the combined list.
contains(Object) / containsAll(Collection)	How do you determine if one or more elements are contained within a collection?	Use the methods `contains(Object)` or `containsAll(Collection)`.

Collections (cont.)

Pattern Name	Answers the Question	Solution
Detect	How do you extract the first element of a collection that meets a condition?	*Procedural:* Iterate through the collection using a `while()` loop, extracting each element within. Return the first element that meets the specified criteria. *Object-oriented:* Create a `detect()` method in the list that takes a closure as a parameter. `detect()` iterates over the collection and sends a message back to the closure for each element. The closure returns true if the element meets the specified criteria. Upon receiving the first true result from the closure, `detect()` returns the associated object.
Do	How do you perform an operation using each element in a collection?	*Procedural:* Iterate through the collection using a `while()` loop, extracting and processing each element within. *Object-oriented:* Create a method called `forEachDo()` in the collection that takes a closure as a parameter. This method encapsulates the iteration over the collection and sends a message back to the closure for each element.
Duplicate Removing Set	How do you remove duplicates from a collection?	Use a temporary set to determine which elements are duplicates.
Enumeration	How do you process a collection?	Use an Enumeration or Iterator object to iterate across its elements.

(continued)

Collections *(cont.)*

Pattern Name	Answers the Question	Solution
Equality Method	How do you provide a method to test whether or not two objects are equal?	Code an `equals(Object)` method to return true if the Object parameter is equal to this object.
Hash Map	How do you provide fast keyed access to a collection of elements?	Use a HashMap (JDK 1.2) or Hashtable (JDK 1.1) object.
Hashing Method	How do you specify where an element will be located within a HashMap?	Provide a `hashCode()` method to return an integer based on the key values of the object.
Inject Into	How do you manage a running value as you iterate over a collection?	*Procedural:* Declare a variable to hold the running value. Iterate through the collection using a `while()` loop, adding to the running value by processing each element within. *Object-oriented:* Create an `injectInto()` method in the list that takes a closure as a parameter. `injectInto()` iterates over the collection and sends a message back to the closure for each element. The closure processes the element and returns a value to be added to a running total stored within `injectInto()`. `injectInto()` returns the final running value after all elements have been processed.
isEmpty()	How do you determine if a collection does not have any elements?	Use `isEmpty()` instead of checking the collection's size.
Linked List	What do you use when elements are frequently added to/removed from the middle or beginning of a collection?	Use a LinkedList object.

Collections (cont.)

Pattern Name	Answers the Question	Solution
List	How do you store a collection where elements can be added and removed?	Use a List object.
Lookup Cache	How can you optimize expensive serial searches against a list?	Create a HASH MAP that will store elements as they are found in the list. For each lookup, search first in this HASH MAP.
Map	How do you map keys to values?	Use a data structure that implements the Map interface.
Queue	How do you maintain a list of elements in which the first element added to the list is the first element processed?	Use a LinkedList to emulate the standard operations. Add elements to the end of the LinkedList; remove elements from the beginning of the LinkedList.
removeAll(Collection)	How do you remove one collection of elements from another?	Use removeAll() to specify the elements to be removed.
retainAll(Collection)	How do you delete all but a specified list of elements from a collection?	Use retainAll(Collection).
Reverse Enumeration	How do you iterate through a list in reverse order?	JDK 1.1: Code a for loop to count down from the size of the collection to 0; access each element of the list directly using the index of the for loop. JDK 1.2: Use the hasPrevious() and previous() methods available in the ListIterator interface.

(continued)

Collections (cont.)

Pattern Name	Answers the Question	Solution
Select/Reject	How do you derive a subset of a collection?	*Procedural:* Create an empty list. Iterate through the collection using a `while()` loop, extracting each element within. Add each element that meets the criteria to the new collection. *Object-oriented:* Create `select()` and `reject()` methods in the list class. Each method takes a closure as a parameter. `select()` and `reject()` iterate over the collection, sending a message to the closure for each element. The closure returns a boolean value indicating whether the object should be added to a new list created in `select()` or `reject()`. The `select()` or `reject()` method returns a new list that is a subset of all elements in the original list.
Set	How do you create an unordered collection where there are no duplicate elements?	Use a Set object.
Stack	How do you store a collection of elements so that the last element stored is always the first element removed?	Use a Stack object.
Temporarily Sorted Collection	How do you dynamically demand a collection in sorted order?	Use the JDK 1.2 collections utility method `Collection.sort(Collection)`.
Tree Map	How do you implement a Map whose keys remain in sorted order?	Use a TreeMap object.
Tree Set	How do you create a sorted collection where there are no duplicate elements?	Use a TreeSet object.

Classes

Pattern Name	Answers the Question	Solution
Qualified Subclass Name	What name do you give to a subclass?	Use the superclass to provide a more specific name that implies the relationship to the superclass.
Scoping Package Name	What name do you give to a package?	Create a package hierarchy that goes from general to specific, starting with an organizational name and moving to the name of a component package to which similar classes will belong.
Simple Superclass Name	What name do you give for a class that will be inherited by a subclass?	Use a concise name that imparts the role the superclass will play as the root of an inheritance hierarchy.
Typing Interface Name	What name do you give an interface?	Use the SIMPLE SUPERCLASS NAME pattern to derive a name for your interface.

Formatting

Pattern Name	Answers the Question	Solution
Conditional Expression	How do you code conditionals in which the return value of the result is required in an assignment, return value, or longer expression?	Use the ternary operator to eliminate unnecessary if/else statements.
Guard Clause	How do you format control flow when an alternate condition is encountered?	Have exceptional conditions return directly out of the method as soon as they occur.
Left-Aligning Block	How do you format the braces in a block statement?	Left-align both braces so that they are flush with the first character of the block-enclosing statement.
Message Send	How do you format an invocation of a method or constructor?	If the parameters are unclear, put each parameter on a separate line and annotate it with a line comment. Otherwise use EXPLAINING TEMPORARY VARIABLES to clarify the role of a parameter in a message send.
Method Signature	How do you format a method signature?	Put the complete signature, minus the throws clause (if any), on a single line.
Role-Suggesting Parameter Name	What do you name each parameter in a method?	Name each parameter after the role it plays in the method. Use an underscore to distinguish SETTING METHOD parameters from the instance variable they are setting.
Simple Enumeration Variable Name	What do you call the temporary variable that holds each element extracted via an ENUMERATION?	Name it each.

INDEX